The Gift of Reading:
Part 2 – A Biblical Perspective on Hermeneutics

J. Alexander Rutherford

Unless otherwise indicated, all Scripture quotations are from The Holy Bible, English Standard Version® (ESV®), copyright © 2001 by Crossway Bibles, a publishing ministry of Good News Publishers. Used by permission. All rights reserved.

ISBN-13: 978-1-9990172-8-6

2nd Printing

Cover Design: Stephen Joshua Arriola

Copyright © 2019, 2021 J. Alexander Rutherford
Teleioteti publishing, Vancouver BC
All rights reserved.

To contact Teleioteti publishing for information or to provide feedback, please visit us at **https://teleioteti.ca** or email us at **info@teleioteti.ca**.

DEDICATION

This book is dedicated to all the teachers who have taught me to read and love the Bible. To Noel Sterne, who was the first to teach me that reading the Bible takes hard work. To Kerry Pretty, who first introduced me to hermeneutics, thinking about how we come to understand and apply the text. To Brad Copp, whose passion for Scripture inspired me to read and love it more and whose careful attention to the text taught me many of the skills I use every day in devotions and study. To Fred Eaton, who helped me solidify the doubts I had about some approaches to biblical interpretation and helped me pursue a whole-Bible approach to interpretation. To Rikk Watts, who helped me to think through the issues concerning the New Testament's use of the Old. To Iain Provan, who showed me how to think carefully and critically about my own assumptions in reading the text. And to Phil Long, who showed me how to pay careful attention to the way the stories of the Bible are told and observe the details of the text.

CONTENTS

Dedication iii
Contents v
Analytical Outline vii
Acknowledgments xi
Series Introduction xiii
Introduction 1
1. Approaches to Hermeneutics 7
PART 1: The Role of the Bible 49
   2. The Bible as Self-Interpreting 51
   3. The Bible and Meaning 69
   4. The Bible and Genre 81
PART 2: The Role of the Reader 97
   5. The Reader and Meaning 99
   6. The Audience of Scripture 103
PART 3: The Role of the Author 109
   7. The Author and Meaning 111
   8. The Bible in History 117
   Conclusion 125
APPENDICES: Theory in Application: Exegetical Essays 129

A1. The Sovereignty of God Over the Repentance of Man: Re-Reading Deuteronomy 30:1-14 131

A2. I Will Make them like the Calf: An Examination of Jeremiah 34:17-22 in Its Literary Context 143

A3. The Lament of the Afflicted: A Translation of Job 30 153

A4. Do Not Say In Your Heart: An Exposition of Romans 10:1-8 in the Context of 10:1-13 165

A5. 2 Thessalonians and Hell: Separation from or Wrath Coming Forth From God? 177

A6. Convinced of Better Things: An Exposition of Hebrews 6:1-12 ... 183

Works Cited 199

About Teleioteti 211

ANALYTICAL OUTLINE

I. INTRODUCTION
   1. CHAPTER 1: APPROACHES TO HERMENEUTICS
      A. Hermeneutics in Pre-Modernism
         a. Irenaeus and the Rule of Truth
         b. Allegorical Interpretation
         c. The Reformation
      B. Hermeneutics in Modernism
         a. Critical Hermeneutics
            i. Source Criticism
            ii. Form & Tradition Criticism
         b. Grammatical–Historical Exegesis (GHE)
            i. The Goal of Grammatical-Historical Exegesis
            ii. The Method of Grammatical-Historical Exegesis
               - Excursus: Mirror Reading
      C. Hermeneutics in Postmodern
         a. Structural Exegesis
         b. Feminist Interpretation
         c. Theological Interpretation
            - Excursus: The Narrative turn
      D. Conclusion
II. PART 1: THE ROLE OF THE BIBLE
   1. CHAPTER 2: THE BIBLE AS SELF-INTERPRETING
      A. Analogy of Faith
      B. Closure
      C. Linguistic Sufficiency
      D. External Sufficiency

- E. Conclusion
- 2. CHAPTER 3: THE BIBLE AND MEANING
  - A. The Meaning of Meaning
  - B. The Text and Meaning
  - C. Conclusion
- 3. CHAPTER 4: THE BIBLE AND GENRE
  - A. Genre and Its Problems
    - a. The Issue of Genre and Audience
    - b. The Issue of Composition
    - c. The Issue of Identification
  - B. Classification and Interpretation
  - C. The Generic Categories
    - a. Language Pattern
    - b. Manner of Communication
    - c. Form
    - d. Function
  - D. The Function of Generic Categories
- III. PART 2: THE ROLE OF THE READER
  - 1. CHAPTER 5: THE READER AND MEANING
  - 2. CHAPTER 6: THE AUDIENCE OF SCRIPTURE
    - A. The Audience of the Bible
    - B. Our Distance from the Text
- IV. PART 3: THE ROLE OF THE AUTHOR
  - 1. CHAPTER 7: THE AUTHOR AND MEANING
    - A. The Author as Originator
    - B. The Authorship of Scripture
  - 2. CHAPTER 8: THE BIBLE IN HISTORY
    - A. The Uses of Extra-Biblical Evidence
    - B. The Challenge of Using Extra-Biblical Data
    - C. Objections
- V. CONCLUSION
- VI. APPENDICES: THEORY IN APPLICATION: EXEGETICAL ESSAYS
  - 1. APPENDIX 1: THE SOVEREIGNTY OF GOD OVER THE REPENTANCE OF MAN: RE-READING DEUTERONOMY 30:1-14
    - A. Identifying the Apodosis of The Condition in Verse 1
    - B. Translating the Conjunction Ki

    C. The Time of Verses 11-14
2. APPENDIX 2: I WILL MAKE THEM LIKE THE CALF: AN EXAMINATION OF JEREMIAH 34:17-22 IN ITS LITERARY CONTEXT
    A. Jeremiah 34:1-16
    B. Jeremiah 34:17-22
    C. Vv. 17-22 in Context
    D. Conclusion
3. APPENDIX 3: THE LAMENT OF THE AFFLICTED: A TRANSLATION OF JOB 30
    A. JOB 30
        a. Strophe 1 – I Am Mocked by Wretches
        b. Strophe 2 – I Am a Byword to the Unrestrained
        c. Strophe 3 – I Am Afflicted by God
4. APPENDIX 4: DO NOT SAY IN YOUR HEART: AN EXPOSITION OF ROMANS 10:1-8 IN THE CONTEXT OF 10:1-13
    A. Exegesis
        a. Israel Needs Salvation, Having Rejected God's Righteousness (10:1-4)
        b. God's New Covenant Righteousness Ended the Law (10:5-8)
            - Excursus: Deuteronomy 31:11-14 in Context
    B. Conclusion
5. APPENDIX 5: 2 THESSALONIANS AND HELL: SEPARATION FROM OR WRATH COMING FORTH FROM GOD?
6. APPENDIX 6: CONVINCED OF BETTER THINGS: AN EXPOSITION OF HEBREWS 6:1-12
    A. Exegesis
        a. Hebrews 6:1-3
        b. Hebrews 6:4-8
        c. Hebrews 6:9-12
    B. Conclusion

ACKNOWLEDGMENTS

The completion of this project and the ideas found within owe themselves to a great many people. Above all, I am completely dependent upon the Spirit of God in all that I have done and do. Without his daily sustaining grace, I would not have pushed through the various trials that arose and continued throughout the writing process. Without his guidance, I know there would be nothing of profit found in this little book. Without his action in my heart, I never would have turned to God and desired to rightly interpret his Word. For all my life and work, I am indebted to the grace of God poured out by Christ Jesus through the Spirit.

God works through means, and there are many people he has placed in my life who have contributed to this volume. First, without the patience of my lovely wife Nicole, I would not have had the time and space—literally, my desk and bookshelves take up a massive chunk of our small home—to finish this project. She has also shown great faith in allowing me to set aside one day of a week to devote to ministry. I am thankful for her faith in this and God's continued provision. Second, without the many friends who have challenged me in my thinking and raised good questions over the years, I never would have been able to complete this work. Among others, this includes Jonathan Hawes, Raphael Haeuser, Daniel Supimpa, Brad Copp, Fred Eaton, Phil Long, Eliezer Arriola, Joel Nafziger, Andre Roberge, and surely many more. I am especially thankful for Brad, who looked at an early manuscript and offered feedback on the whole project and its details. I pray that this book will be of profit to all those who helped shape it and many more. To God be the glory, to him alone. *Soli Deo Gloria.*

SERIES INTRODUCTION

> His divine power has granted to us all things that pertain to life and godliness, through the knowledge of him who called us to his own glory and excellence. – 1 Peter 3:3

God has not left his people without help in the day of trouble—or in the day of prosperity, for that matter. The Bible is God's gift to his people, revealing to them Jesus Christ and the salvation he has accomplished. But the gift of Scripture does not end in revealing our need for salvation and God's provision for it; Scripture is sufficient for the entire Christian life. In his first epistle, Peter tells us that God's divine power has given us everything for life and godliness (1 Pet 3:3, cf. 2 Tim 3:16-17).

In *God's Gifts for the Christian Life*, J. Alexander Rutherford unpacks how God through the Bible has given us what we need to live faithfully in his world. Each volume unpacks the Scriptural teaching against the background of contemporary culture and shows how the Bible provides a firm foundation for our lives. Each volume is intended to be short, around 110-150 pages, and accessible to the interested reader. The primary audience is theologically interested lay Christians (Christians who are not in paid ministry and have no formal theological training), students, and pastors. Several parts are planned, but only the first is in progress.

Part 1, the Christian mind, addresses some of the questions raised by philosophy, especially how humans know anything and gain knowledge. Part 1, Volume 1 addressed epistemology, particularly how God has equipped humans to know him and his world. This is Volume 2, Part 2: this volume, in two parts, considers how God's word functions authoritatively in our lives, namely the nature of reading and applying the Bible (hermeneutics). Volume 3, *The Gift of Seeing*, will present a biblical perspective on metaphysics (the limits and nature of knowledge).

INTRODUCTION

If the Bible is God's gift to guide his people, then no more important question can be asked than this: "how do we interpret it?" If the Bible is God's gift so that we may know him and his world, we need to have an answer. For this reason, I wrote *The Gift of Reading – Part 1*. However, it was beyond the scope of that work to address many secondary questions it would raise, especially for those who have studied hermeneutics before. My goal in that book was to give a foundation for a life-long reading of Scripture rooted in the idea that God gave us a clear word—that Scripture is perspicuous. I argued this point from the explicit teachings and from the implications of Scripture. However, most approaches to hermeneutics today, far from supporting the perspicuity of Scripture, explicitly or implicitly deny it.[1] They make reading the Bible far more difficult than the Bible indicates it should be. That is not to say Scripture claims to be an easy read, it does not (e.g. 2 Pet 3:16), but Scripture does teach that it is written for all Christians and intended by God to be understood by them. It is this claim that I believe many approaches to hermeneutics today deny, that God intends his Scriptures to be understood by all his people, not just scholars in the 21st century.

Consider the words of the Christian scholar George H. Guthrie,

---

[1] In his essay "Is the Doctrine of *Claritas Scripturae* Still Relevant Today?" D. A. A. Carson argues that perspicuity is important but sees the primary challenge to this doctrine coming from Postmodern trends. Though D. A. Carson has done much to make the Word of God accessible to pastors and students worldwide, I will argue below that his own approach to interpretation—Grammatical Historical Exegesis—is equally a danger for this doctrine. D. A. Carson, "Is the Doctrine of Claritas Scripturae Still Relevant Today?," in *Collected Writings on Scripture*, ed. Andrew David Naselli (Wheaton: Crossway, 2010), 179–193.

discussing the work of biblical scholarship,

> The process of learning, at its most basic, involves a deep study of the text of Scripture itself, and for the scholar, a deep study of Scripture calls for the hard work of biblical studies research…. To begin with, we must be able to engage the biblical languages with competence, as well as modern languages that facilitate our dialogue with others in the field. The study of the history of the ancient Near East and the Roman Empire, as well as a wide variety of cultural backgrounds, is mandatory. Since we are dealing with texts in a world of other texts, the ability to access and analyze ancient Near Eastern literature for Old Testament scholars or Second Temple Jewish literature and Greco-Roman literature for those studying the New Testament is mandatory, and increasingly, various aspects of modern linguistic theory play a part in our work as well. To understand and enter into dialogue with others in the field, we also must have some familiarity with the dizzying array of "criticisms," both higher and lower, in the history of investigating the biblical literature. Further, since texts are always interpreted, we need an awareness of what is going on in the areas of philosophical hermeneutics and biblical theology. On top of all this, we must keep up with developments in our own areas of focus—and bibliography has become daunting in almost all specializations.[2]

There are few scholars who have laboured more than George Guthrie in furthering the understanding of the Bible among Christians outside of Academia,[3] and his zeal for God and his Word is clear in his work. However, the methodology Guthrie has adopted in his reading of Scripture subtly undermines this labour. In this quote, Guthrie is discussing the work of the Christian biblical scholar, not the average Christian reading their Bible, yet it is disingenuous to think that such work is necessary for the scholar alone and not for everyone else.

Christian biblical scholars do all this work because they want to properly understand the text before them. They study modern languages so they can interact with the relevant scholarship in other fields. Among these other fields, they must study the history of the Ancient Near East, the Roman

---

[2] George H. Guthrie, "The Study of Holy Scripture and the Work of Christian Higher Education," in *Christian Higher Education*, eds. David S. Dockery and Christopher W. Morgan, (Crossway, 2018), 83.

[3] Cf. https://georgehguthrie.com/

Empire, and other cultures because the biblical texts were written within these cultures. To understand and dialogue with these and other fields, the scholar must learn the various criticisms used to analyse the production and meaning of the biblical text. Indeed, the very question of the possibility of interpretation and the appropriate way to do it must be investigated: how can anyone hope to interpret the text if they do not have an idea of what "interpretation" means? Moreover, they need to study the ins and outs of Old Testament studies, New Testament Studies, of each book, of each corpus (The Torah, Prophets, Gospels, etc.), and of the relevant extra-biblical literature. This is a mountain of work, but the Christian scholar only undertakes it because they think it will help them understand the text. In some fields, the Bible might be studied in conjunction with these fields in order to learn more about the Ancient Near East or the Roman World, but Guthrie is claiming that the biblical scholar needs to study these things to learn more about the Bible—to interpret it. If God has given Scripture to guide his people and this guidance only comes through the right interpretation of Scripture, then every Christian needs to do what is necessary to properly interpret the Scriptures. Think about the implications if this is true.[4]

If pastors and lay Christians cannot hope to learn and master the materials necessary for sound biblical studies, they are left dependent on the scholarly commentaries. Yet there are dozens of commentaries on each biblical book, commentaries that not only disagree in the details but in their entire approach to interpreting a book. How can anyone—including the scholars themselves—have sufficient understanding of the necessary materials to properly weigh the arguments presented for specific interpretive approaches and then for a particular interpretation of a passage. And the lay Christian cannot just rely on their pastor's preaching alone for access to the Word of God. Pastors have a limited time each week and an entire congregation to whom they minister, but Christians are called to teach their children the word of God and to live their entire lives in light of Scripture. The preaching of the Word plays an essential role in the life of a Christian, but it cannot be the

---

[4] I address some of the problems with such thinking in my book *The Gift of Knowing*, but I intend to address it more thoroughly in an upcoming book on training Christian teachers.

only access a believer has to God's Word.

If this is truly what is necessary to interpret Scripture properly, no one—not even the scholar—has a hope of arriving at a confident conclusion concerning the text's meaning. This is disastrous if the Bible is our only hope to know anything in this world, as I argue in my book *The Gift of Knowing*. If the Bible is our only access to the saving Gospel of Jesus Christ, then a failure to understand it means that we have lost access to the very message that can save us. If the Bible is God's guide for life before him, equipping us for every good work (2 Tim 3:16-17), but is inaccessible, what hope do we have for living a life pleasing before Him?

If this is true, if the present approach(es) to biblical interpretation leads to nihilism concerning the text's meaning, then we need an alternative approach to reading the Bible, a way of reading the Bible that is rooted in its own authority. I have argued for such an approach in *The Gift of Reading Part I*.

In this book, I do not intend to revisit that same territory; instead, I hope to consider more closely the alternate approaches to hermeneutics among Evangelicals and biblical scholars. First, in doing so I hope to prove the above assertions, namely, that present approaches to hermeneutics undermine the perspicuity of Scripture and lay impassable barriers before the interpreter. Second, I hope to unpack some of the theory behind the hermeneutical approach presented in the first book. Namely, I hope to address to a greater extent the questions of the Bible's role in its own interpretation, of meaning, and of the Bible's relation to history.

To do this, to show the hopelessness of the contemporary hermeneutical endeavour and to flush out the approach of the first book, we will first survey the history of hermeneutics. This will be an unfortunately brief survey, for my strengths lie elsewhere, yet I hope it will lay a solid foundation for the following discussion. In the three main parts of the book, we will consider the role of the Bible (Part 1), particularly the question of authority and the textual aspect of meaning; the role of the reader (Part 2), particularly the nature of the biblical audience and the reader's contribution to meaning; and the role of the author (Part 3), particularly the author's role in meaning and the relationship between the Bible and history.

I pray that this book will help us to better understand our contemporary circumstances and point us back to the Word of God as a firm anchor for our lives. It is my prayer that this book would point us back to Scripture as a clear, sufficient, and authoritative foundation for life and ministry. Scripture has such a breadth and depth that it demands from the scholar a life of rigorous study yet simultaneously beckons the thirsty child of God, come, be quenched with the glory of God shining forth and his all-sufficient wisdom graciously given to his people. May God grant to us the blessings that come from being firmly rooted in his Word:

> Blessed is the man
> > who walks not in the counsel of the wicked,
> nor stands in the way of sinners,
> > nor sits in the seat of scoffers;
> but his delight is in the law of the LORD,
> > and on his law he meditates day and night.
>
> He is like a tree
> > planted by streams of water
> that yields its fruit in its season,
> > and its leaf does not wither.
> In all that he does, he prospers.
> The wicked are not so,
> > but are like chaff that the wind drives away.
>
> Therefore the wicked will not stand in the judgment,
> > nor sinners in the congregation of the righteous;
> for the LORD knows the way of the righteous,
> > but the way of the wicked will perish. (Ps 1:1-6)

1

APPROACHES TO HERMENEUTICS

Throughout the history of the Church, Christians (and the Jews before them) have wrestled with God's authoritative revelation in Scripture and how to interpret it. They have wrestled with how to apply God's words to and through the Old Testament prophets and New Testament apostles to a people living hundreds—even thousands—of years later. It can be disheartening to consider all the different approaches that have been taken to biblical interpretation—to hermeneutics—throughout the history of the Church.

However, despite the dozens of approaches we witness in the literature, it is encouraging to observe that throughout the ages, the Bible has been understood. That is, whether the method consciously adopted was "allegorical" or "literal," Christians have consistently confessed the teaching of Scripture, that Jesus is fully God and fully man, that there will be a resurrection from the dead when Christ returns, that Jesus was crucified under Pontius Pilate and rose again on the 3rd day, etc. There is debate, yet it is clear when we study the history of God's people that his Word is getting through, that it is being understood and responded to. That is, whatever our method may or may not say about the clarity (or perspicuity) of Scripture and our ability to read it, men, women, and children have understood the Word of God read and proclaimed for several millennia. Indeed, until recent years, the debate over the interpretation of Scripture has not been whether the words on the page can be understood but whether or not there is additional meaning beyond these words.

Closely related to this debate over additional meaning is the question of application, namely, how do we relate the words of Scripture to our lives? What do we do with them? Specifically, what do we do with difficult texts or those that are hard to apply? This is where, in my judgment, the confusion begins, yet this is also where Scripture speaks most clearly.

The Bible does not provide us with a definition of "meaning," though it has implications for our definitions. It does not give us a treatise on its relationship to history, though it does give us ample guidance in this regard. Yet, Scripture is clear on whom it was written for and how they are to respond to it—as I have attempted to show in *The Gift of Reading – Part 1* and will continue to argue here. Furthermore, Scripture is clear that it bears ultimate authority, authority to define good and bad, right and wrong (see *The Gift of Knowing*). Thus, Scripture is abundantly clear concerning how it ought to be used, concerning its application. More often than naught, the diversity of hermeneutical approaches throughout the history of the church emerges out of confusion over these two points, the authority and audience of Scripture. It seems, therefore, that Scripture has something to say on the topics where interpretation is most contentious.

As we briefly survey the history of hermeneutics, keep these things in mind, the question of audience and authority. For convenience's sake, we will consider the various approaches to hermeneutics according to their relationship to three major movements in Western philosophy, Premodernism, dominated by the Greek philosophers; Modernism, dominated by the empirical sciences and enlightenment philosophy; and Postmodernism, dominated by relativism or the authority of the thinking person.[1]

A. <u>Hermeneutics in Pre-Modernism</u>

We could begin our discussion with the early Jewish forms of interpretation, such as is found in the early Pesher commentaries and later Midrash, but I think it will be more fruitful to begin with early Christian hermeneutics. Among the many reasons for this, the Christian writers are more explicit about what they are doing, so it is easier to discuss their methods, and much of what the 1st century Jews did in interpretation is echoed in later Christian

---

[1] It may be appropriate to observe a certain chronological arrogance in the way contemporary philosophy and historical studies consider the world, as if Modernism is the defining moment in the history of the world. Modernism is not so different from pre-modernism and is guilty of as much ignorance and wrong as its predecessors. Nevertheless, these categories remain useful.

works.[2]

a. *Irenaeus and the Rule of Truth*

There was much fruitful discussion among the apostolic and early church fathers about particular hermeneutical issues, such as how the Old Testament relates to the New—specifically prophecy and typology (an issue we considered briefly in *The Gift of Reading – Part 1*). Attention was particularly given to the role of Scripture in its own interpretation. The early Church Fathers were quick to identify and emphasize the importance of Scripture for its own interpretation, namely, its authority over us to lead us in interpreting it. Irenaeus argued that Scripture functioned as a "rule of truth," a guide to its own interpretation; he argued that the Valentinian Gnostics missed the meaning of the Scriptures by arguing from individual snippets of text and in doing so disregarding "the order and connection of the Scriptures, and so far as in them lies, dismember[ing] and destroy[ing] the truth."[3] he describes their practice like this,

> Their manner of acting is just as if one, when a beautiful image of a king has been constructed by some skilful artist out of precious jewels, should then take this likeness of man all to pieces, should rearrange the gems, and so fit them together as to make them into the form of a dog or of a fox, and even that but poorly executed; and should then maintain and declare that *this* was the beautiful image of the king which the skilful artist constructed, pointing to the jewels which had been admirably fitted together by the first artist to form the image of the king, but have been with bad effect transferred by the latter one to the shape of a dog, and by thus exhibiting the jewels, should deceive the ignorant who had no conception what a king's form was like, and persuade them that that miserable likeness of the fox was, in fact, the beautiful image of the king. In like manner do these persons patch together old wives' fables, and then endeavour, by violently drawing away from their proper connection, words, expressions, and parables whenever found, to adapt the oracles of

---

[2] E.g. Philo practiced allegorical interpretation like many church fathers. Both are dependent on the Greek allegorical tradition for their methods.

[3] This is from *Against Heresies*, 1.8.1 according to the translation in Philip Schaff's *Ante-Nicene Fathers*.

God to their baseless fiction.[4]

Here, Irenaeus charges the Valentinians with wrenching the Scriptures from their textual connections—from the context in which they should be read—and jamming them together to prove their point.[5]

Later in the work, he speaks of the need to interpret the parables in light of the clear teaching of Scripture, by doing so he "he who explains [the parables] will do so without danger, and the parables will receive a like interpretation from all, and the body of truth will remain entire, with a harmonious adaptation of its members, and without any collision [of its several parts]."[6] Elsewhere, in his *Demonstration of the Apostolic Preaching*, he summarizes this rule according to various doctrines concerning the Father, Son, and Holy Spirit (par. 6). Adriani Rodrigues is surely right when he summarizes Irenaeus thought in this way;

> In these considerations, the rule of faith seems to be described as a framework or system that serves as the correct set of presuppositions or preunderstanding for the activity of biblical interpretation. However, this rule does not appear to be distinguished from Scripture.[7]

This rule seems to be the Scripture, its canonical shape and teaching, applied to its own interpretation. This is a profound insight into the function of Scripture in its own interpretation, an insight that lies at the heart of my project in these two books. In Irenaeus and many of the early fathers, Scripture was given a preeminent role in its own interpretation.

In the following centuries, the rule of Scripture interpreting Scripture continued to be employed, yet it sometimes took on a function that undermined Scripture's own authority to confront and challenge the

---

[4] Ibid.

[5] Their twisting of Scripture would be like taking Jesus' words, "relax, eat, drink, be merry" as a command to be practiced instead of the foolish words of the rich man in Jesus' parable (Luke 12:19).

[6] The first note is my own, the second is from Schaff. This is again taken from Schaff's *Ante-Nicene Fathers*.

[7] From his article, "The Rule of Faith and Biblical Interpretation in Evangelical Theological Interpretation of Scripture," Themelios 43.2 (2018), 259-260.

presuppositions of its readers.⁸ Moving past Irenaeus, we see this in the most (in)famous approach to interpreting Scripture among the early Christians, allegorical or spiritual interpretation.

b. *Allegorical Interpretation*

Allegorical interpretation is often associated with the Alexandrian Catechetical school (its most prominent figures being Clement of Alexandria and Origen) but can be found throughout the writings of the Church Fathers. Moisés Silva reminds us that it is too simplistic to associate allegorical interpretation with the Alexandrians alone, but it is also simplistic to think that allegorical interpretation was the only hermeneutic used by these Fathers. To the contrary, even Origin—infamous as he is for his allegorizing—believed that much of the biblical narrative is historical and that there is a literal meaning. However, as we will see, this literal sense was for the simple believer; allegorical interpretation was for the more spiritual Christian.⁹

Allegorical interpretation was a practice the early Christians and 1st-century Jews adopted from the Greek philosophical schools. For the Greeks, allegorizing was a way to find the principles of their philosophy in the ancient Greek epics; for the Philo the Jew, it was a way of finding Platonic philosophy in the writings of Moses and the Old Testament. For the Christians, allegory was a tool used to find Spiritual truths of Christianity and Christianised Greek philosophy in Scripture. Loosely, allegorical interpretation mirrored the Greek philosophy it evolved out of, "in Platonic thought, earthly things are inferior to the heavenly forms and only shadows of them. In the same way, the literal sense of the Bible is inferior to the spiritual sense."¹⁰ I would add, "and the literal sense is a shadow of the spiritual sense." Allegorical interpretation sought to look through the historical or literal sense to a greater

---

⁸ I deal with presuppositions in the first book of this series, *The Gift of Knowing*. We could define a presupposition as, "one of our foundational beliefs by which we automatically—without deliberate thought—interpret all our experience and from which we do all our reasoning" (16).

⁹ Moisés Silva, *Has the Church Misread the Bible?* in Moisés Silva, ed., *Foundations of Contemporary Interpretation* (Grand Rapids: Zondervan, 1996), 48–54.

¹⁰ Graeme Goldsworthy, *Gospel-Centered Hermeneutics: Foundations and Principles of Evangelical Biblical Interpretation* (Downers Grove: InterVarsity Press, 2006), 95.

spiritual or philosophical truth. Clement, for example, was able to identify in the story of the prodigal son several spiritual truths, such that "the robe that the father gave to the prodigal represents immortality; the shoe represent the upward progress of the soul; and the fatted calf represents Christ as the source of spiritual nourishment for Christians."[11] In particular, allegorical interpretation was seen as a way to resolve apparent difficulties in Scripture. In fact, not all passages of Scripture were to be interpreted allegorically.

Saint Augustine was a careful reader of Scripture and argued that careful attention to the text would yield its meaning. Indeed, he was so bold as to claim that it is "very rare and very difficult to find any ambiguity in the case of proper words, as far at least as Holy Scripture is concerned, which neither the context, showing the design of the writer, nor a comparison of translations, nor a reference to the original tongue, will suffice to explain."[12] However, there are places in Scripture where "figurative words" are used and where taking them as literal, or according to their normal historical sense, would be dangerous. From the example he uses and the evidence of his practice, what he intends is not metaphorical speech, which is probably considered part of the ambiguous language made clear in context, but texts meant to be read allegorically:

> For he who follows the letter takes figurative words as if they were proper, and does not carry out what is indicated by a proper word into its secondary signification; but, if he hears of the Sabbath, for example, thinks of nothing but the one day out of seven which recurs in constant succession; and when he hears of a sacrifice, does not carry his thoughts beyond the customary offerings of victims from the flock, and of the fruits of the earth. Now it is surely a miserable slavery of the soul to take signs for things, and to be unable to lift the eye of the mind above what is corporeal and created, that it may drink in eternal light.[13]

---

[11] William W Klein, Craig L. Blomberg, and Robert L. Hubbard Jr., *Introduction to Biblical Interpretation*, ed. Kermit A. Ecklebarger (Dallas: Word Publishing, 1993), 34.

[12] Saint Augustine, *On Doctrine*, Book 3, chapter 4 in Philip Schaff, *A Select Library of the Nicene and Post-Nicene Fathers of the Christian Church: St Augustin's City of God and Christian Doctrine*, vol. 2, A Select Library of the Nicene and Post-Nicene Fathers of the Christian Church (Buffalo: The Christian Literature Company, 1887).

[13] Ibid, Book 3, chapter 5. Notice the Platonic language here.

For Origen and Augustine, allegory was not a hermeneutic for reading all Scripture but a writing strategy used by the biblical authors, a writing strategy that only the more spiritual and learned readers of Scripture would discern.

They thought that allegorical reading was recognized by difficulties in the text, by moral truths that seemed unpalatable or historical events that could not have happened, according to their judgment. "Allegorical reading is pursued in addition to the literal exegesis, which is seldom wholly eliminated. It is almost never applied to whole biblical books; rather, it is used only for problematic, that is incomprehensible, morally objectionable or seemingly nonsensical passages."[14]

This is ultimately a problematic approach, for by addressing apparent difficulties in Scripture with such a hermeneutic, the reader is able to avoid submitting his or her intellect and judgment to Scripture in the very place it is being challenged. A similar phenomenon happens today when readers committed to naturalism readers the miracles of Scripture in terms of purely natural phenomenon: because God—if he exists—cannot interfere in the natural world, miracles must be merely coincidental events explained by the regular working of the world.[15] In his book *On the First Principles,* Origen explains in some detail the phenomenon that revealed to him an allegorical passage,

> But since, if the usefulness of the legislation, and the sequence and beauty of the history, were universally evident of itself, we should not believe that any other thing could be understood in the Scriptures save what was obvious, the word of God has arranged that certain stumbling blocks, as it were, and offences, and impossibilities, should be introduced into the midst of the law and the history, in order that we may not, through being drawn away in all directions by the merely attractive nature of the language, either altogether fall away from the (true) doctrines, as learning nothing worthy of God, or, by not departing from the letter, come to the knowledge of nothing more divine… the Scripture interwove in the

---

[14] Therese Fuhrer, "Allegorical Reading and Writing in Augustine's Confessions," in *In Search of Truth. Augustine, Manichaeism and Other Gnosticism,* ed. Jacob Albert van den Berg et al. (Leiden, The Netherlands: Brill, 2010), 27.

[15] One thinks of cable documentaries on biblical events, one of which attempted to explain the pillar of fire by which God led his people in the Exodus as oil fields burning.

history (the account of) some event that did not take place, sometimes what could not have happened; sometimes what could, but did not. And sometimes a few words are interpolated which are not true in their literal acceptation, and sometimes a larger number. And a similar practice also is to be noticed with regard to the legislation, in which is often to be found what is useful in itself, and appropriate to the times of the legislation; and sometimes also what does not appear to be of utility; and at other times impossibilities are recorded for the sake of the more skilful and inquisitive, in order that they may give themselves to the toil of investigating what is written, and thus attain to a becoming conviction of the manner in which a meaning worthy of God must be sought out in such subjects.[16]

Two things should be observed in Origen's argument here. First, interestingly enough, his argument presupposes Scripture's inerrancy while apparently undermining it. That is, he assumes that Scripture cannot make errors, so when he discerns an error, it must be an intentional cue to seek a deeper meaning. This reveals a more serious concern: for Origen, Augustine, and those who adopt a similar approach to discern an error in Scripture, they must assume they have authority over Scripture to determine its truthfulness. That is, they must have a standard other than Scripture by which to discern what is tenable in their reading. If Scripture were their standard, it would be impossible to observe an error or incongruity, for if Scripture is the highest authority, then apparent errors reveal error only in the reader.[17]

In sum, though they rightly identified a literal sense in Scripture and even confessed that this literal sense was almost always attainable, Origen and Augustine struggled with some areas of application and subtly rejected the Scriptures own claims to absolute authority with their allegorical interpretation.

c.   *The Reformation*

The same trends observed in the church fathers continued throughout the middle ages; centuries of Christian teachers continued to interpret the

---

[16] Origen, *De Principiis* (Greek), Book 4, chapter 15 in A. Roberts and J. Donaldson, *Ante-Nicene Christian Library: Translations of the Writings of the Fathers Down to A.D. 325*, Ante-Nicene Christian Library: Translations of the Writings of the Fathers Down to A.D. 325 v. 10 (T&T Clark, 1895).

[17] See further *The Gift of Knowing*.

Scriptures allegorically, yet they often maintained that their allegories must be grounded in the literal sense of Scripture. There was at this time push back against allegorizing, with some significant teachers elevating the literal sense of Scripture above the allegorical sense.[18] Albert the Great and Thomas Aquinas both moved away from allegorical interpretation towards the words of Scripture:

> Albert assumed that "that [sic] there was but one genuine exegesis worthy of the name; that which explains the sense intended by the author and is indicated by the text itself": the literal sense, therefore, provided the basis for the three spiritual senses, which Albert understood as pedagogical extensions of the letter. Aquinas built on this assumption and moved away from the method of the postils or annotations toward an analysis of the text in terms of its logical divisions and their relationship to one another.... Aquinas' commentaries are "almost exclusively occupied" with the exposition of the literal sense, which he also identified as the *fundamentum historiae* [the sense based in history]. Indeed, Aquinas commented with some frequency that the *primus sensus* [the first sense] and *prima expositio* [the best explanation] was *magis litteralis* [the more literal],[19] and that the purpose of exegesis was to identify the "intention" of the words, of the book, or of the

---

[18] Klein, et al., claim that Thomas Aquinas argued for the literal sense of Scripture. Klein, Blomberg, and Hubbard Jr., *Introduction to Biblical Interpretation*, 39.

During the middle ages, the view appears to have emerged of a fourfold sense of Scripture, in addition to the literal or historical, there was also the moral and anagogical senses. A short rhyme supposedly circulating at this time expresses what is intended by these quite clearly; "The letter shows us what God and our fathers did; the allegory shows us where our faith is hid; the moral meaning gives us rules of daily life; the anagogy shows us where we end our strife." Ibid., 38.

In the work *Glossa ordinaria*, the senses where defined in this manner, "*historia*, which tells what happened (*res gestae*); *allegoria*, in which one thing is understood through another; *tropologia*, which is moral declaration, and which deals with the ordering of behavior; *anagoge*, through which we are led to higher things that we might be drawn to the highest and heavenly." Richard A. Muller, *Post-Reformation Reformed Dogmatics Volume 2: Holy Scripture: The Cognitive Foundation of Theology*, vol. 2 (Grand Rapids: Baker Book House, 1987), 17.

[19] "Literal" here means something like my definition below, the clear sense of the text whether it is metaphorical or plainer.

writer.[20]

In the pre-reformation ages, we see that the so-called "literal" sense remained important, though allegorizing was frequent. The rules for attaining the literal sense were much the same as those Augustine expressed in *On Doctrine*, yet Aquinas added that this literal sense was singular and associated with "intention." These ideas prove to be highly influential in the modern era yet are fraught with difficulties. However, for Aquinas these are firmly rooted in the grammatical or literal sense of the text. Continuing with our brief history, it was in the Reformation that the literal sense rose to forefront of biblical interpretation, though allegorizing was still present.

Steeped as he was in the monastic traditions, it was hard for Luther to set aside allegorical interpretation completely, and so it is present in his work. However, with the other reformers, his teaching concerning biblical interpretation set aside allegorical interpretation for the literal meaning. Where he did allegorize, he sought to find truths about Christ and the Gospel in the Old Testament. Setting aside the practice of allegorizing among Luther and the reformers, I want to consider their development of the interpretation of the literal sense of Scripture.

At this point, we should probably clarify what we mean by "literal sense." As I believe is clear from Origen and Augustine, the literal sense does not mean "literal" as opposed to "metaphorical," but literal as the plain sense of the words of Scripture. The literal sense is what is said, interpreted appropriately in its context, not anything we might discern behind or above the words of the text. "Literal" may thus encompass literary conventions such as symbolism, intentional allegory, or metaphor but excludes all meaning that is not indicated by the written context of words, phrases, sentences, paragraphs, etc., which are the object of our interpretation. Luther's allegories are not "literal" in this sense because there is nothing in the context to connect his interpretations with the text,[21] unlike, for example, Paul's

---

[20] Muller, *Post-Reformation Reformed Dogmatics Volume 2: Holy Scripture: The Cognitive Foundation of Theology*, 2:18–19.

[21] Consider his allegory of the doves in Genesis 8:6-12, which can be read here http://henrycenter.tiu.edu/2016/01/luther-allegory-doves/. Luther interprets the raven and doves sent forth by Noah as pictures of the Law and Gospel, respectively.

"allegorical" argument in Galatians 4. We could define the literal sense as the meaning of the text as determined by its linguistic and literary context.[22] We will consider "meaning" to a greater depth in a later chapter.

Returning our attention to the reformers, several key emphases emerge in their writings concerning Scripture and interpretation. For both Calvin and Luther, the Holy Spirit had an essential role in guiding the reader in the right reading of Scripture and confirming it to them. This was called by Luther "internal perspicuity," whereby the Spirit's internal witness allows the Christian to discern and recognize God's voice in Scripture and to evaluate the teachings of man.[23] This internal work was necessary but not sufficient; Scripture also had an external perspicuity. The radical reformers, from whom the Anabaptist tradition derives, went farther than the magisterial reformers in arguing that the Spirit was the sole arbiter of meaning, even claiming that the Spirit revealed meaning beyond the letter of the text. The reformers responded that the Spirit helped the believer discern the meaning that was clear in the text.[24] Thus, external perspicuity was a partial answer to the extremes of the radical reformers: Luther considered Scripture to be reasonably clear in its meaning so that Christians—those who have the internal testimony of the Spirit—can argue and resolve disputes of the

---

[22] Following Kevin J. Vanhoozer, Iain Provan brings authorial action into the definition of "literal." Against the sort of literalism that misses the point of a text, Provan argues that a "truly literal reading pays attention to the 'speech acts' of the author, and not just the words themselves... The literal sense of a text is discovered, then, not only by consulting a dictionary about what a word... typically means in the language spoken by the author (which is indeed important), but also by paying attention to how the word is used in a particularly speech act." As will become clear later, the language of "speech act" is less than helpful for understanding the meaning of biblical texts. However, this understanding of literal is very similar to what I have proposed, in that "literal" encompasses all forms of literary communication. Iain W. Provan, *The Reformation and the Right Reading of Scripture* (Waco, Texas: Baylor University Press, 2017), 87–88.

[23] Martin Luther, *The Bondage of the Will*, ed. J. I Packer and O. R Johnston (Grand Rapids: Fleming H. Revell, 2003), 124; Klein, Blomberg, and Hubbard Jr., *Introduction to Biblical Interpretation*, 41.

[24] Cf. Kevin J. Vanhoozer, *Biblical Authority after Babel: Retrieving the Solas in the Spirit of Mere Protestant Christianity* (Grand Rapids: Brazos, 2016), 116; Provan, *The Reformation and the Right Reading of Scripture*, 286.

meaning of Scripture.[25]

Over-against the Catholic counter-reformers' emphasis on Tradition as the interpreter of Scripture, Luther and the rest of the Reformers also reaffirmed the early church teaching that Scripture interprets Scripture, which we saw in Irenaeus.[26] The later English Puritan, William Ames, wrote that the Scriptures "give light to themselves, which should be uncovered diligently by men and communicated to others according to their calling."[27] In the Westminster Confession, the English divines wrote that "The infallible rule of interpretation of Scripture, is the Scripture itself; and therefore, when there is a question about the true and full sense of any scripture (which is not manifold, but one), it may be searched and known by other places that speak more clearly" (1.9). One of the key ways the later reformers unpacked this "infallible rule," was through a biblical theology of covenants, through which the relationship between New and Old Testaments could be understood.

Lastly, they appealed to the text of Scripture, interpreted in the context of Scripture and according to its grammar and context, as the basis of meaning. According to Ames, "Some knowledge, at least, of [the original languages] is necessary for a precise understanding of the Scriptures, for they are to be understood by the same means required for other human writings, i.e. skill and experience in logic, rhetoric, grammar, and the languages."[28] The Scriptures, according to Luther, are clear in their meaning, in its literal sense; any unclarity comes from our own confusion or lack of knowledge.[29] At least for Ames, this literal sense was singular; "there is only one meaning for every

---

[25] Luther, *The Bondage*, 125; William Ames, *The Marrow of Theology*, trans. John D. Eusden (Grand Rapids: Baker Books, 1997), 188.

[26] Cf. Luther's letter to the Catholic Emers, "Dr. Martin Luther's Answer to the Superchristian, Superspiritual, Superlearned Book of Goat Emser of Leipzig."

[27] Ames, *The Marrow of Theology*, 188.

[28] Ibid., he makes the exception that the Spirit is necessary.

[29] Ibid., 125. Cf. Martin Luther, *Sermons by Martin Luther: Volume 1; Sermons on Gospel Texts for Advent, Christmas, and Epiphany*, ed. John Nicholas Lenker, vol. 1 (Albany, Ore: AGES Bible Software, 1997), 330; Martin Luther, "Dr. Martin Luther's Answer to the Superchristian, Superspiritual, Superlearned Book of Goat Emser of Leipzig," in *Works of Martin Luther*, trans. A. Steimle, vol. 3 (Albany, Ore: AGES Bible Software, 1997), 255–256; Mark Thompson, *A Sure Ground on Which to Stand: The Relation of Authority and Interpretive Method in Luther's Approach to Scripture* (Carlisle; Waynesboro, GA: Paternoster, 2004), 204, 208.

place in Scripture. Otherwise, the meaning of Scripture would not only be unclear and uncertain, but there would be no meaning at all—for anything which does not mean one thing surely means nothing."[30]

B. Hermeneutics in Modernism

After the Reformation, the Western world underwent tremendous change. When the ashes settled, a new movement came on the scene. Out of the Renaissance and Reformation emerged the Enlightenment (17th-18th centuries) and the worldview of Modernism after that. During the Enlightenment, philosophy and the scientific revolution were transforming the world. Within the scientific and philosophical world, there was a significant departure from the biblical presuppositions of the Reformation—that the Bible was the ultimate authority for all human life—and a renewed commitment to the autonomy and rationality of humans. As the Modern world emerged after the Enlightenment, there was an intense interest in the scientific study of history or "historical criticism," the objective study of the history behind texts. (I have covered this period to some extent in *The Gift of Knowing* and in *The Gift of Seeing;* the philosophical movements covered there shed light on the related evolution of biblical studies at this time.)

Biblical studies became the subject not only of Christian study but of intense scholarly scrutiny from both the orthodox and non-orthodox, the Christian and atheist (or deist). The variety of approaches to the biblical text that developed during this time are too numerous to account for here, but we can consider three broad trends of biblical interpretation during the Modern period (19th-20th centuries). There was the critical approach that flourished among rationalistic Protestantism and atheistic biblical studies; the Evangelical or orthodox approach that followed the Reformers and culminated in the so-called "Grammatical-Historical" approach; and various anti-modern views, such as the anti-rationalist approach taken by Martin Kähler and his disciples.

a. *Critical Hermeneutics*

Among the universities in post-reformation Europe, the default approach to

---

[30] Ames, *The Marrow of Theology*, 188.

studying the Bible was that of historical criticism, the objective study of the text and the world in which it was formed. As an "objective study," historical criticism was to be done apart from theological commitments, without prejudicing the potential outcomes of biblical study. This represents the first time in "Christian" (loosely conceived of course) biblical studies that the principle of "Scripture interprets Scripture" was outright rejected. Richard N. and R. Kendall Soulen in their *Handbook of Biblical Criticism* outline the presuppositions of this model as follows;

> (1) that reality is uniform and universal; (2) that it is accessible to human reason and investigation; (3) that all events historical and natural occurring within it are in principle interconnected and comparable by analogy; and (4) that humanity's contemporary experience of reality can provide objective criteria by which what could or could not have happened in the past can be determined.[31]

This approach was not really the "objective" study of Scripture but the atheistic study of Scripture, the study of the Bible and the events it records on the presuppositions that God either does not exist or that he does not interfere in his creation (i.e. deism). Not only did the historical-critical approach reject the principle of Scripture interpreting Scripture, but it also rejected the necessity of the Spirit for interpreting Scripture rightly and the search for the literal meaning of the text.

That is, no longer were scholars interested in the meaning—singular or plural—of the text and its contemporary application; they were interested in the events recorded in the text and the history of the text's formation. Biblical studies thus moved away from application (whether theological or practical) to description. Commentaries at this time and onward came to be dominated with the description of text history, the background of the text, and the nuances of language and text criticism (the study of what manuscript reading represents the original).

This broad approach of historical criticism generated a myriad of criticisms, specific approaches to the historical study of the Bible. "Criticism" in biblical studies after this point has come to refer to a specific scholarly

---

[31] Richard N. Soulen and R. Kendall Soulen, *Handbook of Biblical Criticism: Now Includes Precritical and Postcritical Interpretation*, 3rd Revised and Expanded. (Louisville; London: Westminster John Knox, 2001), 78.

approach to the Bible (such as feminist criticism, rhetorical criticism, etc.). Considering three of the early approaches to historical criticism should serve to illustrate this general approach.

i. Source Criticism

Source Criticism may be the preeminent form of Historical criticism in the history of biblical studies. Many theorists in the 19th century contributed to this approach, but its most significant contributor may be Julius Wellhausen, whose *Prolegomena to the History Israel* set the agenda for Historical Criticism for the next century. By reading the biblical text carefully, primarily the Pentateuch (Genesis – Deuteronomy), source critics thought they could delineate the original sources that were used to compile the Pentateuch. Classically, critics identified four sources behind the Pentateuch, each source named after its distinguishing features; J, the Jehovist or Yahwist; E, the Elohist; D, the Deuteronomist; and P, the Priestly source. For example, J was supposed to use the divine name Jehovah (or Yahweh) while E employed the divine name Elohim. It was thought that two sources were indicated by the interweaving of these names throughout the biblical text. In other cases, supposedly contradictory accounts were thought to betray different sources.

It was argued, for example, that Genesis 1 and 2 represented two creation accounts from different sources juxtaposed in the final source. Source criticism, especially JEDP, loomed over the following century of biblical studies, only going out of fashion in the 80s and 90s. In some circles, it still finds favour (e.g. some volumes of The Word Biblical Commentary). Source criticism sometimes appears in New Testament studies as a tool for textual criticism in the Gospels, but its Modernist and unorthodox starting assumptions have led to its rejection by secular postmodern interpreters and orthodox Christian interpreters.[32]

---

[32] Many of its assumptions are also plainly false. In addition to the atheistic presuppositions quoted from the Soulens above, OT source critics also rejected inerrancy and biblical authority—which is how they could view Genesis 1 & 2 as contradictory—and gave the biblical authors far less credit than is due. Many of the supposed contradictions and discrepancies are actual rhetorical and literary devices used to recount the biblical narrative, other supposed contradictions simply do not exist. This view also does not see Scripture as an authoritative document delivered by God and addressed to present believers.

ii. Form & Tradition Criticism

Another historical-critical movement that has loomed large over the history of interpretation is that of Form Criticism and its child Tradition Criticism. Essentially, Form Criticism seeks to delineate the different types of literary forms used by the biblical authors—such as legendary stories, myths, legal cases, etc. Herman Gunkel, for example, argues that Genesis is composed of "legends." A legend is a poetic and subjective account of a historical event that begins orally; it is a crafted historical account meant to teach an idea. Because legends originated as oral traditions, interpretation must concern the original oral form, not the final written form.[33]

Tradition criticism sought to trace the evolution of literature through the process of its oral transmission. While neither of these criticisms necessarily rests on atheistic presuppositions, their value for Christian biblical studies is questionable. Regarding Tradition criticism, even if its starting presupposition that biblical literature began in an oral form were true and the outline of its transmission accurate—a very big if—this would not have any effect on Christian biblical interpretation, which involves interpreting Scripture as a canonical document written by God to govern his covenant people. Form criticism can be helpful at times, but as we will see in chapter 3, "form" and "genre" are slippery terms. Though their study has yielded some fruit, much of the product of form criticism is speculative and unhelpful for the study of the Bible as God has given it to his people.

In New Testament Studies, form criticism became associated with the existential interpretative approach of Rudolf Bultmann. Bultmann argued that the biblical stories could not be the substance of God's revelation, for the progress of science in the modern age has revealed a world far different from that described in the New Testament; "We cannot use electric lights and radios and, in the event of illness, avail ourselves of modern medical and clinical means and at the same time believe in the spirit and wonder world of the New Testament."[34] his brand of form criticism involved identifying the form of the text and performing demythologization, looking through the objectifying presentation of the NT—i.e. the way it cloths existential truths

---

[33] Cf. Herman Gunkel, *Genesis*, trans. of the 1910 ed. (Macon: Mercer University, 1997).

[34] Rudolf Bultmann, *New Testament and Mythology and Other Basic Writings*, trans. Schubert Miles Ogden (Philadelphia: Fortress Press, 1989), 4.

in mythological language—for the "understanding of existence that expresses itself in them."[35] Only in this way would the message of the NT be accepted in the modern scientific age.[36]

Though the outcomes of historical criticism have sometimes been adopted by more conservative biblical interpreters, such approaches could not serve as the basis for theology and church teaching. For this, the biblical text needed to be read to discern how God was speaking to his people through it. Continuing in the same interpretive tradition as the reformers, conservative biblical scholars formulated the rules of interpretation more clearly in response to historical criticism and its bedfellows. This arc of serious conservative engagement with Scripture reached its peak in what is often called grammatical-historical interpretation.

b.   *Grammatical-Historical Exegesis (GHE)*

The growing debate over the historicity of the biblical text, its accuracy, and the proper interpretation of difficult passages and language led to the production of technical commentaries among conservatives as much as it did among liberal or atheistic scholars. Conservatives approached the Bible with generally conservative theological presuppositions, so their conclusions were significantly different than their contemporaries, yet the style of technical commentary—commenting on the historical background and linguistic nature of the text—grew to be the predominant scholarly genre of commentary, differing from the more theological and application-oriented Reformation era commentaries (such as Calvin's biblical commentaries).[37] In the mid to late 20th century, the principles of a conservative scholarly approach to biblical interpretation were expressed in various ways under the heading "grammatical-historical interpretation."

As the name indicates, such an interpretation revolves around two major

---

[35] Ibid., 10.

[36] This interpretive approach seems to have made a minor resurgence in the teaching of Psychologist Jordan Peterson, see my review of his *12 Rules for Life*. https://teleioteti.ca/2018/10/11/review-of-12-rules-for-life/.

[37] A helpful example of this conservative critical commentary is the commentary series written by Karl Fredreich Keil and Franz Delitzsch, which remains helpful today.

axes, the text and history. Originating as it has among conservative scholars, grammatical-historical interpreters also tend to employ the ancient principle of the analogy of faith, or Scripture interprets Scripture.[38] We could thus summarize this approach to Scripture as a theologically informed, historical investigation of the meaning of the text. The goal for evangelical grammatical-historical interpretation is to apply the meaning of the text to contemporary circumstances. Let us consider, first, this goal of GHE Interpretation and, second, the method usually used to attain it.

i. The Goal of Grammatical-Historical Exegesis

The goal of GHE is to identify the *meaning* of the text, often with the goal of then applying the meaning of the text to our contemporary context. At the core of what makes GHE unique is its view of meaning, from which its method is derived. If a text's meaning is found in the reader, then the study of a text would focus on a reader; if it is found in the text, it would focus on the text alone. Proponents of GHE argue that there is only one meaning for each text, the same meaning for any reader; that it is propositional; and that this meaning is equivalent to the author's intention.[39] Thus, the meaning of a text is historical because it is the intention of a historical author. However, the only access we have to the author's intention is the text he has given understood as a product of the world within which it was produced—in its cultural context. By studying a text in interaction with what we can

---

[38] This principle is used to differing degrees among such exegetes. The work by Goldsworthy places a particularly strong emphasis on this aspect of Grammatical-Historical Exegesis. Goldsworthy, *Gospel-Centered Hermeneutics*.

[39] Though not an Evangelical, Benjamin Jowett summarized this well when he wrote in 1869, "Scripture has one meaning—the meaning which it had in the mind of the Prophet or Evangelist who first uttered or wrote, to the hearers or readers who first received it." Quoted in David C. Steinmetz, "The Superiority of Precritical Exegesis," in *A Guide to Contemporary Hermeneutics: Major Trends in Biblical Interpretation*, ed. Donald K. McKim (Grand Rapids: Eerdmans, 1986), 65. Francis Watson writes that the literal sense of Scripture consists of "verbal meaning, (ii) illocutionary and perlocutionary force, and (iii) the relation to the centre." "Illocutionary" and "perlocutionary" force are terms borrowed from speech-act theory, meaning what one does by the act of speaking (i.e. warning, answering a question) and the effect one intends to achieve with an act of speaking. The "centre" here is the canonical context focusing on Jesus Christ. Francis Watson, *Text and Truth: Redefining Biblical Theology* (Edinburgh: T&T Clark, 1997), 123.

reconstruct of the thought-world and events of its historical context, it is possible to uncover the intention of the author, or at least that is the claim of GHE proponents.

ii. *The Method of Grammatical-Historical Exegesis*

We could identify the Grammatical Historical school as a moderate or conservative form of what John Sailhamer calls "event-centered" exegetical method.[40] That is, Grammatical-Historical interpreters are concerned with the historical communicative event, or speech-act, represented by the text.[41] A book is the creation of an author who seeks to communicate something to an audience. The author's intention is that which he wants to communicate to this audience. On this view, the text is the code by which the author transmits his intended communication. It is assumed his audience would have the necessary knowledge to decode this communication, a position we cannot presume to share by default. We must work to decode the transmission in the text we have because of our cultural distance and roles as observers of this communicative act.

---

[40] John H. Sailhamer, *Introduction to Old Testament Theology: A Canonical Approach* (Grand Rapids: Zondervan, 1995), 36–85.

[41] "Speech-act" is a specific phrase use by some philosophers to describe the nature of human communication. This analysis focuses on language as an action, as such meaning is found in the context of communicative action and not just the text—which is only a piece of a speech-act. Kevin J. Vanhoozer may be the most prominent Evangelical to employ speech-act theory in his hermeneutical and theological theory. Yet even where this language is not present, speech-act provides a good summary of the way GHE views communication. Kevin J. Vanhoozer, *Is There a Meaning in This Text?: The Bible, the Reader, and the Morality of Literary Knowledge* (Grand Rapids: Zondervan, 1998); Kevin J. Vanhoozer, *The Drama of Doctrine: A Canonical-Linguistic Approach to Christian Theology*, 1st ed. (Louisville: Westminster John Knox, 2005). Cf. Watson, *Text and Truth*, 98–106.

This involves the threefold study of the author, text, and audience. Because we do not have direct access to the author and audience, the method to regain their perspective is again threefold. We can read the text and attempt to discern the events and positions that have necessitated it, an effort known as *mirror reading*), we can read the rest of the Bible to learn more about the author and his audience, and we can study extra-biblical accounts of the culture and thought world in which the text was composed. For the biblical authors, a scholar could understand them better by studying all their writings (e.g. "The Pauline corpus," Paul's letters) and the 3rd and 1st person accounts given of them in the rest of Scripture (we can learn more about Paul from Acts and autobiographical comments such as Gal 1:11-24 and Phil 3:1-11). For the audience, the primary way a scholar could understand them better is through mirror reading and by studying the cultural context. Broadly, this context would be the Ancient Near East (Old Testament) or the Greco-Roman world (New Testament). Narrowly, this involves the study of the particular geography, social climate, and thought world where the audience of the biblical books lived (e.g. Thessalonica, Galatia, Ephesus, Philippi, etc.). Such study is through to help us understand the thought world presupposed by the text.

i. *Mirror Reading*

Andreas Köstenberger and Richard Patterson define mirror-reading as, "the (often doubtful) interpretive practice of inferring the circumstances surrounding the writing of a given text from explicit statements made in the text."[i] As a staple of historical critical methodology, mirror-reading is often criticized and even rejected outright. However, despite Patterson and Köstenberger's rightful caution towards the excesses of this approach, it seems to me that all historically rooted methodologies involve an element of mirror reading: as the scholar attempts to identify a correspondence between the text and known circumstances, they are forced to identify circumstances implied by the text to test against the historical data. Clinton Arnold, another Evangelical interpreter, seems admit this—though rejecting the title "mirror-reading"—in an interview with Andrew Naselli, "It is not 'mirror reading,' however, to examine explicit features of the so-called heresy in light of the religious and cultural environment. In other words, when Paul says, 'Let no one disqualify you, insisting on asceticism and worship of angels, going on in detail about visions' (Col 2:18), this is a specific indicator of what the opponents were teaching that calls out for historical examination. We need to look at all such explicit indicators and attempt to discern what the church was facing."[ii] It seems that some level of understanding concerning the circumstances against which the author writes is required in order to understand his intentions, and this implies some level of reading the text to discern such circumstances. But the excesses are evident when authors create elaborate background scenarios to explain the meaning of a text—as exemplified in several works in recent memory.[iii] So, though qualifying it against some excess, GHE implies a form of mirror-reading as an aspect of its historical methodology. The difference is that GHE measures its mirror reading by history, comparing what is said and implied by a text with historical data. I have argued elsewhere that even this form of mirror reading is unhelpful; in its place, I suggested mirror-reading as a tool for better reading texts—as a form of the analogy of faith:

> Mirror reading, when used this way, takes the data from a reading of the letter and then correlates it with the rest: it asks, what in the letter best explains this feature? What features of the letter fit together? Reading [Colossians] this way, we see a correlation between Christ's creation of and authority over the rulers, their defeat, the elemental spirits (note the inclusio in 2:8, 20), and the worship of angels. These details are mutually interpreting, making sense of each other when read together. Therefore, this form of mirror reading is not an attempt to read each individual part against a reconstructed background but each part against each other. To read the parts by the whole is a normal part of interpretation; mirror reading is a tool for doing this. With it, we correlate the parts and use the resulting synthesis in our reading of the letter (e.g. that Christ created the rulers in 1:16 is probably meant to address the problem of spirit worship in 2:18).[iv]

---

[i] Andreas J. Köstenberger and Richard Duane Patterson, *Invitation to Biblical Interpretation: Exploring the Hermeneutical Triad of History, Literature, and Theology* (Grand Rapids: Kregel Publications, 2011), 842.

[ii] Quoted from "Mirror Reading," *Andy Naselli*, last modified May 30, 2011, accessed April 26, 2019, http://andynaselli.com/mirror-reading.

[iii] E.g. Richard Clark Kroeger and Catherine Clark Kroeger, *I Suffer Not*

a Woman: Rethinking 1 Timothy 2:11-15 in Light of Ancient Evidence (Grand Rapids: Baker, 1992).

[iv] James Alexander Rutherford, "Christ Is Preeminent over False Religion: An Investigation of the Colossian False Teaching," August 29, 2016, https://teleioteti.ca/resources/papers.

Thus, grammatical study tells us what the text says, and historical study helps us to understand what that would have meant when the original author wrote it. For example, Craig Blomberg, in his commentary on 1 Corinthians, argues concerning 1 Corinthians 11:2-16 that Paul may be referring to a shawl or covering but probably hair length; this is the grammatical aspect of interpretation, what the text says. On the other hand, he argues that in light of the 1st-century world in which Paul wrote this letter, Paul's intention was to instruct men to act in culturally appropriate ways as males and women as females, not to use their freedom in Christ as an opportunity cast of traditional values. He offers many suggestions as to why long hair on a man or short hair on a woman would have been culturally inappropriate.[42] he writes, "most interpreters agree that one timeless principle that may be deduced from this passage is that Christians should not try to blur all distinctions between the sexes."[43] he then argues that none of the verses commands a specific "timeless" custom, such that hair length or a heading covering should be used, only

> When in a particular culture, appropriate honor to God and husband cannot be maintained without certain head coverings, such coverings must be used. When covered or uncovered heads and long or short hair imply nothing about one's religious commitment or marital faithfulness, worrying about the appearance of one's physical head in these ways becomes unnecessary.[44]

Having identified the probable meaning of the words and the syntax of the text, Blomberg then uses historical background to explain why Paul says what

---

[42] Eg. Craig L. Blomberg, *1 Corinthians*, NIVAC (Grand Rapids: Zondervan, 1994), 210–211.

[43] Ibid., 214.

[44] Ibid., 215. I argue for a different approach in my article, https://teleioteti.ca/2018/02/15/is-a-covering-long-hair-or-veil-interpreting-1-corinthians11/.

he says and is used to guide application.

One college-level textbook uses the analogy of a journey to explain this method. First, the interpreter grasps the text in the "town" of the original audience, using grammar and historical context to discern what it would have meant to them.[45] Second, the interpreter identifies the width of the river separating that "town" from their own: they seek to identify the differences between the original audience and themselves (e.g. redemptive-historical context, cultural, historical setting, situation, linguistic background, etc.).[46] Third, the interpreter "crosses the principlizing bridge," identifying the universal theological truth that connects their town to the interpreters. "As God gives specific expressions to specific biblical audiences, he is also giving universal theological teachings for all of his people through these same texts."[47] Fourth, this theological principle is then applied in the interpreter's own town; the journey is complete when the meaning is brought from the audience's town to the interpreter's—when the text is applied to its contemporary audience.[48]

Though Conservatives responded to the challenge of Modernist historical criticism by becoming better historians and linguists, studying the history behind the biblical texts and the languages in which they were written to counter the challenge of Modernism, not all scholars adopted this response. Others retaliated against Modernism by seeking to separate God's revelation in Scripture from the sphere of history and grammar within which the challenges of historical criticism were raised.

---

[45] Grammatical Historical exegetes often interchange what the author intended with what the audience would have understood. Though practically these are not identical, in hermeneutical theory they are treated as the same.

[46] D.A. Carson describes the step of leaving one's own town as "distanciation." Distanciation describes the act of critically examining a text and oneself as a reader, discerning the differences in presuppositions between the two so that the text can be read on its own terms. In *Exegetical Fallacies* (Grand Rapids: Baker Books, 1996), 22–24.

[47] J. Scott Duvall and J. Daniel Hays, *Grasping God's Word: A Hands-On Approach to Reading, Interpreting, and Applying the Bible*, 2nd Ed (Zondervan, 2005), 23.

[48] Ibid. 21-25

c. Existential Hermeneutics

This is the approach taken by a school of interpretation we could call "Existential." By existential I do not mean to identify these thinkers with the Existentialist school of Philosophy (identified with Heidegger, Sartre, Bultmann and Tillich), though there are significant parallels in their thinking and a common historical root. Instead, I identify them as an "existentialist" school of hermeneutics because they identify God's revelation (which is the goal of Christian biblical interpretation) with a personal experience and not the text's meaning, however that may be conceived.

The originator of this approach was a German theologian name Martin Kähler. In his book, *The So-Called Historical Christ and the Historic Biblical Christ*, Kähler attempts to guard Christian theology against the attack of historical criticism by separating God's revelation in Christ from the historical events and grammatical meaning of the text.[49] *Historie*, the events and people of history which are the subject of historical-critical science, was to be distinguished from the way people receive or are affected by historical events, *Geschichte*.[50] Against historical criticism, Kähler argued that their goal of an unbiased picture of history—*Historie*—was unattainable: the historical task is itself interpretive and employs historical materials which are themselves interpreted. Because *Historie* was unattainable, the historical-critical task of rooting Christianity in objective facts was doomed to fail. Furthermore, the conservative approach, as embodied in Grammatical-Historical Exegesis, was likewise doomed to fail. On the one hand, it depended on vast theological structures or systems that were beyond the

---

[49] Martin Kähler, *The So-Called Historical Jesus and the Historic, Biblical Christ* (Vancouver: Regent College Pub., 1998).

[50] Students of philosophy will notice striking parallels between the position developed by Kähler and Barth and the philosophy of Immanuel Kant. To protect the hard sciences from the scepticism of David Hume, Kant developed a two-fold picture of the world. On the one hand, there was the *phenomenal* world, the world of our experience. This realm is wholly subjective, created by our minds, yet it is completely knowable and subject to consistent laws; it is the realm of science, where we can attain knowledge. On the other hand, there was the *noumenal* world, the world that actually exists apart from our mind's interpretation. This world is wholly unknowable. Its existence is the presupposition of the sciences and knowledge, but it cannot actually be known. In the same way, *historie* is the real events of history that must have happened for *geschichte*, our interpretation, yet we cannot know anything about *historie*—it is not accessible to us.

grasp of the average Christian, and by competing with historical-critical scholars to show that the Bible is indeed factual, they anchored their theology to *Historie,* which was unattainable. A better way was needed, an approach that recognized the Gospels as subjective responses to the historical events of Christ's life—as *Geschichte*—and grounded theology in this. In the place of these historical approaches, Kähler offers an existential hermeneutic. God does not use Scripture to communicate propositions (statements of truth) or theological systems to Christians. Instead, Scripture paints a picture of Christ. We see Christ in Scripture and so recognize the Bible as authoritative, as God's revelation. The whole Bible is needed for us to get this picture, yet this picture does not rest on any detail; whether Scripture errs or not, it infallibly presents a picture of the "historic" (*geschichtlich*) Christ. Thus, our reading of Scripture concerns our subjective perception of Christ in Scripture and does not involve wrestling with the grammar and history of the text.[51] Kähler himself is not well known today, but his students are some of the most influential scholars who wrote under the banner "Christian" in the 20th century, including Karl Barth and Paul Tillich. Karl Barth is the author that most obviously and most influentially represents an existentialist hermeneutic.

To vastly simplify Karl Barth's approach,[52] we could say that for him, Scripture is God's chosen avenue of revelation. God has freely chosen to use this one book to reveal himself to man. Yet God has not bound himself to this book, as if humans were able to grasp and manipulate his revelation as they see fit. Instead, God reveals himself in Scripture at his pleasure through a personal, existential encounter. To say the Bible is the Word of God is to say that the Bible becomes the Word of God in so far as and when God allows it to be so.[53] The Christian meets God as he or she reads Scripture; this encounter is, as with Kähler, non-propositional (it does not reveal

---

[51] This is based on my review of Kähler's book on Teleioteti, "Review of the So-Called Historical Jesus and the Historic Biblical Christ," *Teleioteti,* July 25, 2018, accessed April 26, 2019, https://teleioteti.ca/2018/07/25/review-of-the-so-called-historical-jesus-and-the-historic-biblical-christ/.

[52] In my opinion, Karl Barth's theology is on the whole unclear and confused.

[53] Karl Barth, *Church Dogmatics*, vol. 1.1 (Peabody, Mass: Hendricksen, 2010), 11–17, 115–124, 174–175.

anything *about* God). Instead, it is personal.⁵⁴ Textual meaning and authorial intent are not, therefore, the subjects of Christian theological investigation; they are the objects of historical-critical study. Therefore, despite what the historical critics may say, God's revelation through Scripture is unhampered, for it does not rest on what is said but in God's free decision to encounter his people there.⁵⁵

In some ways, existential interpretation anticipates postmodern interpretation in the second half of the 20th century, but a key difference is evident. Though Postmodern interpretation rejects objective truth in significant ways, it does not deny that a reader comes away from a text with a meaning or with meanings—with statements that can be formulated as propositions. Instead, it makes this meaning dependent on the reader and separates it from the text and author who wrote it. Existential interpretation, on the one hand, has gone farther than Postmodern interpretation by saying that the biblical text does not communicate *anything*. But, on the other hand, in moving meaning into the reader, Postmodern interpretations often go further than existential interpreters like Barth and even Kähler, denying not only the possibility of accessing historical events but also the ability of texts or authors to communicate.⁵⁶ That is, we can walk away from a text with

---

⁵⁴ We would, of course, debate the bifurcation of propositional and personal knowledge or encounters, as if you could meet and know someone without knowing anything about them. Though, it is true that we can know things about someone without being able to succinctly express them. Cf. *The Gift of Seeing*.

⁵⁵ Cf. Karl Barth, *The Word of God and the Word of Man* (New York: Harper & Row, 1957); John M. Frame, *A History of Western Philosophy and Theology* (Phillipsburg: P&R Publishing, 2015), 364–383; Cornelius Van Til, "Has Karl Barth Become Orthodox," *The Westminster Theological Journal* 16, no. 2 (May 1954): 135–181.

Barth does not argue for a "special hermeneutic," a unique way of reading the Bible over against all other literature. Instead, the differences between the interpretation of the Bible and every other book rest in the difference of subject matter. Because the subject matter of the Bible is the sovereign Lord Jesus Christ, who is ultimately free, the meaning of the text can only be grasped if and when the sovereign subject allows this to happen. See Thomas E. Provence, "The Sovereign Subject Matter: Hermeneutics in the Church Dogmatics," in *A Guide to Contemporary Hermeneutics: Major Trends in Biblical Interpretation*, ed. Donald K. McKim (Grand Rapids: Eerdmans, 1986), 241–262.

⁵⁶ I address this briefly in the previous volume in this series, *The Gift of*

propositional knowledge, yet this knowledge is a product of our own activity as we interact with the text not the text or the author's intentional activity.

C. Hermeneutics in Postmodern

In the 20th century, philosophy entered a new movement, known as Postmodernism. Though it is sometimes thought that Postmodernism is a response to Modernism, it appears to be Modernism come of age. In Modernist philosophy, there was an irreconcilable tension between the objective world and the subjective interpreter. Postmodernism drew out this tension and drove it to its extremes, turning the emphasis from the objective world to the subjective interpreter.[57] In language, this produced several different movements. As far as its impact on biblical hermeneutics, the most significant impact of Postmodernism has been expressed in the flourishing of "exegeses," of which Structural interpretation and reader-response criticism are worthy of notice.

Before the 20th century, the question biblical hermeneutics sought to answer was, "How do we properly interpret the Bible?" This implies, of course, that there are right and wrong ways to read the Bible, that there are right and wrong interpretations and, therefore, right and wrong interpretative methods. Within Postmodernism the emphasis is not on how to properly interpret the Bible but how we can interpret the Bible. That is, the Bible can be studied historically, to understand how it was shaped and its historical role (historical criticism and sociology of religion). The Bible can be studied as a product of a community, understanding how it functions to shape the life of and came to be as a product of a particular society (Canonical criticism, analysis of the interpretive community).[58] The Bible can be studied as a product of and a tool for the flourishing of Patriarchy but also as an agent for the liberation of women (Feminist criticism).[59] A socio-literary, political

---

Knowing, and in an article on Teleioteti, https://teleioteti.ca/2017/11/20/the-moral-act-of-reading-a-response-to-deconstructionism/.

[57] Cf. *The Gift of Knowing*, 7-18; Frame, *A History*, 500–504; Goldsworthy, *Gospel-Centered Hermeneutics*, 130–138.

[58] Cf. Brevard S. Childs, *Introduction to the Old Testament as Scripture* (Philadelphia: Fortress, 1979).

[59] Cf. Letty M. Russell, ed., *Feminist Interpretation of the Bible* (Philadelphia: Westminster John Knox, 1985).

reading of the Bible might use the opposition of "empire," those in power, and "periphery," those exploited, as the lenses through which to read and apply Scripture, as Ched Myers has in his commentary on Mark.[60] The list goes on and on, but it is important to observe that in postmodernism, these differing exegeses are not mutually exclusive; they are all legitimate approaches to the text.

Because of the mutual toleration these exegeses have for one another and their almost unanimous focus on the reader, we could identify behind postmodern exegeses a unified Postmodern hermeneutic. For the most part, the question of "how do texts communicate" and "what is meaning" are answered by looking at the reader. The reader of a text is, in one way or another, the arbiter of meaning.[61] The various approaches of exegesis are only different ways that a reader or recipient of the text might respond to or interact with the text they study. An example of this is some forms of structural exegesis.[62]

a. Structural Exegesis

Structural exegesis takes its cues from Structuralism, a movement in linguistics deriving from the work of the Swiss linguist Ferdinand de Saussure (1857-1913). The ways structural linguistics has been applied to biblical

---

[60] Ched Myers, *Binding the Strong Man: A Political Reading of Mark's Story of Jesus* (Maryknoll, N.Y.: Orbis, 1988).

[61] Jonathan Culler writes, "If the reader always rewrites the text and if the attempt to reconstruct an author's intention is only a particular, highly restricted case of rewriting, then a Marxist reading, for example, is not an illegitimate distortion, but one species of production." Jonathan Culler, *On Deconstructionism: Theory and Criticism after Structuralism* (Ithaca, N.Y.: Cornell University, 1982), 38. That is, once the arguments of scholars like Kähler is accepted, that all attempts to recover *historie*—in this case, the author's intention—are actually *geschichte* (interpretation or subjective reception), then it makes sense to argue that various interpretations or subjective receptions (reader responses) are acceptable. If the "author's intent" is a subjective interpretation—even a creation of the interpreting mind—then what claim to pre-eminence can it have over explicitly ideological interpretations such as Marxist reading? If *historie* is inaccessible—if the author's intention is lost—then it seems to follow that all sorts of reader responses are acceptable.

[62] Structuralism is in some ways a predecessor of Postmodernism more than an example itself, for it places meaning in the text not the reader. However, there is greater continuity than is sometimes granted. Cf. Ibid., 17–30.

exegesis are manifold, but it fits into the Postmodern turn in hermeneutics as one of many different exegetical approaches that are considered compatible.[63] It also fits into the Postmodern turn in philosophy in that meaning is moved away from history, even the author. However, the role of the reader in Structural exegesis is not creating meaning but discovering the meaning found in the text. In some forms of structuralism, meaning (or signification) is imposed upon the author rather than a creation of the author.[64] However, more Evangelical approaches to structural exegesis identify the author as the originator of meaning. In such approaches, meaning is identified with the deeper structure of a text. The Evangelical Old Testament scholar K. Lawson Younger serves as a good example of this form of structural exegesis.

In his book *Ancient Conquest Accounts*, Younger argues that the conquest accounts in Joshua can be understood as a form of ideological communication. That is, they are carefully structured to communicate an ideological message shared among other Ancient Near Eastern conquest accounts of the same form.[65] What distinguishes his approach from other exegeses is that he wants to look beyond the details of the text to the underlying structure, the *trellis*, which he claims communicates meaning.[66] he argues that this communicative structure is made up of a series of syntagms or individual syntactic entities (phrases, clauses, etc.—textual units— understood to have stereotyped functions) structured in a specific way.[67] Thus, by identifying a parallel structure of such syntactic entities (syntagms), Younger claims to identify the same *trellis*, or form, in similar Ancient Near Eastern conquest accounts, arguing that this structure communicates the same ideological message in all these accounts. Though he does not reject the

---

[63] Cf. K. Lawson Younger, *Ancient Conquest Accounts*, Journal for the Study of the Old Testament Supplement 98 (Sheffield: Sheffield Academic Press, 1990), 57; Daniel Patte, *What Is Structural Exegesis?* (Philadelphia: Fortress, 1976), 1–3.

[64] Daniel Patte explains that Structural exegesis presupposes a dialectical view of man and language, where man is both the creator of signification (or meaning) and has signification imposed upon him by the very nature of language. Ibid., 3.

[65] For Younger, "ideology" is a pattern of beliefs and facts claimed to be explanatory of a range of social phenomena. Cf. Younger, *Ancient*, 46, 51, 56.

[66] Ibid., 55–56, 63.

[67] Cf. Ibid., 70.. I examine Younger's approach to a greater extent in my paper, "Not a Single Survivor," available at https://teleioteti.ca/resources/papers/.

historicity of the events recounted, he does argue that the existence of an underlying ideological structure should make exegetes cautious about coming to historical conclusions about the details of the text.[68] Furthermore, he contends that this ideological pattern is the meaning of the text; whatever historical details may be present are secondary. That is, the historical events are merely an opportunity for textual performance, for the ideological message to be communicated.

This implies that the events themselves are not meaningful apart from the meaning given to them by the human interpreter; meaning is found in the structural form into which the events are fit.[69] This allows Younger to dismiss some of the details of the text as products of the underlying structural pattern. Particularly, he claims that the statements of complete destruction found in Joshua 9-12 (e.g. Josh 10:28-43) are instances of stereotyped language used in conquest accounts: the language serves a structural function as part of the underlying *trellis* that communicates the text's meaning.[70] Therefore, the reader is not to understand these statements as literal descriptions of what happened.[71] In this way, the historical emphasis of Modernism gives way to an emphasis on suprahistorical communication, history as a means of communicating and not the communication itself.

More extreme than structuralism are the various forms of criticism that separate meaning from both the author and the text, placing it in the interpreter. Feminist interpretation is a significant reader-response and deconstructionist literary movement today that does this.

b.   *Feminist Interpretation*

In the book *Feminist Interpretation of the Bible*, edited by Letty M. Russell,[72] the authors provide a litany of examples of such exegesis. In her essay,

---

[68] he explicitly brackets out or ignores the historical aspect of the text from his investigation, but he then says, "The fact that there are figurative and ideological underpins [sic] to the accounts should not make us call them into question *per se*—it [sic] should only force us to be cautious!" Ibid., 256.

[69] Ibid., 55–56, 63.

[70] Ibid., 227–228, 323.

[71] Ibid., 243.

[72] Russell, *Feminist Interpretation of the Bible*.

"Feminist Interpretation: A Method of Correlation," Rosemary Radford Reuther seeks to explain what is meant when feminist theology is said to draw upon women's experience as a source of knowledge.[73] She delineates "women's experience" and its relevance for interpretation. Against traditional theology, she defends experience as ultimately authoritative. Tradition is verified by its explanation of experience; experience collects and provides interpretive keys (tradition) that are, dialectically, further refined by experience.[74] Feminist hermeneutic is new not because it asserts the authority of experience, for all interpretation does this (the presupposition of reader-response hermeneutics). Instead, it is new because it invokes the experience of women.[75] She defines women's experience as that experience of women in a patriarchal society with its interpretation of their distinctive biology. This experience is interpretive when women become aware of this society's false paradigm and take a differing stance rooted in their experience: they begin to interpret texts and reality not according to the pattern of the reigning society but according to the paradigm provided by "women's experience." As an interpretive principle, she posits that only what affirms the full humanity of women is authoritative. This interpretive principle denies every form of chauvinism in interpretation. To give biblical sanction to her approach, she correlates the feminist hermeneutic with Scripture's prophetic-messianic tradition. For Ruether, this is Scripture's process of ever reconsidering what

---

[73] Rosemary Radford Ruether, "Feminist Interpretation: A Method of Correlation," in *Feminist Interpretation of the Bible*, ed. Letty M. Russell (Philadelphia: Westminster John Knox, 1985), 111.

[74] Ibid., 111–112. "Dialectically" refers to the back-and-forth interchange characterized by this interaction. Tradition is an accumulation of experience which is interpreted by further experience.

[75] A particularly confusing point in feminist interpretation is what is meant by "women's experience." Feminists do not mean the experiences of particular women; instead, what is intend is an abstract "women experience" that is not equivalent to every experience of women. Some experiences are consistent with and thus embody this "women's experience," yet not all things a woman experiences are characteristic of "women's experience." This "experience" is thus a scholarly abstraction. Jonathan Culler describes it like this (revealing the incoherence of the idea), "For a woman to read as a woman is not to repeat an identity or an experience that is given but to play a role she constructs with reference to her identity as a woman, which is also a construct, so that the series can continue: a woman reading as a woman reading as a woman." Culler, *Deconstructionism*, 64. "Construct" here refers to an abstraction, an identity that is not equivalent to any specific experiences of a particular person

is truly liberating (the Word of God) and discarding what was distorted in tradition. This prophetic tradition faces similar distortion and so requires refinement also. This, she writes, affirms feminist principles, which measures Scripture by their experience of oppression to discern in it what is truly liberating and so authoritative.[76]

With Feminist interpretation, we touch upon the extremes of Postmodern hermeneutical approaches. To conclude this chapter, let us pull back from the fringes and turn to a final hermeneutical approach that has far more of a following among Evangelicals, theological interpretation.

c.   *Theological Interpretation*

Theological interpretation does not refer to any single approach to interpreting the Bible but to a group of approaches that share some similarities. Theological Interpretation rejects the myth of neutrality perpetuated by historical criticism, that interpretation of the Bible could be done from a neutral, unbiased perspective. Instead, it recognizes that all interpretation is "theological," influenced by the theology of the interpreter. Theological interpretation seeks to be explicit about these presuppositions and—among its Evangelical proponents—seeks to be explicitly confessional, rooted in the tradition or traditions of the church (that is, the so-called "great tradition" or different denominational traditions). In this broad sense, the exegetical approach I am developing in this series is a form of theological interpretation. Indeed, there are some brands of theological interpretation that operate within the confines of Grammatical-Historical Exegesis, as discussed above. But many theological interpreters identify themselves with the pre-critical or pre-modern allegorical interpretation, which we also considered above. David C. Steinmetz, for example, wrote an essay arguing for the superiority of pre-critical exegesis over Grammatical-Historical Exegesis that focuses on a single meaning for biblical texts.[77] Because our discussion above has already covered these two branches of theological interpretation, I want to discuss theological interpretation as it is practised in ways distinctly Postmodern.

---

[76] Ruether, "Feminist Interpretation: A Method of Correlation," 111–124.

[77] Steinmetz, "The Superiority of Precritical Exegesis," 65–77.

As we saw above, the pre-modern approach of the Early Church was not radically different than that practised by the reformers and even shared many similarities with the Grammatical-Historical approach of Modernism. In my opinion, the reformers and Protestant's rejection of allegorizing practised by the Fathers was merely taking the bibliology of the Fathers and allowing it to reform their hermeneutical practice, rejecting any external authority that could identify a Scriptural passage or teaching as "difficult." Even the focus on the single meaning and authorial intention among Grammatical-Historical Exegesis was anticipated in Thomas Aquinas and Albert the Great. However, theological interpretation, in its most postmodern form, has not followed this stream of biblical exegesis but has taken the excesses of Medieval Exegesis and run with them. As an example of this tendency, we could look at what we could call dogmatic allegorical interpretation.

Allegorical interpretation, as we saw earlier, was reading scripture as an allegory, where events and persons signified another reality. For Augustine and Origen, allegory was a form of writing the biblical authors used. The biblical authors signalled the presence of an allegory through the insertion of difficult doctrines or events. This could be called allegory as a genre, which fits into the overall textual approach these interpreters took. However, what I am calling "dogmatic allegory" is allegory of a different sort. Instead of looking for places where authors intended allegory, this form of allegory is free to find additional meaning in every text. For example, Hans Boersma writes in his book *Heavenly Participation* that he does not believe that there is any "objectively given, historical meaning that one can discover and solve as one does scientific problems" in the biblical text.[78] he does not reject the insights of historical-critical study but points to spiritual or theological interpretation as a way of going beyond historical-critical exegesis and avoiding the Postmodern scepticism towards meaning.[79]

The literal sense or senses are the starting point for this interpretation, but spiritual interpretation will look for the greater Christological reality that this sense points to. The difference between this approach and genre-based allegorising lies in the rejection of any objective meaning or basis for the

---

[78] Hans Boersma, *Heavenly Participation: The Weaving of a Sacramental Tapestry* (Grand Rapids, Mich.: W.B. Eerdmans Pub. Co, 2011), 152..

[79] Ibid. Cf. Hans Boersma, *Sacramental Preaching: Sermons on the Hidden Presence of Christ* (Grand Rapids: Baker Academic, 2016).

allegory. For Augustine and Origen, they thought that the authors intended to write allegorically, so they looked for clues to the allegorical meaning in the text. Boersma, on the other hand, writes approvingly of the approach taken by Henri de Lubac,

> He recognizes that different readers might well come up with different interpretations *within* the same level. In other words, two exegetes might well present two (or more) different allegorical or Christological readings of the same passage. This hardly presents a problem for de Lubac. Convinced that interpretation is a sacramental entry into the infinity of the spiritual realm, he maintains that the sacramental reality (*res*) of the biblical text cannot possibility be captured by one particular allegorical rendering of the text. Therefore, plurality of meaning is not a danger to be avoided and does not constitute an argument against spiritual exegesis; plurality of meaning is something to be *expected*, precisely because exegesis is the Spirit-guided means that enables human participation in heavenly realities.[80]

This multiplicity of meaning is not bound by the author's intention but is bound up in the reception of the text by the reader. There is an interchange between the text and tradition, allowing further meaning to be identified over time. Indeed, "the church's historical interpretation of the text has entered into its meaning, sometimes in enormously significant ways."[81] Because the meaning of a text is bound up in Christ, as the one to whom it points, the meaning of any text is infinite. Christ and his actions have infinite implications for the Christian life, so the interpretation explores this wealth of meaning. Tradition sets the trajectory of this exploration; "As long as (1) allegory centered on Christ and his church and (2) one allowed for real participation of the historical in the spiritual, one could hardly go wrong with allegory."[82]

---

[80] Boersma, *Heavenly Participation*, 140.

[81] Ibid., 141.

[82] Ibid., 151. For a further discussion of the language of "participation" and "sacrament," see my paper "Sacramental Ontology and Augustine's Platonism" on https://teleioteti.ca/resources/papers.

The parallels between this approach and postmodernism are, I think, clear. As with postmodern interpretations, Boersma conceives of meaning as plural, not singular; he identifies meaning in the reader (here it is the reader's imaginative exploration of the Christological anchor of Scripture); and he sees his approach as parallel to and not in conflict with other exegeses.

ii. *The Narrative Turn*

It is worth observing that there has been a turn in recent interpretation towards the importance of narrative in Biblical interpretation. On the one hand, there is the Reformed emphasis on Redemptive History, which I discussed as an essential part of interpretation in *The Gift of Reading Part 1*. But there has been another emphasis on narrative that has emerged in recent years, what we might call sociological or epistemological narrative. There has been an increasing interest in narrative as a key aspect, if not the key aspect, of human self-understanding. In the early chapters of his book *The New Testament and the People of God,* N.T. Wright states that "Stories are one of the most basic modes of human life" and that "the stories which characterize the worldview itself are thus located, on the map of human knowing, at a more fundamental level than explicitly formulated beliefs, including theological beliefs."[i]

In Biblical studies, the role of this emphasis on narrative or story has come to the forefront in two ways. First, the Bible has been identified as a narrative and so narrative becomes the primary lens through which to read it. Second, and closely related, many scholars have attributed narrative (more precisely, story) with prominence in the formation and content of a worldview. In *The Gift of Reading Part 1* I acknowledged the essential role of narrative for understanding the Bible and the Christian life, something I intend to expound further in the third volume of this series (*The Gift of Seeing*). However, I want to take issue with some aspects of this narrative turn in theology and interpretation.

First, regarding the significance of the Biblical narratives in Christian spiritual formation, I am not qualified to comment on the merits of the psychology present here—that story is essential to human identity and self-understanding—but in as much as this emphasis detracts from the non-narrative parts of Scripture and the non-narrative role of narrative, I think this is a danger. That is, narrative is important yet so are the didactic prose and prophetic—i.e. non-narrative—parts of Scripture. Some scholars claim that the Bible is a narrative, yet I have seen no compelling evidence in this regard nor is it evident to me that this is the case. As I discuss in *The Gift of Reading Part 1,* the Bible tells a narrative—it explains the true meaning of history—but does so as a covenant document, not a narrative. It does not do justice to the unique ways the different parts of Scripture inform and shape Christian life and doctrine to subsume them all under the overarching category of narrative—as both Reformed and narrative-theological interpretations are sometimes guilty of doing.

Furthermore, as I believe V. Phillips Long has argued persuasively, narrative has a profoundly didactic function. Phil shows that narratives are artfully shaped to convey interpretations of historical events, to give an interpretation of what happened.[ii] That is, sometimes this narrative focus is used to diminish the propositional authority of Scripture, its ability to tell us true and false and to teach truth about God and man. This is contrary to the very nature of narrative; the difference between didactic prose—such as this book—and narrative is not that one communicates truth that can be summarized as propositional statements (i.e. God is all-powerful) but that they represent two different approaches to teaching truth and eliciting different responses to it. Narrative has the power to show us truth in a way logical arguments cannot and to make us feel the emotive import of these truths. It is also uniquely suited to telling us *what happened.* Didactic prose, on the other hand, is especially suited to convincing us of truth and debunking falsehood and for explaining *why something happened.* Thus, didactic prose and narrative—as well as poetry—are complementary approaches to teaching truth.

Second, I think the epistemology presupposed in this narrative turn is questionable. These are issues I have touched upon already in *The Gift of Knowing* and will deal with more thoroughly in *The Gift of Seeing,* but a few words would be fitting here. I believe that the use of "story" is confused in these views, that the role of "stories" in knowledge is misunderstood, and that the idea of story in Biblical studies is used—

whether intentionally or unintentionally—to undermine the authority of Scripture over every aspect of our thinking. Regarding the use of "story," what is intended is not clear. "Narrative" refers the literary form used to tell stories, where a story is developed through a temporal succession of events (a plot) recounted by a narrator.[iii] "Story" naturally refers to "plot," or the basic—that is, non-literary—interpretation of the relationship between temporally successive events, or history. "Story" is an interpretation of these events and narrative the recounting of this story.[iv] According to Wright, "story" is irreducible to anything else, such as a proposition, and is the essential nature of Scripture.[v] However, story begins to be stretched beyond reasonable bounds in these examples. Scripture is clearly not narrative and though it tells stories, it is not a story. Paul's letters draw on the Biblical metanarrative, or interpretation of history and events, yet does not tell many "stories." Paul's ability to interpret and apply events, which naturally fit a story form, in prose seems to me to lay bare the epistemological weakness of Wright's position.

That is, Wright argues that theological "abstractions," such as "Monotheism," are shorthand for stories. He also dismisses the ability for stories to be reduced to anything else. To anticipate the argument I will present in *The Gift of Seeing*, and have anticipated in *The Gift of Knowing*, stories—and their narrative presentations—are better understood as one part of the subject's interpretation of objects—namely events. That is, we can look at an event and deduce truths from it and we can interpret in relation to other events. This is what a story is, an interpretation of events in relation to one another. Narratives presuppose a story, for they recount a specific relation between events. Narrative is the natural form for recounting a story and a story may be the best way to interpret the relationships between events; however, it is not the only way. We can also interpret these relations as confirmation of universal laws; we interpret the cause-effect relationship between two pool balls as confirmation of the laws of motion and causality. Furthermore, stories are often used not only to interpret the relationships between events but also to teach the meaning of things and to illustrate or prove abstract ideas such as laws. I can illustrate what is meant by causality by telling a story about events that demonstrate causality. I can illustrate what is meant by God's power through stories about God's actions. Stories are essential to human knowledge, for we experience a temporal succession of events throughout our lives and interpret them. And stories are indispensable for pedagogy, for teaching truth. But stories are not irreducible; the fact that we can talk about stories in non-narrative forms and discuss them demonstrates this to some extent. Furthermore, to embrace story at the expense of the role of abstraction in human thinking is to stumble into the same epistemological dilemma as empiricism. Empiricism bases all knowledge upon the senses, so all knowledge is limited to telling what has happened. Such knowledge cannot guarantee what will happen or will always happen; it can only say what has happened (the objects of experience). Such an epistemological position can tell you what it means for God to have acted faithfully but cannot tell you that God's faithfulness means he will always act in this manner. It can tell you that God is powerful but not that God is all-powerful. Indeed, abstractions such as laws are more ultimate than stories in the sense that they are the principles by which we interpret events, producing stories. All that to say, human knowledge is complex and cannot be reduced to "story," no matter how significant that category proves to be and how pedagogically effective narrative is.

Which brings us to one final point concerning the narrative turn. Wright, and others to different extents,[vi] have sought to explain the authority of narratives or the role of theology in new terms, terms other than that of epistemic normativity (ability to tell us what is right and wrong, good and bad, etc.).[vii] Wright argues that the authority of Scripture is like an unfinished play, setting the trajectory and establishing the parameters and characters for later actors—us—to improvise with. He disavows the ability to "look up the right answers" in Scripture.[viii] However, as I argued in *The Gift of Knowing* and *The Gift of Reading Part 1*, the Bible makes no such claims. Indeed, the Bible claims complete normative authority over all areas of our life and is a covenant document meant to *legislate* the Christian life. That narratives can have normative authority in this sense is demonstrated by the Old Testament case laws, which were not merely suggestions for improvisation but concrete examples to use in making future judgments. There is an aspect of improvisation to be sure, for we must draw analogies. Yet this improvisation is grounded in normative commands and truths that shape our perspective of the world. I think John Frame is right when he writes, "To base ethics on a narrative devoid of revealed commands leaves us with no ethical standards except those derived from would-be autonomous thought."[ix] I do not find Wright's suggestions helpful at all for understanding the Christian life and the role of Scripture within it.[x]

---

[i] N.T. Wright, The New Testament and the People of God, Christian Origins and the Question of God 1 (Minneapolis: Fortress, 1992), 38.

[ii] V. Philips Long, "The Art of Biblical History," in *Foundations of Contemporary Interpretation*, ed. Moisés Silva (Grand Rapids: Zondervan, 1996).

[iii] Jean Louis Ska, *"Our Fathers Have Told Us": Introduction to the Analysis of Hebrew Narratives*, Subsidia Biblica 13 (Roma: Editrice Pontificio Instituto Biblico, 1990), 21.

[iv] This is something I will unpack further in my book *The Gift of Seeing*, but seems congruent with Wright's presentation of "story," cf. Wright, *The New Testament*, 79.

[v] Ibid., 38, 79, 139–143, 371; cf. N. T. Wright, *Scripture and the Authority of God* (Society for Promoting Christian Knowledge, 2005).

[vi] Cf. Vanhoozer, *The Drama of Doctrine*; Kevin J. Vanhoozer, *Faith Speaking Understanding: Performing the Drama of Doctrine*, First edition. (Louisville: Westminster John Knox Press, 2014). Vanhoozer's model of theodrama is very similar to Wright's understanding of the authority of narrative.

[vii] Wright, *The New Testament*, 139–144.

[viii] Ibid. 141. Cf. Wright, *Scripture and the Authority of God*.

[ix] John M. Frame, *The Doctrine of the Christian Life*, A Theology of Lordship 4 (Phillipsburg: P&R Publishing, 2008), 326. n. 2.

[x] Cf. John M. Frame, *The Doctrine of the Word of God*, A Theology of Lordship (Phillipsburg: P&R Publishing, 2010), 517–524.

D. Conclusion

Throughout the history of the Church, Christians have been reading the Bible. Despite the different ways they have approached the Scriptures, every generation has arrived at and confirmed the same doctrines. Despite the hermeneutical obfuscation, God's voice has been heard clearly. A significant reason for this, I believe, is that we have all been looking at *the text*. Though we differ in our approach to reading, we cannot deny what is before our eyes. Though the Bible admits that it contains difficult texts, even here, the emphasis falls on the corruption of those who stumble over these hard-to-understand passages (2 Pet 2:9).

I think this much has been clear in our survey: through each generation, some Christians have often fallen into the trap of reading the Bible according to the agenda of the culture. For the early Church fathers, their Neo-Platonic philosophy often influenced their perception of textual difficulties and justified their allegorical readings. For the Reformers, the temptation was to read their struggles into the text, such as identifying the Pope as the Antichrist. Under Modernism, the Church fought to justify the historicity and moral authority of the text in light of the progress of the Enlightenment. Under Postmodernism, Christians have fought to maintain the universal authority of Scripture against the relativizing tendencies of Postmodernity. I suggested in the introduction to this chapter that it is worth observing the role of audience and authority in these different hermeneutical approaches. Sometimes in subtle ways and at other times in explicit ones, the different approaches we have seen have let the ultimate authority of the Bible slip.

In the early Church fathers, they relied on external standards of morality and philosophy to judge what was a difficult teaching or text. For the Modernist interpreters, the canon of human reason was dominant in epistemology, giving the standard of morality and truth by which the Bible was to be read and judged. The influence of this thinking has even been seen within the Grammatical Historical camp, as proponents have sought to justify the Bible's inerrancy and authority on the basis of human reason as their epistemological authority.[83] In Postmodernism, the authority of the Bible has been radically dismissed by those who claim that it cannot even speak apart from a reader giving it meaning, that it cannot communicate and so cannot have authority, or that its authority is not the sort that can tell us what to believe and what not to believe. Alongside these struggles with the question of biblical authority has been confusion over the audience of the Bible.

Though it is present to some extent in the early church, the struggle over the question of the audience has come to the fore since the Reformation.

---

[83] In *The Gift of Knowing*, I try to show that a key tension throughout human history has been the authority of God versus the authority of man. Christian theology and philosophy, even by those who are otherwise orthodox, has been heavily influenced by non-Christian philosophy which has attempted to interpret the world form the standpoint of autonomous, human authority.

Under Modernism, the historical nature of the Bible came under close scrutiny, and great attention was paid to the original context of the individual books of which it is composed. Specifically, by looking at the Bible as a historical document recording a communicative act—a transmission from an author to an audience—much thought was given to the role of the original audiences in this communication. When Modernism matured into Postmodernism, the role of the audience was almost entirely eclipsed by the reader. That is, the intended audience of the author and his intentions were eschewed in exchange for the response of the present reader. In its most extreme forms, the text becomes merely an opportunity for a reading performance—for the reader to imaginatively create meaning. The questions of authority and audience—along with the author, meaning, and text—will play a key role in my hermeneutical proposal. In the following pages, I am striving to acknowledge the Bible's authority over every area of the hermeneutical task, as I attempted in *The Gift of Reading Part 1*. By doing so, I think we can see why God's Word has always been heard despite the din of hermeneutical theories, and we can see how God has equipped us through the Word with the tools necessary to read it well. We will begin here, with the role of biblical authority in the hermeneutical task in Part 1. We will look at the role of the Bible in its own reading. Then we will consider the role of the reader in Part 2. Finally, in Part 3, we will consider the role of the author.

Further Reading

Graeme Goldsworthy - *Gospel-Centered Hermeneutics,* 87-180
Moises Silva – *Has the Church Misread the Bible*

—Part 1—
The Role of the Bible

2

THE BIBLE AS SELF-INTERPRETING

When your son asks you in time to come, "What is the meaning of the testimonies and the statutes and the rules that the Lord our God has commanded you?" then you shall say to your son, "We were Pharaoh's slaves in Egypt. And the Lord brought us out of Egypt with a mighty hand. And the Lord showed signs and wonders, great and grievous, against Egypt and against Pharaoh and all his household, before our eyes. And he brought us out from there, that he might bring us in and give us the land that he swore to give to our fathers. And the Lord commanded us to do all these statutes, to fear the Lord our God, for our good always, that he might preserve us alive, as we are this day. And it will be righteousness for us, if we are careful to do all this commandment before the Lord our God, as he has commanded us." – Deuteronomy 6:20-25

Throughout this series, I have argued that the Bible is the ultimate authority for a Christian. As God's very words given to govern and guide his people, Christians are obligated to obey the Bible. In *The Gift of Knowing*, I argued that the rejection of God's authority undermines any claim to knowledge, that submission to God as he has spoken through the Scriptures is essential to the task of living within and understanding God's world. In *The Gift of Reading Part 1*, I argued that the Bible is shaped as a covenant document, explicitly communicating with God's authority. The authority of God expressed in the Bible is not a word for bygone generations nor a word for this generation alone; the Bible was intended by God to govern his covenant people until his return. God breathed out the Scriptures in order that they might be useful, available to equip his people for the good works for which he created them (2 Tim 3:16-17, cf. Eph 2:10). Surely Yahweh—the God who created the heavens and the earth by his very words (Genesis 1), who struck Egypt with might plagues (Exodus 1-12), and who raised Jesus Christ from the dead (Eph 1:19-21)—could ensure such an end if that were truly what he desired. Isaiah affirms that when God sets his mind to do something, when he speaks to accomplish a goal, it is accomplished (Isa 55:10-11).

If God truly intended his Word to govern his people and equip them for the very purpose he created them—as Paul affirms in 2 Timothy 3:16-17—then surely he will have given his people not only a text but a means to interpret this text. And if he has invested the Bible with ultimate authority, the authority of his own word, then it must be self-interpreting—for if interpretation relied on another court of appeal, that interpreter would be the ultimate authority. This is an issue I take with many of the hermeneutical approaches we saw in the previous chapter: they have not taken into consideration the Bible's own claims and have produced hermeneutical models that imply one generation—either the first generation or us today—has a privileged position for interpreting the Bible. But if God has given us the Bible to be read and profited from, we must presuppose in our hermeneutic that the Bible is self-interpreting. I want to outline in this chapter several ways God has shaped the Bible to be self-interpreting. But first, let's look closer at the problem that would emerge if the Bible was not self-interpreting.

The goal of the Bible is truly ambitious, to govern God's people over a period of roughly 3300-3400 years and counting. When the Torah was first written, it was intended to legislate the Old Testament people of God. This covenant remained in effect until the 1st century AD. The New Testament was finished by the end of the 1st century AD and was given to govern God's people until Christ's return—almost 2000 years now. To illustrate the difficulties that are involved in such a project, think of all the cultural changes that have happened in Western Culture over the last 600 years. Roman Catholicism has lost its dominance in Europe, Protestantism became a force to be reckoned with, North America and South America were colonized by European countries, most Western monarchies have been replaced by alternate forms of government or have been radically transformed, the influence of Christianity on public life is waning, technology has exploded in unimaginable ways, etc. Not only has culture shifted, but language has also shifted, consider the preface to John Owen's *The Doctrine of the Saints*

Perseverance (1654),

> *The Wiſe man tells us, that* no man knoweth Love or hatred, by all that is before him. *The great variety wherein God diſpenſeth outward things in the World, with the many changes and alterations,* which according to the counſell of his will, *he continually works in the diſpenſations of them, will not all them nakedly in themſelves, to be evidences of the fountaine from whence they flow. Seeing alſo, that the* want, *or* abundance *of them, may equally by the Goodneſſe and Wiſdome of God, be ordered and caſt into an uſefull* fubferviency, *to a Good* infinitely tranſcending *what is, or may be contained in them, there is no receſſity....*[1]

In the 360 or so years since this edition was printed, the English "ſ" has been replaced by the "s," at least one word has passed out of usage (I do not know what "fubferviency" means), verbal forms and spelling has changed, and stylistic standards have also changed (though Owen was never exemplary in his time). This is, nevertheless, recognizably English. Imagine trying to learn 17th century French today; you would not only be wrestling with the changes in language but also the challenges of moving from one language to another. This is similar to what we find in the Old and New Testaments. The Old Testament was written in Hebrew and Aramaic, intended to be read by an audience for hundreds of years. But by the 1st century, Hebrew was replaced as the common language in Judea with Aramaic and Greek. So readers in the 1st century were dealing with texts in a non-native tongue written up to 1,400 years prior. From the time of the New Testament until now, the Greek language has undergone massive changes as well, and Hebrew was not a living language until it was resurrected recently. So a challenge has faced interpreters since the Bible was penned, understanding the language of the Bible as those who are fluent in an altogether different language or a language that has changed significantly.[2] If the original texts or *autographa* are authoritative, then we need a way to be sure that we can understand the language of the

---

[1] Taken from the digitized copy on the John Richard Allison Library website, see The Puritan Project.

[2] Though I think the differences are less significant than are often claimed, Hebrew scholars differentiate between Archaic, Classical (Pre-exilic), and Late Biblical Hebrew (Post-exilic). These categories describe the Hebrew found in different parts of the Bible; the Hebrew texts found in Qumran also demonstrate differences and the Rabbinic Hebrew of the Mishnah even more so.

Bible to interpret it correctly—despite the differences.[3]

In addition to the problem of language-distance, there is also a problem created by the size and scope of the Bible. As we discussed in *The Gift of Reading Part 1*, to read any part of the Bible we need to understand the whole teaching of Scripture. We saw earlier in this book that the early church practised such contextual reading (reading parts in light of the whole) in the form of the analogy of faith. The Bible is massive and complex; it would be a lifelong endeavour to come to a sufficient understanding of the whole Bible by oneself. So, for the Bible to be self-interpreting in the sense discussed above, it must be able to function as its own standard for its language, it must be sufficient to allow us to learn its languages and verify our interpretations,[4] and it must be sufficient in scope to present an interpretive lens for the parts.

However, sufficiency in this internal sense is not enough: even if the Bible were perfectly sufficient in its content, this would not ensure that it was self-interpreting. If we had no knowledge of the Bible and, given internal sufficiency, it fell from heaven into the midst of our culture, we would still not be able to interpret it. That is, we would have no knowledge of the language to begin interpreting, and without knowledge of the whole, we would not have a solid beginning point to interpret it.[5] To be self-interpreting, the Bible also needs to have what we could call *external sufficiency*. What I mean by external sufficiency is this: it must have the capacity and means in itself to create an interpreting community through which an understanding of the whole can be passed on to succeeding generations.

So in our discussion of the sufficiency of Scripture for its own self-interpretation, we can distinguish between *external* and *internal* sufficiency. For the rest of this chapter, I want to consider several features of the Bible

---

[3] Translations do not solve the problem, for we need to be able to have confidence that our translators can accurately understand the original texts to produce accurate translations.

[4] "Verify" corresponds to the category of validity developed in *The Gift of Reading Part 1*.

[5] If, somehow, we knew the languages in which it was written, we could eventually come to an understanding of whole by reading and re-reading, constantly re-evaluating our understanding of each part. Yet, as mentioned above, given the scope and complexity of the Bible, this would take far more than a single lifetime.

that provide internal sufficiency and the role of external sufficiency, how the Bible creates an interpreting community sufficient to ensure its interpretation throughout the generations. Regarding internal sufficiency, I want to consider the role of the analogy of faith, the role of narrative/textual closure, and linguistic sufficiency.

A. <u>Analogy of Faith</u>

We saw earlier how the analogy of faith was the appeal made by the earlier church fathers, such as Irenaeus, to all the Scriptures in interpreting the parts. The emphasis of the analogy of faith today often focuses on the role of the narrative told by Scriptures (its interpretation of the created world's past, present, and future)[6] and the role of systematic theology in interpretation (e.g. we interpret the biblical passages in which God is said to change his mind in light of those passages where he is said not to change his mind and vice versa, coming to a more nuanced understanding of God).[7] Both of these approaches are seen throughout this series; I have argued so far that we need to read the Bible according to its own theology and worldview—the worldview it teaches—and that we need to interpret it and the world through its metanarrative, or interpretation of all history. These are important aspects of the analogy of faith, but we can point to two other ways Scripture interprets itself. It provides a robust context for interpretation and is often explicitly self-interpreting.

Beginning with context, consider what would happen if you only had the ending and the beginning of a book. You may understand the argument of the book, but you will not know whether to believe it or not or understand what any specialized terms mean, for these are often defined and worked out in the body of a book. Alternatively, consider if you found the middle chapter of a book. What could you understand of it? You would not know the necessary details about the characters, you would not know where they came

---

[6] E.g. Peter John Gentry and Stephen J. Wellum, *Kingdom through Covenant: A Biblical-Theological Understanding of the Covenants* (Wheaton: Crossway, 2012); Goldsworthy, *Gospel-Centered Hermeneutics*.

[7] E.g. Vern S. Poythress, *Reading the Word of God in the Presence of God: A Handbook for Biblical Interpretation* (Wheaton, Illinois: Crossway, 2016), 36–37; Goldsworthy, *Gospel-Centered Hermeneutics*.

from, why their present circumstances are important, and what end this is all working towards. Furthermore, you may be missing key details about the setting, language, or others features that are only revealed when you read the whole book. To put it simply, a text deprived of context is meaningless. It is not meaningless because it says nothing, but it is meaningless because it could mean anything.[8]

Without the author telling you what you should think about the circumstances and characters in the story, you are "free" to create all manner of circumstances, scenarios, storylines, and details. However, such freedom is ultimately a curse, for you will never understand what the author wanted you to know. To understand a text as it is meant to be understood, we need context—a beginning, middle, and end. We need to know the vocabulary an author is using, his characters, and his story. This is not only true of novels, but it is also true of books that recount historical events. In these cases, there are characters—nations and individuals—and circumstances that the reader must be familiar with.

Consider the book of Revelation; what would Revelation 20-22 communicate if we were missing the rest of the Bible? What would we think of final judgment and Satan if we did not understand the nature of sin and the enemy of God's people? What would we make of the massive city descending from heaven if we did not have the rest of the Scriptures to identify Jerusalem with the people of God? What would we do with Jesus's promise to come quickly? Would we assume that he already came or broke his promise? Only context, the rest of Scripture, can answer these questions. God has shaped Scripture as a cohesive whole to provide such a context, a sufficient context to interpret all the events and characters involved so that we might understand them. This enables us to rightly understand the parts of Scripture by reading them in light of the whole Bible, in light of what has come before and what comes after.

This is the case for symbolism as well. A reader of the Gospels for the first time, for example, would probably be lost as to the significance of Jesus referring to the "cup" his Father has prepared for him (e.g. Luke 22:42, John 18:11). However, someone familiar with the Old Testament will recognize in this language—especially in the context of the crucifixion—the symbolic use of "cup" in the Old Testament. In the prophets, God's judgment against

---

[8] We will look at this further in the chapters on meaning.

nations and people was often expressed as drinking from the cup of God's wrath (Isa 51:17, 22; Jer 25:15; Hab 2:15-17; Job 21:20; Rev 14:10). Thus, reading Jesus words in the context of the Bible, we understand that Jesus is about to drink full the wrath of God towards the sins of his people.

Having a context that explains the features of a text is important if it is to be self-interpreting, yet knowing the context—knowing the story and characters—will not necessarily help us resolve pressing difficulties in an individual text. Sometimes we need a word from the author, a little bit of a hint or help to resolve a pressing difficulty.

A good author is aware of this. A good author pays attention to the clarity of his or her work and anticipates confusion, providing interpretive clues along the way to help the reader grasp the point. It is a serious understatement to say this, but God is a good author. He is the best author. He knows that his children are going to get confused over some point or another, so he has provided us with the canon to give us clarity. There is a lot of overlap with the previous category, for context often provides this interpretive clarity. Often, reading a bit further reveals the necessary details to understand what came before. But, at other times, the Bible specifically comments on itself to help us understand it. This is frequent in books of prophecy, where the prophets provide God's interpretation of their vision (e.g. Dan 7:15-28, Dan 8:15-27; Rev 7:14). These interpretations often serve double duty because the imagery is shared between books—e.g. the interpretation of Daniel's visions helps us understand the visions in Revelation. More significantly, the revelation of Jesus Christ in the New Testament sheds immense light on the Old Testament (e.g. Luke 24:25-27, Acts 8:25-35). The New Testament authors often quote the Old Testament; by doing so, they help us understand what was meant: this goes both ways, for the Old Testament also helps us understand what the New intends (e.g. Hab 2:4 sheds light on Rom 1:16-17, Gal 3:11, and Heb 10:36-39 and vice versa; Gen 15 helps us understand Rom 4 and Gal 3, and vice versa; etc.). God has given us the canon we have in order that it might be self-clarifying, that is, in order that it would give us all the tools necessary to interpret difficult texts.

The analogy of faith describes the role of the teaching and context of Scripture for interpreting the parts. Scripture provides a sufficient context to be self-interpreting so that we might understand the persons, events, symbols, etc. in order to apply Scripture to our lives. Now, as we saw in *The*

Gift of Reading Part 1, Scripture is sufficient to interpret it as God intended but not to indulge all our curiosities. There are passages in Scripture that hint at events and persons about which I would love to know more, such as the responses of people to the mass resurrection when Jesus died and what happened to those resurrected, but it gives no more details than is necessary to understand the role of these events in their context—the resurrection of these saints testifies to the new reality that began with Christ's death and resurrection, namely that the new creation and end times resurrection have begun (cf. Matthew 27:52-53).[9]

The analogy of faith has functioned since the Scriptures were first delivered in order that God's people would be able to interpret and apply God's word. Yet throughout the Old Testament period, revelation continued. Scripture had a sort of sufficiency, but because of rebellion, God's people required continual rebuke and reminders: they needed continuing prophetic words. Full sufficiency for interpretation can only be attributed to a final document, one that will not receive any more supplementation. Thus, in its full sense, it is only an attribute of the completed Bible, New and Old Testaments together. Not only is finality a precondition for something to be "sufficient" and so self-interpreting, but it is also a condition that makes it self-interpreting.

B. Closure

Though the Bible began with a core set of covenant documents—the Torah, Genesis through Deuteronomy—it expanded throughout the Old Covenant period. This period ended with the death of Jesus, at which time a New Covenant was inaugurated. This covenant was accompanied by a new revelation from God, a new covenant document to supplement the Old Testament. Only this final product, the Bible—the Old and New Testaments together in one covenant document—could be called final. This is God's final word for his people until Christ returns. Theologians will often say that Canon is "closed"; this closure is necessary for Scripture to be self-interpreting for God's people from the 1st century until Christ returns.

---

[9] That is, the new creation and end times resurrection have begun with Christ but will not be finished until his return. In New Testament studies this is called inaugurated eschatology: the end times have begun but have not fully arrived.

Let me try to illustrate this point. Imagine finding a novel lying on a bench outside your home. It is a book you have never read before, and it is missing the last chapter. Ignoring the existence of the internet and bookstores, what would happen if you read through the whole book only to discover that the last chapter was missing? Besides your frustration, several consequences would result. On the one hand, you would be deprived of the ending you longed for. But more significantly, you would not understand what you had read. Your mind might go wild imagining all the possible endings the story could have, but you would never have certainty as to which of these possible endings was intended—was true. If it were a good story, you would not really understand anything at all. That is, many good stories wait until the very end to supply the key interpretive insight that sheds light on all that preceded it. When you reach the end of a good story, your mind speeds back over all that you have read and re-interprets it in light of the final revelation or twist (think of the movie, *The Sixth Sense*). In the case of such a story, the lack of an ending—of closure—means that the rest of the story is ultimately shrouded in mystery, awaiting the revelation that will reveal its meaning.

What if the ending of your book was missing, yet it was cut off at such a point that you were unsure if it was missing or not? What if you got to the end and were left questioning if that was all there was? You are forced to decide; do you interpret the book in light of the ending you have or conclude that you are missing the ultimate interpretive key to the book?[10]

In both cases, what is needed is closure. To rightly interpret a book, you need to have its ending and know that what you have is, in fact, the ending. The canon as we have it provides the necessary closure we need to interpret it. Scholars will argue from various pieces of evidence throughout the New Testament to show this, but the most significant evidence is the very shape

---

[10] The book of Mark provides an interesting illustration of this point. The book of Mark ends on a cliff-hanger, it recounts the angels' report of Christ's resurrection but ends there. At some point, it appears that scribes were not satisfied with this cliff-hanger and tried to fill in the ending of Mark from the other Gospels and Acts. The several endings that appear in the manuscripts provide different interpretations of the whole book, with the short ending printed in our English Bibles strongly supported by the rest of the book and our manuscript evidence. The point is this: if you read Mark with the short ending, you interpret the book one way; if you read it with the long ending, another interpretation presents itself. Only one is correct, so having a right knowledge of the ending is highly important.

of the canon itself. Good stories, good books, share many things in common. One of these things is resolution: the tension invoked in the beginning is resolved in the end. There are various ways of presenting this, but two significant ways are *mirroring* and *summarizing*. As you may remember from High School or college, the way to understand a book is to study its beginning and its end. A book that makes an argument will present a thesis or a question at the beginning, raising a problem or stating its solution to a problem; throughout the book, various arguments will be made; and in the conclusion, these arguments will be summarized and the thesis or problem restated. The beginning and end give you two different perspectives on the same thing, the meaning of the book.

Sometimes, especially in a narrative, this is done artfully by mirroring. The conclusion will reverse the structure and content presented in the introduction, providing answers instead of questions. The book of Revelation both mirrors and summarizes Genesis. A careful reading of the last chapters of Revelation and the first chapters of Genesis reveals that the problems raised in the beginning are answered in the end, and the language and structure mirror their counterpart. Genesis recounts God creating humanity for a garden and being exiled from it because of the Fall; Revelation recounts the answer to the Fall and the return of the exiles to a new Eden, a holy city occupied by God himself. Because the Bible is closed, we can expect to find a resolution to its narrative tensions, to the problems it raises. Knowing that the Bible is closed or completed should lead us to seek answers to problems we find in our reading, expecting them to be resolved later in the Bible. Closure is necessary for a book to be understood, providing both the ground for believing that tensions are resolved and the motivation to seek their resolution. Where such an endeavour concludes in an apparent paradox, we are led by canonical closure to accept that this is the resolution God intended for us to have. Canonical closure, along with the analogy of faith, describe significant ways by which God has made Scripture self-interpreting. Before turning to *external sufficiency*, I want to consider a specific application of the analogy of faith, how the Bible is linguistically sufficient.

C. <u>Linguistic Sufficiency</u>

I raised at the beginning of this chapter the problems for the sufficiency of Scripture and interpretation when it comes to language. To some extent, these problems are resolved by Scripture's external sufficiency, a tradition of interpreting Scripture in light of the original languages that has continued throughout the history of the Church. However, this sense of sufficiency does not make Scripture self-interpreting unless Scripture also has an internal sufficiency such that it can be the authority for its linguistic interpretation—for interpreting the words, grammar, and syntax of the original text. Some readers might be thinking at this time that I, as a student of the biblical languages—especially Hebrew—should know better. Archaeological discoveries and extra-biblical textual traditions have shed much light on the languages of the Bible, allowing us to interpret them better. I will postpone a discussion of the role of such discoveries until a later chapter, but I will say at this time that I am not convinced that these discoveries have or can have any normative value for interpreting the Bible: they cannot tell us what a word or grammatical construction mean. Whatever role they have, they will be supplementary to the content of the Bible. We will look at the roles they have later, but let's argue for the linguistic sufficiency of Scripture here.

I argued above that this must be the case theologically. If Scripture is not sufficient to lead us in the interpretation of the grammar, syntax, and meaning of the original language text, then it will not be self-interpreting, for interpretation is built on this foundation. We have seen that the Bible's claims to authority and sufficiency demand that it be self-interpreting, so from this starting point, we must ask how it is so linguistically. I believe we can argue for this in two ways, by showing briefly how the Bible has epistemological priority in its own interpretation—implying what we have already seen—and by considering the scope of the Bible as it has been given to us.

First, consider the epistemic priority of Scripture. To say that the Bible has epistemic priority is to say that the Bible has the ultimate say in its own interpretation. That is, if external evidence suggests one or more interpretations of a text and the piece of literature in which the text is found offers one interpretation, the interpretation provided by the text's context will always have precedence—for textual context is the primary consideration for interpretation (we explored this in *The Gift of Reading Part 1* and will look at it from a different perspective in a later chapter). When it comes to interpreting the Bible, the main difficulties are presented by rare words—including words that only occur once in the Bible (*hapax legomena*)—and difficult syntactic or grammatical constructions (i.e. difficulties in understanding the relationships between grammatical clauses and words). If there is an explanation of any of these difficulties that can be argued from the Bible itself, this explanation takes precedence over any other explanation given from extra-biblical evidence. We can give several reasons for this. First, the Bible is the context given to us for interpreting the text, of which words and clauses are a part. In this sense, it has epistemic priority. Second, textual context gives immediate credibility to an explanation coming from the Bible; extra-biblical explanations are far harder—maybe even impossible—to prove. That is, if you are explaining the meaning of a word from an extra-biblical text, you must show how this text is relevant to the interpretation of the biblical book—how it is geographically, linguistically, culturally, and temporally related (for language changes given different locations, dialects, worldviews, and times). Third—positively—the Bible also takes evidential priority in explaining itself because it provides three bodies of intelligible language that have exerted a shaping influence on themselves.

That is, first, whatever truth is found in the distinction between different stages of Hebrew in the Bible (archaic, classical, late), these involve stylistic changes. The vocabulary and grammar of Biblical Hebrew remain consistent: if you can read archaic Biblical Hebrew, there is a good chance you can read the classical and late Biblical Hebrew and vice versa.[11] So the Bible is demonstrability a single corpus of language, whereas appeals to different Hebrew inscriptions do not necessarily represent the same form of Hebrew (consider the differences between Christian literature from the American South and atheistic literature from England).[12] Considering the New Testament, though different styles are present (compare John with Acts and Hebrews), all the books of the New Testament are examples of the common dialect of the 1st-century world, Koine Greek. I am not an expert in Biblical Aramaic, but from my encounters with the Aramaic sections of the Bible, I believe the same can be said for these sections of the Bible as well. In this way, the Hebrew and Aramaic (for they are closely related) and the Greek

---

[11] Comparing modern English to Old English is not even a good comparison, for the spelling of words is almost identical across these different Hebrew styles. There are some noticeable changes, yet they are encountered once or twice a reader quickly adjusts (e.g. the use of הוא in the place of היא, "she," in Archaic Hebrew, Gen 2:12). The biggest change maybe the preference for different verb types in Classical Hebrew vs Late Hebrew, though even here I believe the differences are sometimes overstated.

[12] Though different dialects existed between the tribes of Israel, especially in pronunciation (cf. Judges 12:5-6), the Old Testament largely comes from the perspective of Judah.

sections of the Bible represent two or three bodies of intelligible literature.

Second, it should be un-objectionable to say that the Bible has exerted a shaping influence on itself. The entire Old Testament is shaped by the Torah, which provides its foundations;[13] the New Testament is shaped by the Old Testament; and the letters are shaped by the Gospels, or at least the teachings of Jesus found in the Gospels. Even stylistically, it has often been argued that the writing styles of the New Testament authors demonstrate the influence of the Hebrew Old Testament. As it is relevant to our argument, that the authors of the Bible are consciously and unconsciously influenced by the rest of the Bible suggests that we should seek to explain not only the meaning of their texts but also the decisions they make in writing by the texts that have shaped them. When we add to these considerations the theological argument that God has intentionally shaped Scripture to be self-interpreting, I think we have a strong case to suggest that this extends to the language in which it is written.

One last observation to make in this regard concerns the scope of Scripture. What I have argued so far would be hard to believe if it were said about any other single text. It is not so preposterous given a large body of texts—a corpus, such as Shakespeare's works, or maybe early 20th century English literature—but not many, if any, single texts could justify such a claim. Unlike the other books, the Bible is massive in its scope and size. Considering its scope, it covers the beginning of the creation to its end, documenting every major event God has deemed essential to interpreting history. It provides an interpretation of all history and of all the creation—giving a lens by which we can see everything (cf. *The Gift of Knowing* and *The Gift of Seeing*). Not only does it have such a broad scope, but it is also very large and is written in many different ways—such as narrative, didactic prose, poetry, and prophecy. Its scope is relevant to the first part of internal sufficiency—the analogy of faith—and its size relevant to the second part—linguistic sufficiency. The Bible provides many examples of grammar, syntax, and word usage to which we can compare difficult passages in order to

---

[13] I have argued elsewhere, for example, that the Torah provides a lens for interpreting the events of Samuel and Judges. Cf. J. Alexander Rutherford, *God's Kingdom Through his Priest King: An Analysis of the Book of Samuel in Light of the Davidic Covenant* (Teleioteti, 2019); "Not a Single Survivor," teleioteti.ca/resources/papers.

resolve them.[14]

Having considered the analogy of faith, canonical closure, and linguistic sufficiency, I think we have seen how God has created the Bible to be internally sufficient for self-interpretation. But as I suggested above, for a text to be self-interpreting, it needs external sufficiency in addition to internal sufficiency.

D. External Sufficiency

By externally sufficient, I refer to the necessity of an interpreting community to realize the self-interpreting nature of a text. That is, unless a text is very small, it is almost impossible to start from scratch—without any knowledge of its language, meaning, story, structure, etc.—and come to a full understanding of it. What is needed is a community that already understands the content and possess the tools to interpret the text so that new interpreters can be equipped to understand it. What separates a self-interpreting text from a non-self-interpreting text is the ability of the former to create and sustain an interpretive community and to serve as the final standard of its own interpretation (it must be internally sufficient for self-interpretation).

First, if a text fails to sustain the interpretive interests of people, after several generations, the meaning of the text will be lost—maybe even the text itself. Second, a self-interpreting text must have the ability to refine and challenge the understanding of the community it creates. That is, it provides the tools and content necessary for its own interpretation by constantly shaping and refining the tools of the community so that they understand it rightly. This process of refining means that the text itself is the ultimate standard of what tools and interpretive lens are appropriate for its own interpretation: this is the distinguishing mark of a self-interpreting text. This process, of coming to the Bible with a pre-understanding (an understanding of the whole) and having it refined under the authority of the text is often called "the hermeneutical spiral."[15] Beginning with some level of

---

[14] See *The Gift of Reading Part 1* for my introductory guide to resolving such difficulties. To see how this works, see the essays in the appendices of this book and my forthcoming commentary *The Book of Habakkuk: An Exegetical-Theological Commentary*.

[15] Grant Osborne named his 1991 introduction to biblical hermeneutics after this

understanding, the interpreter finds their interpretation of the Bible challenged and refined every time they attempt to interpret individual texts in light of the whole.[16]

This is the significance of the passage I quoted at the beginning of this chapter (Deut 6:20-25). Christians, and God's Old Covenant people before them, are profoundly text-centred people. The Bible, as God's very words, places a vital role in personal, family, work, and Church life. Every facet of life is to be brought into conformity with the Bible, so every Christian ought to be able to understand the Word when they read it or hear it read. In the Old Testament, the society of the Israelites was shaped to teach them the proper interpretation of God's word. The festivals—especially the Passover—were lived out parables or celebrations of God's past deeds, meant to point forward towards the demands of the Law (Deut 6:20-25). They provide both a reminder of what happened and an opportunity to reflect upon and learn the significance of the events recounted. The sabbath was a reminder not only of God's initial creation rest but also of the rest God promised his people when he brought them out from Egypt (Exod 20:8-11, 31:12; Deut 5:12). For New Testament Christians, baptism and the Lord's supper have a similar function.

Furthermore, reading Scripture was a regular practice in the Old Testament, demanded especially of the leadership (e.g. Deut 17:18-20; Josh 1:8). In the New Testament, the Apostles and the churches they founded devoted themselves regularly to the reading of the Scriptures (1 Tim 4:13). As amazing evidence to this fact, many of Paul's letters were written to largely Gentile churches—churches full of those who had not grown up with the Old Testament Scriptures—yet he constantly quotes the Old Testament

---

process, *The Hermeneutical Spiral: A Comprehensive Introduction to Biblical Interpretation* (IVP).

[16] J.I. Packer describes this spiral (though he uses "circle") in this way, "I use the phrase 'hermeneutical circle' to express the truth (for truth it is) that our exegesis, synthesis, and application is determined by a hermeneutic—that is, a view of the interpretative process—that is determined by an overall theology, a theology that in its turn rests on and supports itself by exegesis, synthesis, and application.... From this standpoint it might be better to speak of the hermeneutical *spiral*, whereby we rise from less exact and well-tested understanding to one that is more so." J.I. Packer, "Infallible Scripture and the Role of Hermeneutics," in *Scripture and Truth*, ed. D. A. Carson and John D. Woodbridge (Grand Rapids: Baker, 1992), 348.

assuming that his Gentile hearers would understand the quotations (cf. Galatians, Ephesians, Philippians, Colossians, 1 & 2 Thessalonians). In the short time since their conversion, he expects them to have learned—or have access to those who would teach them—the Old Testament. Through its symbolic life and its mandate for the church (cf. Matt 28:18-20), the Bible sustains an interpretive community with the tools necessary to interpret it.

Throughout the history of the Church, those who become Christians are taught the faith that they confess; they receive from pastors and teachers a sketch of the biblical teaching by which they can interpret it when they read it or hear it read.[17] When God created the Church in the 1st century, calling forth Jews and Gentiles into a new covenant community instituted through the blood of Christ, he created an interpreting community that was shaped by the Apostolic teaching canonized in Scripture and was so equipped with a knowledge of its teaching in order to begin the hermeneutical spiral. This is the external sufficiency of Scripture: it was given into and was written to sustain a community that would use its own tools to interpret it. I discuss the role of the Church and tradition more in *The Gift of Knowing* and *The Gift of Reading Part 1*, but it is worth reiterating that Scripture, as the canonized teaching of God's prophets and apostles, is the foundation of Christian life and doctrine. Tradition is a record of the Christian interaction with and application of Scripture to their own cultures and times. It is invaluable—even necessary—for interpreting Scripture but only because it represents the whole counsel of God revealed in Scripture as it has been taught to his people.

E. Conclusion

In this chapter, we began our discussion of the hermeneutical issues concerning the Bible's role in interpretation. Starting with the Bible's role as authority for interpretation, I have argued that the Bible needs to be self-

---

[17] Many catholic interprets or supporters of the normative function of tradition point to Philip's encounter with the Ethiopian Eunuch in the Acts 8:26-40 as an example of the necessity of tradition to interpret Scripture. I would suggest that this is an example of the people of God functioning as an interpretive community, not adding anything to Scripture but helping those unfamiliar to make the connections that already exist. The New Testament does what Philip did in this passage, makes the connection between the Old Testament and Jesus; God's people throughout the ages help us to see clearly how Scripture does this.

interpreting and have attempted to demonstrate several ways God has shaped the Bible to be so. With this as a foundation, I want to begin our discussion of "meaning" with the contribution the Bible, or the text, has in meaning.

3

THE BIBLE AND MEANING

> The "meaning of meaning" is a subject that has frequently been discussed by linguists, philosophers, theologians, and others. As with most terms, there is no single correct definition of *meaning*. Some types of definitions, however, promote misunderstandings and others help to alleviate them. – John Frame[1]

Behind the many different approaches to interpreting the Bible we saw in chapter 1, the question "What is 'meaning'?" or better, "where does meaning reside?" has stood behind their differences. For Postmodern interpreters, meaning rests solely in the text or the reader; for Modernists, meaning rests in the historical communicative act of which the text is a part. In different ways, all the approaches we have seen emphasize either the role of the reader, the author, or the text in meaning. In my attempt to answer these two questions—which are really two different ways of asking the same question—I want to suggest that the author, reader, and text all have a role to play in "meaning." In this chapter, we will consider the role of the text for meaning. In chapter 5, we will consider the role of the Reader, and in chapter 7, the role of the author. In summary, the author is the originator of meaning, the text is the standard or norm for meaning, and the reader is agent in making meaning. In this chapter, we will look at what I mean when I speak of "meaning" and then the role of the text as a standard for meaning in this specific sense.[2]

---

[1] John M. Frame, *The Doctrine of the Knowledge of God*, A Theology of Lordship (Phillipsburg: P&R Publishing, 1987), 93.

[2] Our discussion in this and following chapters is dependent on work published

A. The Meaning of Meaning

When it comes to the definition of terms, there are no right or wrong answers, only helpful and unhelpful ones. When an author uses a word in a non-standard way and fails to explain what is meant, this is unhelpful; but if words are used in their normal way or their use is appropriately explained, there is nothing wrong with different definitions.[3] So I am not arguing that a specific meaning for the word "meaning" is correct; instead, I want to explain why I use "meaning" in specific way and why this is, in my opinion, the best way to use it in the context of hermeneutics.

Of the many ways the word "meaning" is used, I think two are most relevant to our discussion. On the one hand, people will sometimes say "that is not what I meant," "that is not what it means," or "what I meant to say is…." In these cases, "meaning" refers to an application or implication of what someone said. When someone draws a false conclusion from what is said, this conclusion is not what was meant. When people have competing explanations of the text, they debate over which one is what "the text means." Here, meaning is something other than the text; meaning is a right explanation of it. When someone clarifies what they *meant* to say, they often provide the conclusion—the action or belief—they wanted you to draw from what they said. They express the meaning they wanted you to take away from what they said. In all these senses, meaning appears to be an application or use of the text, the result of drawing from it an explanation, an action to take, an idea to believe, etc. John Frame argues, based on the later work of Ludwig Wittgenstein, that "meaning" as the use of a text makes the best sense of how we use the word and is the most helpful for discussions of hermeneutics.

---

in my Master's Thesis, *God's Kingdom Through his Priest King* (Teleioteti, 2019), in *The Gift of Reading Part 1* (Teleioteti, 2019), and in a paper and an article available through Teleioteti.ca. J. Alexander Rutherford, "Towards an Evangelical Hermeneutic: A Critique of the Chicago Statement on Hermeneutics (1982)" (Teleioteti, December 2016), accessed January 23, 2018, https://teleioteti.ca/resources/papers/; J. Alexander Rutherford, "An Investigation into the Role of Context in Interpretation," *Teleioteti*, January 16, 2018, accessed January 24, 2018, https://teleioteti.ca/2018/01/16/investigation-role-context-interpretation/.

[3] Consider the discussion of meaning and terminology in general in Vern Sheridan Poythress, *Symphonic Theology: The Validity of Multiple Perspectives in Theology* (Grand Rapids: Academie Books, 1987); Frame, *Doctrine of Knowledge*, 93–98.

"We must say," he writes, "that the meaning of an expression is its *God-ordained* use."⁴ he summarizes his discussion like this,

> To ask for the meaning of an expression is to ask for an application. When we ask to know the meaning of a word or sentence, we are expressing a problem. We are indicating that we are not able to *use* the language in question. The problem may be relieved in a wide variety of way: synonymous expressions, ostensive definition, references to mental images, intentions, methods of verification, and so forth may all be of help. The goal, however, is not merely to supply one of those; the goal is to relieve the problem, to help the questioner use the language in question.⁵

I generally adhere to this sense of the word "meaning" in what follows: "meaning" refers to a justified use of a text. Because there are many justified uses of a text, we can rightly speak of the *meanings* of a text. I will use the phrase "meaning potential" to refer to all the potential uses a text may have.⁶

However, when it comes to hermeneutics, "meaning" is often used to refer to what the author intended. E.D. Hirsch, Jr. famously defined meaning in contrast with significance. Meaning was "fixed and immutable," but significance or application changed.⁷ This "fixed and immutable" meaning

---

⁴ Frame, *Doctrine of Knowledge*, 97..

⁵ Ibid., 98. This is the definition I (loosely) followed in the first part of this volume. Cf. Ibid., 62–64.

⁶ "Meaning-potential is a justified use of the text, as determined by the criteria of validity, fittingness, and appropriateness. When a new context is added, the text remains the same, but the field of reference, function, linguistic understanding will be affected. Some referents for "redemption" from "Egypt," for example, are removed from the realm of possibility (what may be "fitting" is narrowed). Yet, the justified uses of a text are increased. Without context to provide the fitting referent of "redemption" and "Egypt," a use that assumes the referent is the Exodus of Israel achieved by God is possible but not fitting, and so not justified. But with the addition of context that makes clear the referent, many possible uses are excluded, but this possible use is justified." J. Alexander Rutherford, *God's Kingdom through his Priest-King: An Analysis of the Book of Samuel in Light of the Davidic Covenant*, A Teleioteti Technical Study 1 (Vancouver: Teleioteti, 2019), 99. On justification and its criteria, see *The Gift of Reading Part 1*.

⁷ This is Hirsch's own summary from the article "Meaning and Significance Reinterpreted"; his original work was *Validity in Interpretation*. Eric D. Hirsch, Jr., "Meaning and Significance Reinterpreted," *Critical Inquiry* 11, no. 2 (1984): 202–

was equivalent to the historical intent of the author when he originally spoke or wrote. An immediate problem emerges with such a definition of meaning: what is intended by "intention?" Is it a mental picture the author had, a propositional statement of truth, or a goal he or she hoped to achieve with their communicative act?[8] Furthermore, is it conscious or unconscious intent? To be honest, I cannot tell you what the single, fixed "intent" is of what I am writing here. These are common criticism of such a definition.[9]

There is another problem with this definition that is often not considered; where do we draw the boundaries for a text with a single meaning? I pointed out in my paper "Toward an Evangelical Hermeneutic" that intention could refer to a propositional statement or goal for every word, sentence, paragraph, chapter, and book in the Bible. For a text to communicate, an author intends—at some level—for a metaphor to be interpreted properly, for a syntactic relationship to have a certain function, for a reader to come to believe or do something, etc.[10] So for every element of a text, we can rightly speak of the "author's intention." In which intention, then, does the single meaning lie? Hirsch sought with his definition to uphold the reader's intuitive belief that there are right and wrong meanings or interpretations of texts. His definition of meaning attempted to identify the normative aspect of meaning—that standard by which we judge the validity of interpretations—

225; Eric D. Hirsch, Jr., *Validity in Interpretation*, 9. print. (New Haven: Yale Univ. Press, 1979). Cf. Walter C. Kaiser, "The Single Intent of Scripture," in *The Right Doctrine from the Wrong Texts?: Essays on the Use of the Old Testament in the New*, ed. G. K. Beale (Grand Rapids: Baker Books, 1994); Earl D. Radmacher and Robert D. Preus, eds., "Appendix A: The Chicago Statement on Biblical Hermeneutics," in *Hermeneutics, Inerrancy, and the Bible* (Grand Rapids: Zondervan, 1984); Norman L. Geisler, "Appendix B: Explaining Hermeneutics: A Commentary on the Chicago Statement on Biblical Hermeneutics Articles of Affirmation and Denial," in *Hermeneutics, Inerrancy, and the Bible*, ed. Earl D. Radmacher and Robert D. Preus (Grand Rapids: Zondervan, 1984), 163–190.

[8] Cf. Frame, *Doctrine of Knowledge*, 98.

[9] Cf. C S Lewis, "Modern Theology and Biblical Criticism," *BYU Studies Quarterly* 9, no. 1 (1969): Article 5; Philip Barton Payne, "The Fallacy of Equating Meaning with the Human Author's Intention," in *The Right Doctrine from the Wrong Texts?: Essays on the Use of the Old Testament in the New*, ed. G. K. Beale (Grand Rapids: Baker Books, 1994); Hirsch, Jr., "Meaning and Significance Reinterpreted."

[10] Cf. Rutherford, "Towards an Evangelical Hermeneutic."

with something behind the text, with the author's original intentions. But as John Frame has observed, this raises more problems than it solves. Placing the normative aspect of the text beyond the text, as with Hirsch's "meaning," is an attempt to guard the intuition that there are right and wrong meanings, yet "Instead of increasing the objectivity of our knowledge," Frame perceives, "such an intermediary is a subjective construct that inevitably clouds our understanding of the text itself."[11]

However, we know that texts mean some things and not others, that there is some sort of standard by which we can judge whether a particular use or meaning of a text is right or wrong.[12] If there is no normative meaning, such as Hirsch postulated in his 1967 book, then we are left with the text as the standard for judging whether a meaning is justified or not. With Frame I contend that the text (whether a sentence, paragraph, chapter, or book) is the anchor of meaning, is the standard by which we evaluate if a meaning or use is justified.[13] I refer to the text, limited by context, as either the text or "what is said." "What is said" brings in the added element of intentionality, which we will discuss in chapter 8. As we will see below, a word or sentence taken on its own could say many things, but when placed in a robust context, it says something specific. This is the ground for meaning—words constrained by context. Meaning is the use of "what is said."

Later, when we consider the reader and meaning in chapter 5, we will consider the Reader's role in making and judging meanings. In what follows, I want to discuss how texts possess meaning, laying a foundation for our later discussion of recognizing meaning. In what follows, I will distinguish between "what is said" and meaning.

B. The Text and Meaning[14]

I argued above that context plays an essential role in the way Scripture self-

---

[11] Frame, *Doctrine of Knowledge*, 98.

[12] We are of course assuming that texts have communicated meaning in the past and do so today in the same way. Cf. Vern Sheridan Poythress, *In the Beginning Was the Word: Language: A God-Centered Approach* (Wheaton: Crossway Books, 2009), 37–38.

[13] Frame, *Doctrine of Knowledge*, 98.

[14] This is adapted from my article on Teleioteti.ca, "An Investigation into the Role of Context in Interpretation."

interprets. The study of language and how it works in the 20th century has led to the common view that context is essential to understanding all communication. It will be advantageous for us to discuss here why this is the case. By considering how context creates meaning, we will see how texts are normative for meaning, how they contain a finite meaning potential.

Context, I argue, both limits and reveals textual meaning so that texts can be used. Texts of every sort are "multivalent"; they have a wealth of *meaning potential.* A text says something but could be used in an infinite number of ways; it has numerous potential applications or meanings. A commandment, such as "You shall not kill," can be used to create legislation, command behaviour, describe God's character, state a moral principle ("killing is wrong"), govern one's choices, etc. Texts are thus multivalent in the sense of "use." The words that make up texts, considered on their own, are also multivalent in the sense that they could be used to say many different things.

That texts are multivalent in this sense can be wonderful! The multivalence of biblical texts is the reason they apply to cultures and situations far beyond those in which they were originally written. However, misunderstood, a text's multivalence can lead to its abuse or neglect. If a text has infinite meaning potential, for example, it is practically meaningless. That is, all its meaning is derived from the reader and not the text itself. For example, the three symbols "רוץ" on their own are meaningless; what good would it do to have a document with only "רוץ" written on it? For the person who does not read Hebrew, it could mean anything they want it to—for nothing constrains their reading. For the person who reads Hebrew, it could mean any number of things (to run, flow; one running, something flowing; etc.). Without an appropriate restraint on meaning potential, a text can be used for any purpose or no purpose at all. For any word or text to have meaning, it needs *context*; it needs a larger unit of text in addition to the language with which to understand combinations of symbols (such as רוץ).

Context constrains the meaning of a text, reduces infinite meaning potential to finite meaning potential. This is how texts *mean*: they use symbols to make words in specific morphological forms and give them meaning by putting them into combinations. For a language to have meaning, it needs context. Context constrains the meaning of words and syntactical combinations, producing a text with a finite meaning potential. It is by constraining meaning that context gives meaning.[15]

Where there is context, and therefore meaning, there are valid and invalid interpretations of a text.[16] For example, careful attention to the context of the Ten Commandments, especially the word I rendered "kill" above, reveals that the meaning "killing is wrong" is an invalid meaning of the commandment (deriving the proposition "killing is wrong" is an invalid use of the text). The Hebrew word refers more specifically to "murder."

Because there can be valid and invalid meanings of a text, and these are given by the context, context is essential for understanding and using a text. Context—the surrounding texts and thought in which a text is found—hedges the meaning potential of a text.

Context tells the reader what is being said by restricting the meaning potential a text would otherwise have. Context also excludes potential uses of a text and guides the reader to those that are most relevant.[17] Context can also illuminate for a reader meaning potential that is originally obscure, such as revealing a shade of meaning for a word or structure previously unknown

---

[15] This account of the function of context is from the perspective of the reader, recognizing meaning or justified uses of the text. From the perspective of the author, writing a text is functional—selecting words and syntax in combinations for specific communicative functions, to communicate an argument, a truth, a picture, compel an emotion. Only a small fraction of potential uses is recognized by the author; sometimes a text implies things that the author would otherwise not want, yet this is nevertheless a valid use of the text—often revealing a flaw in the author's own thinking.

[16] It should be observed that not all context is explicit. For example, one liners and short quotes presuppose—if they are to have meaning—a shared context of meaning, such as a similar experience (experience of the same T.V. show) or a worldview in which the words used have the same meaning for the speaker and the listener.

[17] The idea of relevancy qualifies what we mean by valid interpretations. It is possible to have a valid interpretation that is not relevant. For example, it is valid to use the text "you shall not murder" to formulate the proposition, "'murder' is the fourth word in the command 'you shall not murder.'" This is true, yet it is irrelevant to the author's purpose in giving the command: it is a trivial use of the text, an inconsequential and so an interpretation that is irrelevant. Relevancy is not a measure of justification for an application but its worth. (If justification describes the legitimacy of an application, relevancy describes its usefulness.)

or alerting one to a detail that went previously unnoticed.

Consider the following. The four symbols "h-e-a-t" could be one of two words, each with a wealth of meaning potential (1. to cook, warm up, prepare; 2. the attribute hotness or a manifestation of hotness). The sentence, "Tim enfolded an empanada in tin foil in order to heat it up," limits the potential meanings of "heat" substantially. It is now clear what these four symbols (h-e-a-t) mean here. However, though what is being said is clear enough, how it could be used ("application") is vague: who is Tim, and why does it matter that he heated his empanada in tin foil? The uses at this moment are near infinite: any Tim may be the subject of the action, and his action could have infinite applications. Adding further context, however, will restrict the uses we could make of this sentence significantly and illumine the relevant uses (I concede that the following is preposterous):

> A doctor is treating a victim with substantial burns over his upper body. Readying the admission form, he reads the description of the incident that led to this hospital visit as recorded by Tim's mother. Apparently, during his lunch break, "after coming home, Tim enfolded an empanada in tin foil in order to heat it up; he then put it in the microwave for 10 minutes!! Shortly thereafter, Tim opened the microwave to investigate his food and flames and sparks burst forth, covering the poor boy!"

This sheds much light on the word "heat" and on the sentence as a whole. We now know how it can be used and how we should not use it. We can imagine another scenario where "heat up" indicates that the action in a basketball game is intensifying. For one who is unfamiliar with this idiomatic use of "heat," the context of a sports game will reveal what was, up to this point, unknown meaning potential.

Therefore, the primary function of context is limiting: it restricts meaning (as in the case of Tim and the empanada). A secondary function is illuminating: it reveals meaning (as in the case of a sports game). Reading within properly defined contextual boundaries will achieve both purposes. Because context has such control over meaning, placing a text within a new context can have significant effects on its meaning potential. We will consider this further when we consider the relationship between the author and meaning.

C. Conclusion[18]

In sum, as John Frame observes, in practical use, we use meaning in a way indistinguishable from application.[19] Therefore, meaning naturally refers not to the propositional "sense" behind the text but all the legitimate uses we make of a text, uses that (when justified) demonstrate our understanding of the text.[20] As an example, someone has only understood or grasped the meaning of "you shall not murder" when they can explicate the appropriate situation in which this command applies: he only understands it when he can use it.[21]

Instead of the single-proposition view of meaning, we can build on Frame's conclusion and posit that meaning is not a singular objective

---

[18] This is adapted, with permission, from an excurses in my Master's thesis, Rutherford, *God's Kingdom*, 93–102.

[19] Not being too much of a stickler for terminology, Frame offers as an alternative to identifying meaning with application the possibility of identifying meaning with the text and application with its uses. Frame, *Doctrine of Knowledge*, 98.

[20] Vern Poythress's account of meaning, which has some similarities to Frame's, reveals the fundamentally confused nature of the propositional or single-sense view of meaning. Poythress argues for a position that is both similar to yet more sophisticated than the usual single-sense view: he contends that the "sense" of a text is the objective anchor of application which can be paraphrased or communicated in different languages. It is this objective basis that leads us to conclude when we compare a paraphrase with the original that "they say the same thing." Yet he concedes that such a paraphrase represents a loss: it can never communicate the fullness of the original text. Yet, if meaning is this objective sense and the sense is appropriately embodied in both the paraphrase and the original, what is lost? The answer is that we lose some of the potential applications of the original. Thus, we are faced with a loss of meaning: the paraphrase is not as usable or rich as the original.
We can make more sense of this situation if we adopt Frame's view. We recognize in an accurate paraphrase continuity with the original: this text has been applied appropriately to a new context. In the case of a paraphrase, someone has explained part of the original. Yet as an application, the paraphrase is a restriction of the original; it cannot be used in as many ways as the original. In fact, it is impossible to recapture the full range of a text's appropriate applications by recommunicating a text in any other manner—that is, without reproducing the text in its full context. Thus, it is the text as restricted by its context that is the objective anchor of meaning, defined as legitimate uses of the text. Vern Sheridan Poythress, *God Centered Biblical Interpretation* (Phillipsburg, N.J.: P&R Publishing, 1999), 69–92; Poythress, *In the Beginning Was the Word*, 163–185.

[21] Frame, *Doctrine of Knowledge*, 66–67.

universal idea that can be instantiated in new contexts and languages but the sum-total of the possible legitimate or justified uses one could make of a text. That is, the "objective" aspect of a text is the text itself delimited by its context, not a mysterious proposition that lies behind it.[22] On this understanding, we could define meaning as *every justified use of a text as determined by its literary and linguistic context*.[23] The question that remains

---

[22] We could argue, in addition, that there is no reason to believe God's thoughts about a text are propositions; it would cohere more with our experience of texts (we read texts and use them) to think that God perfectly knows the text in its context and all the real and potential implications that derive from the text. There is no reason to believe that behind the text there lies a singular proposition, either in the mind of an author (I can assure you none of what I am saying can be fully summarized in a proposition) or in the mind of God. This is significant if, as I contended in *The Gift of Knowing*, truth is correspondence between our interpretation of the creation and its Creator and God's interpretation.

[23] "Literary" refers to the textual body (book, anthology, etc.) in which a text is to be read and "linguistic" to the rules and nature of the language in which it was composed. Where does this leave history? As it regards the text—not situations to which the text will be applied—historiography (encompassing social history) and archaeology could be understood as parts of the linguistic context. That is, they help us to better understand the language of the text and the texts field of reference (referential meaning). However, caution must be taken in both regards.

Consider reference: though texts have what we could call "implied referents"—that is, referents that are described within the textual body—textual reference also extends beyond bounds of a text to the actual objects, persons, and events it recounts. A similar relationship exists between implied and historical referents as with implied and historical authors. Though an implied referent corresponds in the case of historical narrative to a historical referent, it is an intentional representation of the latter. Therefore, one must be careful about reading extra-textual knowledge of the historical referent into the implied referent. We will address this issue more in chapter 9. Cf. Carson, *Exegetical Fallacies*, 63–64; Moisés Silva, *Biblical Words and Their Meaning: An Introduction to Lexical Semantics*, rev. and expanded ed. (Grand Rapids: Zondervan, 1994); Rutherford, *God's Kingdom*, 115–116.

Linguistic understanding—specifically vocabulary and grammar—can be considered similarly. There exists a historical Hebrew language that has a close relationship with the historic languages of Ugarit, Syria, Aram, Egypt, and other peoples. Yet, the language of the Bible (and, indeed, the language of each author) is an implied language. That is, no author has a full understanding of his or her own language, therefore we must reckon in interpretation not with the historical language to which they were related but the implied language that they used. Consider, for example, the apostle John: he uses grammar in Rev 1:4 that does not reflect appropriate Greek usage (ἀπό ὁ ὤν, *apo o ōn*, from he who is). The "error" is part of the implied language of John but not the historical language of Koine Greek. See

yet unanswered is, what qualifies as a justified use of a text?

A meaning would be justified if it makes a valid use that is appropriate to the function of the text and fitting for its field of reference.[24] A use is valid if it is part of the text's meaning potential as delimited by context; it is appropriate if it corresponds to the function of the text so that it would be inappropriate to use a text intended to lead one in right behaviour to counsel wrong behaviour (because God says murder is wrong, go murder!); and it is fitting if the use does not equivocate on the relationships between the text and referents (thus, to use a text about Israel's exodus from Egypt to make historical conclusions about the going forth of an unrelated people group from an unrelated location named Egypt would not be *fitting*). Validity, appropriateness, and fittingness in these senses are co-inherent and thus different perspectives by which the whole meaning potential of a text could be viewed, each depending upon the others and determined by a text's context.[25]

---

further our discuss of linguistic sufficiency above.

That God has exhaustive knowledge of each valid use of a text means that there is a true boundary to all textual meaning; it is not potentially infinite from a divine perspective. Poythress observes that at some point, a consideration of application "must somewhere along the way appeal directly to God's knowledge, authority, and presence." Vern Sheridan Poythress, "Divine Meaning of Scripture," in *The Right Doctrine from the Wrong Texts?: Essays on the Use of the Old Testament in the New*, ed. G. K. Beale (Grand Rapids: Baker Books, 1994), 87–88.

[24] "Validity," "appropriateness," and "fittingness," are similar to Poythress's three perspectives on textual meaning—sense, application, and import. Poythress, God Centered Biblical Interpretation, 72–74. They differ in that, with Frame, I identify sense with the original text itself and not something that could be equally expressed by a paraphrase. Therefore, I extend "application" to cover re-expression of the text, such as paraphrase or translation. Cf. Frame, *Doctrine of Knowledge*, 93–98; Poythress, *God Centered Biblical Interpretation*, 72.

[25] That each of these is a co-inherent perspective on the meaning of a text means that the entire meaning potential of a text could be described from each of these perspectives. If a list of every valid use were provided, it would imply every appropriate and fitting use. The same is true of an exhaustive list of appropriate or fitting uses. On the use of "perspective in this sense," see Frame, *Doctrine of Knowledge*, 89–90, 191–193; John M. Frame, *Perspectives on the Word of God: An Introduction to Christian Ethics* (Eugene, Or.: Wipf and Stock, 1999); John M. Frame, *The Doctrine of the Christian Life*, A Theology of Lordship 4 (Phillipsburg: P&R Publishing, 2008), 33–37; Poythress, *Symphonic Theology: The Validity of*

Each text, therefore—whether it is a symbol, word, syntagm, sentence, etc.—has finite meaning potential (or a semantic range) that is delimited by the relevant contexts (textual, linguistic, cultural, etc.). If a context is expanded, there is a change to the meaning potential of a text, as I explained above.

According to the single-proposition view of meaning, meaning is in the text and discovered through the context. Therefore, context is only able to reveal the meaning of the text—what the author intended when he composed it. With reference to the biblical canon, this context is only capable of illuminating the meaning already in a text. In contrast, on the meaning-potential view of meaning, a consideration of the canonical context expands the meaning-potential of a text. No longer are the appearances of gentiles among David's mighty men (e.g. Uriah the Hittite) or reference to the redemption from Egypt (2 Sam 7:23) merely descriptive of historical events or the self-understanding of Samuel's characters, but they become rich with the meaning of the redemptive-historical story they reflect (e.g. Gen 12:1-3; Exod 15). The context does not change what the author said but expands greatly the potential uses of what he said. We will probe the implications of this view further in chapter 8. There remains, however, one more hermeneutical issue pertaining to the role of the Bible that we must address before turning to the role of the reader, namely, the relationship between meaning or interpretation and genre.

Multiple Perspectives in Theology.
    From a human perspective, which does not simultaneously grasp the whole range of validity-appropriateness-fittingness, it could be said that meaning is found at the nexus of validity, appropriateness, and fittingness. Yet from a divine perspective, these are co-inherent, thus their nexus excludes no valid, appropriate, or fitting uses of a text.

THE BIBLE AND GENRE

> That same day Jesus went out of the house and sat beside the sea. And great crowds gathered about him, so that he got into a boat and sat down. And the whole crowd stood on the beach. And he told them many things in parables, saying: "A sower went out to sow. And as he sowed, some seeds fell along the path, and the birds came and devoured them. Other seeds fell on rocky ground, where they did not have much soil, and immediately they sprang up, since they had no depth of soil, but when the sun rose they were scorched. And since they had no root, they withered away. Other seeds fell among thorns, and the thorns grew up and choked them. Other seeds fell on good soil and produced grain, some a hundredfold, some sixty, some thirty. He who has ears, let him hear." – Matthew 13:1-9

If you open most introductions to biblical interpretation written in the last 50 years, you will find a large section on the genres of the biblical texts and the role of these genres in interpretation. Grant R. Osborne, in his work *The Hermeneutical Spiral*, devotes an entire part (110 pages) to "genre analysis." Klein, Blomberg, and Hubbard devote 115 pages to the subject. Despite the significance granted to it, the question of what genre is, let alone its function in exegesis, is not an easy one to answer. Among evangelical works, the definitions of "genre" are not always compatible, if the word is even defined. A glance at the history of genre study, especially in the last 100 years, reveals that it is far more complicated than it might appear. From Plato to the Postmodern study of literature, genre has been analysed, yet no consistent definition or understanding of the concept has emerged.[1] The loose consensus that exists among Evangelical interpreters emphasizes the historical side of grammatical-historical hermeneutics and raises a challenge for the form of biblical sufficiency I have argued for it in this book. I have argued so far that the Bible is our ultimate authority for reading and presents itself as self-interpreting. In this chapter, I want to raise several theoretical problems I see in the present emphasis on genre and suggest that the insights of genre criticism are properly subsumed under what we have been discussing so far as the analogy of faith, reading Scripture in light of Scripture.

A. Genre and Its Problems

We can consider genre according to its definition and the features of a text to which it refers. In the contemporary discussion of genre, a genre is a specialized form of communication that presupposes specific hermeneutical rules. We have discussed general rules of reading so far in this and the previous work; in addition to these rules, genre is thought to provide specialized interpretive rules for specific types of literature. The analogy often used today, taken from Ludwig Wittgenstein (an influential 20th-century philosopher) is that of a game: "genre provides a set of rules that further refine the general exegetical principles ... and allow the interpreter greater precision in uncovering the author's intended meaning,"[2] "Literary genres, then, are like language games. The interpreter's task is to determine which game (e.g. epic, history, chronology, prophecy, parable, etc.) is being played; only then will the individual 'moves' make sense. Hirsch agrees, 'Coming to understand the meaning of an utterance is like learning the rules of a game.'"[3]

Genres function on several different levels; there are genres for book-sized literature and genres employed within these books. Poythress defines the classificational side of genres—how a genre is recognized—as "a group

---

[1] Cf. Osborne's helpful though very brief survey in his essay, Grant R Osborne, "Genre Criticism: Sensus Literalis," *Trinity Journal* 4, no. 2 (1983): 1–27.

[2] Grant R. Osborne, *The Hermeneutical Spiral: A Comprehensive Introduction to Biblical Interpretation* (Downers Grove, Ill.: InterVarsity Press, 1991), 151.

[3] Vanhoozer, *Is There a Meaning in This Text?*, 338. Quoting from E.D. Hirsch, Jr., *Validity in Interpretation*. Cf. Klein, Blomberg, and Hubbard Jr., *Introduction to Biblical Interpretation*, 260.

of pieces of literature with similar organization or style."[4] This classificational aspect of genre (the features which define it) appears to this author to be at odds with the function genre is thought to have, to govern reading.

"Style" and "organization" may have interpretive implications, but they may not. For example, while writing this book, dozens of different organization schemes have bounced around in my head, all of which would lead to the same result. My choice of this particular organization was purely pedagogical, how best to communicate the content I hoped to communicate and to make the argument I am trying to make—supporting the hermeneutic of biblical self-interpretation argued for in *The Gift of Reading – Part 1*. On the other hand, style may have interpretive implications, as we saw in that book, yet other elements of style—such as style of language (e.g. popular or academic)—do not require specialized rules of interpretation.

From the literature concerning genre and those things that are identified as genres, it becomes clear that more than style and organization are involved in generic categories. We could add to style and organization—or "**form**" as it is usually called—**function**, what a text is intended to do. For example, a *rîb* prophecy is supposed to be a legal indictment or prophetic lawsuit; a thanksgiving psalm is defined by its function to give thanksgiving; a historical narrative communicates historical events, but a parable does not seem to do so. We could also be more specific with "style," dividing this into **language pattern**—prose (whether narrative or didactic) and poetry—and **manner of communication**, consider whether it communicates through logical argument, description, or symbolism. These four considerations (form, function, language pattern, manner of communication) cover the various textual features that make up generic categories. An outlier here is the so-called "apocalyptic" genre, which is thought not only to include style and function but theological perspective—the worldview by which world events are interpreted.[5]

---

[4] Poythress, *Reading the Word of God in the Presence of God*, 207.

[5] As mentioned in *The Gift of Reading Part 1*, a better way to understand the distinctive aspect of "apocalyptic" literature in the Bible is to see it as heightened or intensified prophecy. It bears continuity with the prophetic books in its use of symbolism and metaphor and the weaving together of poetry, didactic prose, and narrative. However, symbolism and metaphor are so intensified that the work of an interpreter is greatly increased with apocalyptic literature verses run-of-the-mill

Having considered how genre is defined and the features thought to characterize a genre, we must consider the function it is supposed to have. As a "language game," genre is said to be a shared interpretive framework between the reader and the author. The author uses a genre to communicate and assumes the audience will recognize the genre in the text they read and interpret it accordingly. This raises several problems that I want to consider here. First, if the intended audience of Scripture as we have received it is not the audience for which they were originally penned but believers today, as I have contended and will argue further in a chapter 6, then the intended readership does not know the language games under which the text was composed. This presents a problem for Scripture as self-interpreting. Indeed, most Evangelical authors argue that it is necessary to study generic categories within their historical context to get a firm grasp of the rules involved.[6] But this raises another problem, what explains the similarities found in different examples of a genre; that is, how does genre function in an author's composition of a work? I believe a consideration of compositional issues requires a revising of the usual understanding of genre. Lastly, genre as defined above falls under the same critique that I will raise in chapter 9 concerning the use of historical background material; to identify a specific text as part of a genre, there needs to be enough features present to prove the same thing an appeal to genre would accomplish. That is, if you are arguing that *Text A*, as an example of *Genre B*, needs to be interpreted according to *Principle C*, you must have enough evidence within *Text A* to justify your use of *Principle C*. Thus, an appeal to *Genre B* is redundant; it can only confirm or reveal what was always present in *Text A*. Let's consider these issues more closely.

a. The Issue of Genre and Audience

The first issues are those of genre and audience. Among evangelical authors, genre is part of the historical aspect of grammatical-historical exegesis. This raises a problem as far as our argument so far is concerned. If genre theory as addressed here is correct, there must be a high level of shared literary

---

prophecy. Cf. G.K. Beale, *The Book of Revelation: A Commentary on the Greek Text*, NIGTC (Grand Rapids; Carlisle: Eerdmans; Paternoster, 1999), 37–69.

[6] E.g. Osborne, "Genre Criticism," 24.

heritage between the author and audience for a text to be understood properly. We may be able to assume this is true when an act of communication is intended for someone from the same area and time, but it cannot be assumed across cultural, geographical, and temporal gaps.

The Bible was written to communicate over thousands of years and across the world, so if genre is a necessary category of interpretation, and God has intended the Bible to be read across this geographical-temporal chasm, then genre has to be something identifiable within the text itself. That is, "genre" must refer to the cues texts give to guide their own reading. We must firmly locate genre in the realm of text, its features, and not in the realm of culture—in a shared understanding between the author and audience. But if we follow this route, identifying generic categories as textual categories not extra-textual interpretative categories, we must re-consider their role in authorial composition and in interpretation.

b.   *The Issue of Composition*

What, we must ask, is the relationship between the author and generic categories? Our answer to this question is very important. At the risk of being overly simplistic, I want to consider two possible answers to this question. The first answer is that genre, like rules for a game, is normative for an author's writing. If genre is normative, it means that an author is under obligation—conscious or unconscious—to conform to the standards of the genre. Once an author selects a genre or the choice of intended communicative function necessitates a certain genre, the style, form, and function of the text are a given. We could call such a view genre-realism, the idea that "genre" refers to an actual thing—a set of rules or perfect example—that is reflected in every instantiation or concrete text. If this were the case, knowing genre would reveal the meaning of the text, for by knowing the rules we could figure out exactly what was intended (cf. the approach of K. Lawson Younger mentioned in chapter 1 under Structural Exegesis). Though genre is often treated as if it were real in this philosophical sense, the problems with such a view are numerous. For one, genres have historical origins and change throughout time (e.g. the emergence of the *Nouveau Roman* style novel in France during the 20th century).[7]

Also, unless someone wanted to suggest that every genre exists in the

---

[7] Cf. Osborne, "Genre Criticism."

mind of God and therefore can be truly "real" (again, in the philosophical sense), the idea of genre-realism is absurd (the only option would be that they exist in their own separate world, free-floating ideas beyond time and space). Finally, such a view could not explain why genres are frequently violated, in addition to changing. For example, it is said that epistles in the 1st-century Roman world are examples of a specific genre.[8] This genre has a specific form, yet Galatians—an otherwise perfect example of this genre—violates this form by omitting the thanksgiving section of a Greco-Roman epistle. Furthermore, the book of Hebrews has some epistolary features yet otherwise breaks from this genre. It seems to be a mixed genre, part letter and part sermon, leading to the often-used moniker "sermonic-epistle."[9]

There is a lesser form of realism I think we can also reject, what we could call "textbook realism." That is, there is no evidence for (and it is quite clear that there were no) style books prescribing genre rules for apocalyptic, 1st-century historical narrative, gospel, epistle, etc. Ruling out realism in either sense, we cannot treat "genre" as if it actually exists, as if there is an abstract body of rules embodied in every related text that can be extracted and used to read similar literature. Instead, we must look for another view for the relation between the author and genre.

In the place of realism, I think imitation is a good term to use for describing the role of genre in composition.[10] Texts are similar to one another because no text emerges in a vacuum. Texts are produced by authors, and authors are influenced by other authors—indeed, they are influenced by the history of literature. At the very least, this truth would produce unconscious similarities between texts. However, we can go further.

When we write or speak, we want to communicate, so we pay attention to how we communicate. We think of what will best communicate our purposes, what will best achieve our purpose. If I wanted to be a successful

---

[8] J. Scott Duvall and J. Daniel Hays, *Grasping God's Word: A Hands-on Approach to Reading, Interpreting, and Applying the Bible*, 3rd ed. (Grand Rapids: Zondervan, 2012), 227–243; Osborne, *The Hermeneutical Spiral*, 252–260.

[9] E.g. Walter A. Elwell and Robert W. Yarbrough, *Encountering the New Testament: A Historical and Theological Survey*, 2nd ed., Encountering biblical studies (Grand Rapids: Baker Academic, 2005), 348.

[10] I do not mean "imitation" in the technical realist or Postmodern sense of *mimesis*.

comedian, I would study the performances of other comedians; if I wanted to write gripping novels, I would study those novelists I appreciate the most. The same goes for writing a dictionary; there is no rulebook that says I could not write a dictionary using the conventions of a novel, but it would be inefficient and unsuccessful to do so. Instead, if I wanted to write a dictionary, I would imitate the practice of those who have come before me. The same is true for history books, textbooks, and books like this one. In writing this book and my previous books, I did not consult a rule book for how to properly format a book; instead, I considered those books I found most effective in their communication and studied what they did. Even style books, which give the rules of how to write a good book or thesis, are based on imitation: they ask how a good thesis or book has been written in the past and consider how to teach others to write in that way.

Moreover, a text is not only an imitation; it is also a creative imitation. When we study other books to learn from them, we must decide between different approaches to determine which one is best for the purpose at hand. We may, in fact, contribute our own insight to the genre within which we are writing, creating a unique text that bears similarities to but is not identical with its predecessors. Imitation seems to me to be the best way to describe genre as it functions for the author.

If generic composition involves creative imitation, an issue emerges for the genre theory. Genre cannot be the rules for rightly reading a body of texts, for both elements—imitation and creativity—involve the breaking and invention of reading conventions. The rules for reading a specific genre only work if one text follows the same rules as another, but the "rules" do not exist outside of any individual text; they are bound up with and unique to every text an author produces. This leads us to our last problem with genre before we consider its positive function.

c. *The Issue of Identification*

The implicit realism of present genre theory yields further issues when it comes to identifying genre in texts and interpreting them accordingly. For example, consider The Book of Jonah. Some authors consider Jonah to be an example of the genre "satire." Part of their definition of satire is the fact that satires are not intended to communicate history. So it is argued that this interpretive principle—satires do not communicate historical events—must be applied to Jonah. Therefore, the book is not meant to teach us about historical events. The problem is this: their definition of "satire" begs the question. If Jonah is satirical and also communicates historical events, then the definition of satire must be expanded to include historical events. Otherwise, Jonah must not be satirical. To argue that Jonah is ahistorical because it is satirical, one must show from the book of Jonah that it is satirical *because it is ahistorical*. That is, the feature that one is trying to prove by an appeal to genre must be observable in the text itself, making an appeal to genre redundant. The problem is this; if genres are a body of rules, then we would expect very little variation from the rules; the presence of significant variation would invalidate their function. However, in practice, we do not find pure genres; we find narratives with satirical elements and satires with historical elements; letters with sermonic elements and sermons with epistolary elements; etc. Any interpretive rule to be used must therefore be clearly present in the text at hand, for only with evidence of its presence can we be sure that this is a generic feature the author chose to include.

Another example regards the narratives in Genesis. Authors sometimes have argued that the first chapters of Genesis show a stylized form and highly poetic nature; therefore, they cannot be historical. That is, because style and form from an ahistorical genre are present, the function must be ahistorical. Their arguments are usually overstated, but even if they were accurate in their observations, the conclusion does not follow. That is, there is no rule that says one cannot communicate historical events using poetic style; this is done many times in Scripture (e.g. Exod 15, Judg 5). The fact that style does not determine function and that form does not fix interpretation argues against the view that genre describes shared interpretive rules between authors and audiences. Yet the observations made under discussions of genre are often quite helpful—I made many in *The Gift of Reading Part 1*—so we must look for another model for explaining the insights of genre.

B. <u>Classification and Interpretation</u>

As can be seen from the first part of this chapter, there is a lot of overlap between Genre discussions and those of philosophy. Genres are often treated as philosophical abstractions, so it makes sense that the criticisms raised above are quite similar to those raised in Volume 1 of this series *The Gift of Knowing* and the lengthier criticism I will raise in Volume 3 *The Gift of Seeing*. It also makes sense that my answer to the question, "what is genre" looks the same as my answer to the question "what is an abstraction." I will reserve the term "genre" for book-level literature types, such as dictionaries, novels, math textbooks, academic papers, theology dissertations, etc. Such book-level literary types, or text-types, are classifications used to describe related pieces of literature, literature that share similarities in the areas of **form, function, language pattern,** and **manner of communication.** Adapting my definition of abstraction from *The Gift of Knowing*, we can identify "genre" as a relationship identified between particular pieces of literature (Thesis A, Thesis B, etc.) that allows us to better understand other particular pieces of literature that share these commonalities. The relationships in view are those mentioned above (e.g. form); each of these features can likewise be identified as a relationship identified among the particular features of particular pieces of literature.[11] For the rest of this chapter, I want to consider these four categories we can use to see literature better and how they function as part of the analogy of faith.

C. The Generic Categories

a. Language Patterns

In *The Gift of Reading – Part 1,* we spent a chapter considering "Styles of Biblical Writing" (107-133); as the title of that chapter suggests, we considered the stylistic generic categories, namely, language pattern and manner of communication. I identified four broad styles of biblical writing, Narrative, Poetry, Didactic Prose, and Prophecy. In line with our previous discussion, I eschewed the term "genre" in referring to these classes of literature,[12] preferring the more specialized classification of "style." Specifically, these are groups of biblical writings that share a common pattern of language and manner of communication. By pattern of language, I intend

---

[11] Cf. *The Gift of Knowing*, 102-104; "What is Abstraction? – Part 1 & 2, https://teleioteti.ca/2018/09/06/abstraction-part1/, https://teleioteti.ca/2018/09/20/what-is-abstraction-part-2/; and *The Gift of Seeing* (Airdrie AB, Teleioteti 2021).

[12] These are sometimes identified as genres, but this is rarer than identifying what I have called "text-types" (e.g. letter, historical narrative, covenant document) as genres. Cf. Jean Louis Ska, *"Our Fathers Have Told Us": Introduction to the Analysis of Hebrew Narratives*, Subsidia Biblica 13 (Roma: Editrice Pontificio Instituto Biblico, 1990), 6.

the way a literary work, a text, strings together words and clauses (the constituents of sentences) and sentences in order to make a cohesive text.

On the one hand, narrative in the Bible is characterized by coordinating ("paratactic") syntax and actions within scenes. That is, biblical narratives do not often provide logical explanation through subordinating conjunctions such as "for" or "in order that"; instead, scenes are connected with the coordinating and contrasting conjunctions usually translated "and" and "but." This is closely related to the way narrative structures units of text; instead of being grouped in thought units like a prose book or letter, biblical narratives present scenes that are based on actions. Sentences are either explanatory of or provide an action; an action with its circumstances and any explanatory material make a scene. Together, coordination and the action/scene syntax constitute the language pattern "narrative."

This can be contrasted with didactic prose, such as is found in Paul's epistles, which uses a pattern of subordination ("hypotaxis") and sentence/paragraph syntax. In didactic prose, subordination is favoured over coordination; "and" is rarer than in narrative, but "for" and "in order that" (among many other conjunctions) become much more common. Subordinating conjunctions are found because they make explicit logical connections; they function to make an argument and provide explanation. In the place of actions, didactic prose employs a broad range of sentences—such as statements and imperatives—connected by an implicit logical relation ("asyndeton") or explicit logical relation (indicated by conjunctions). This is what I mean by a pattern of language; I go to a greater depth with narrative and didactic prose—along with poetry and prophecy—in *The Gift of Reading Part 2*. Along with such patterns of language, I include in these stylistic classifications the manner of communication favoured in a text.

b.   *Manner of Communication*

One early reader of these books found it odd that I would include "prophecy" along with narrative and didactic prose in my discussion of style, for prophecy does not exhibit any one pattern of language. This is true enough: as I discussed in *Part 1*, Prophecy switches between poetry and didactic prose freely, often blending the two. This blending justifies to some degree my decision to consider Prophecy as its own style, but language pattern alone does not constitute a style—as I am using the term. In addition to language pattern, there is the manner of communication a text favours; it is here that prose prophecy and poetic prophecy cohere and so become identifiable as a single style. By manner of communication, I intend the predominant means a text uses to communicate. In this book—an example of didactic prose—I am mainly communicating through argument and description. This is the standard manner of communication for didactic prose. At times I will use metaphor and story to make my points clearer, yet these are rare enough to be exceptions. Hence, manner of communication refers to the favoured or default means of communication.

In a narrative, the primary manner of communication is showing or displaying events. That is, a narrative portrays events in such a way that leads the reader to a conclusion: it usually does not tell the reader what to think; it shows them.[13] Poetry favours metaphor and picturesque language in its communication, yet we can be more specific here. Biblical poetry often employs concrete imagery, imagery that has a strong correspondence with the experience of the reader (e.g. Psalms 23; 84:3, 6). Prophecy similarly uses metaphorical language, yet the language of prophecy is far more abstract or symbolic.[14]

We witness the extreme form of this more abstract metaphor in apocalyptic literature, such as Revelation and Daniel (cf. Daniel 2:31-45). It takes more than wisdom to interpret such imagery, so interpretations are often provided. Prophecies such those found within Isaiah and Jeremiah are less abstract than the apocalyptic books, yet they are still distinct from poetry in their abstract symbolism.[15] Whether employing a poetic or didactic prose language pattern, this manner of communication remains prominent in Prophetic literature, hence why I identify it as its own style.

Now, caution is in order here. When we speak of narrative style, we are not talking about the style found in narrative text-types; we are talking about a specific style that is prominent in such text-types, yet narratives such as

---

[13] Literary theorists often of state that narratives "show," they do not "tell."

[14] By "abstract" I refer to the fact that the referents and meaning of the symbols used in prophecy are not as readily discernible as in poetry. Poetry is intended to elicit an immediate emotive response, to carry you along with its rhythm. Prophecy, on the other hand, is didactic; it is meant to teach significant truths about the world, the events of history, and God. The symbolism it uses to communicate sometimes requires careful thought; at other times, interpreting prophetic symbolism requires an explicit word from God.

[15] See the discussion in *The Gift of Reading – Part 1*.

Samuel include poetic and didactic prose sections (e.g. 1 Sam 2; 2 Sam 7). The same can be said of the prophetic books such as Isaiah; it contains prophetic style, but it also contains didactic prose and narrative. Habakkuk is a prophecy, yet its style is more poetic than prophetic, especially in chapter 3. In Isaiah and Habakkuk, prophetic style, as I have defined it, is present in those areas that combine poetic and didactic prose language patterns with abstract symbolism.

c. Form

The next generic category, text form or organization, has received a lot of attention over the last 100 years. In the late 19th century, form-criticism emerged, giving significant attention to literary form; afterwards, rhetorical criticism turned the spotlight onto the organization of material according to rhetorical patterns. More recently, narrative criticism has given significant attention to the organization and form of narratives. "Form" can be considered on several levels; there is the macro-structure of large text units, such as a book, and there are the smaller structures that characterize text units within a larger text. These small structures may be the forms of psalms or story-types. Despite the emphasis form has received in recent literature, I do not think form is critical to understanding many texts, though it remains very important for some text-types.

All texts have some form of structure; the demands of writing require that some thought be given to structure. However, though there will always be structure in a text—a form to its material—not all form has interpretive significance. The primary area where form has great significance is in narrative. Form matters in narratives because there is a standard against which to measure deviation. That is, narratives are based on a plot, a linear-temporal progression. When the form of a narrative deviates from the plot—when it skips a thousand years and focuses on 10, when it re-arranges material (called dischronologization) or interpolates material (when a story is spliced in between another story, such as in 2 Sam 10:1-12:31)—this yields great interpretive insight. However, in letters and many Psalms, the structure is less significant. There is no interpretive significance in placing thanksgiving sections before the body of a letter; this is often the case because of imitation (as discussed above). In many Psalms, their sections are thematically organized. There are some types of Psalms that share a similar structure, yet even in these cases, to rearrange the material would not change the meaning or interpretation of the psalm. For these reasons, because every text has a form and because form is not always of great significance for interpretation, I find it valuable to consider form under two heads—with a bit of a grey area in-between—as indispensable or variable.

In a novel or narrative, form is indispensable—it is fundamental to the text and its communication. However, in a dictionary, form is product of pedagogy, how best to communicate its content to the reader; you could conceivably organize a dictionary in dozens of different ways without changing its meaning (cf. the differences between the BDB and HALOT Hebrew lexicons). In didactic prose, the structure is a way of organizing and putting together an argument; the structure itself is not meaningful but often reveals the train of thought that makes up an argument. I thought about dozens of different ways to organize this book; in the end, the structure I chose was what I deemed best for communicating the content I wanted to communicate in a persuasive manner. If I chose a different structure, the argument may have been less clear or clearer and the book less or more readable, but the meaning potential would largely have remained the same. In between literary works with dispensable structure and those with indispensable structures are those for which structure affects interpretation but the loss of such structure is not catastrophic. I argued in *The Gift of Reading Part 1* that the Bible falls into this category, that the Bible has form and that this form is meaningful, yet if one or two books are rearranged, or the whole thing is shuffled, it is still possible to interpret the Bible correctly. Here, the order has significance for revealing meaning potential but does not create meaning potential.

In light of these considerations, form can be a helpful perspective with which to look at texts, but the most important question will be whether or not form is indispensable. On the one hand, when it comes to a narrative, it is very important to have a right understanding of how the story unfolds and how the author uses form to communicate his intent. But on the other hand, when commentators differ on the form of an epistle, such as Romans, we should not be overly concerned. We can still follow the thought well enough even if we have not divided it into the same sections as last reader. A clue to whether the form is indispensable or not is often given by the text itself. In a narrative, there are various markers that indicate the beginning and end of units and help organize sections of a book: there are clues to the structure given by the author. Such markers are also present in other literature. For example, in Habakkuk, there are two content headings that lead us to break the book into two sections (Hab 1:1, 3:1). But in the early manuscripts of biblical epistles, there were no paragraph breaks, and they did not have section headings; without such visible breaks and without significant syntactic markers of sections, the structure of an epistle's argument given in a commentary represents an effort to help the reader grasp the progression of an author's argument.

d. *Function*

The last generic category that is often considered in discussions of genre is function, what a specific text attempts to achieve. "Function" is often a category of distinction, affirming that a text does one thing instead of another. Every text has many functions, but those that are usually considered under genre are dichotomies: a text may teach theology and history simultaneously, but it cannot be both historical and ahistorical at the same time. Thus, some genres—such as historical narrative—are said to teach history, while others, such as parables, are non-historical narratives. However, because it is possible to use the form and style found in non-historical narratives—such as novels—to tell a historical story, the category of function is not the most helpful.

Function as an aspect of genre is also sometimes used for the way an utterance is used; a *rîb* oracle, for example, is thought to be a formalized prophecy that brings a charge of covenant sin against God's people.[16] But because of the variability implied in the function of genre in composition, we should not assume apart from textual evidence that two prophecies with the same form and style have the same function—to bring a covenant lawsuit. As with all other genre considerations, then, function needs to be identified from the features of the text and not as a corollary of form or style.

D. The Function of Generic Categories

Though I have attempted so far in this chapter to offer a criticism of genre theory as it functions within Evangelical biblical interpretation, I do not want

---

[16] Willem VanGemeren, *Interpreting the Prophetic Word: An Introduction to the Prophetic Literature of the Old Testament* (Grand Rapids: Zondervan, 1996), 400–407.

to disregard the insights that have been revealed through the study of genre. What I suggested above was that we need to reframe the role of genre in interpretation. Instead of interpreting genre in terms of realist categories and historical contexts, I suggested above that the categories usually discussed under genre are better seen as part of the analogy of faith, the way Scripture leads us in its own interpretation. This is where I want to conclude this chapter.

Because there are stylistic, formal, and functional similarities between the texts of the Bible, it is reasonable to believe the in-depth study of one text will help us understand similar texts better. For example, during my studies on the books of Samuel and Habakkuk over the last five years, I have learned much about the way the authors of these books communicate. Turning to other narratives, I see many of the same structural tools used by the author of Samuel in other narratives. By reading the narratives of Kings and Chronicles in light of my in-depth study of Samuel, I have been able to see more clearly how the authors have shaped their stories to communicate a particular view of history and a lesson for their readers. The same is true of Habakkuk; by studying the style used by Habakkuk, I am able to better understand the similar prophetic language employed in the other prophetic books, especially Jeremiah, and the poetic style Habakkuk shares with the Psalms. This is the strength of genre discussions found in most introductions to hermeneutics: they are the result of careful attention paid to particular texts in search of similarities. The resulting categories and generalizations help us to see better features of these texts that we may have otherwise missed (which is the same function abstractions have in other parts of life).

This is how I see the fruits of genre study functioning in biblical interpretation: generic categories are not straight-jackets or hard and fast rules that tell us how to interpret texts or what to expect from them. Instead, genres provide glasses that help us see better what is there in the text. Because of this understanding of genre, not as interpretive rules but as a product of and aid in the exegesis of texts, I believe that genre considerations are not the topic of hermeneutics but of biblical study. Therefore, I intend to include the insights of genre study in the 2nd part of this series, in which I will present a theology of the Bible and an overview of its contents (usually found in NT & OT introductions or surveys).

—PART 2—
The Role of the Reader

5

THE READER AND MEANING

I charge you in the presence of God and of Christ Jesus, who is to judge the living and the dead, and by his appearing and his kingdom: preach the word; be ready in season and out of season; reprove, rebuke, and exhort, with complete patience and teaching. For the time is coming when people will not endure sound teaching, but having itching ears they will accumulate for themselves teachers to suit their own passions, and will turn away from listening to the truth and wander off into myths. – 2 Timothy 4:1-4

In the last four chapters, we have seen that there is much good in the history of the interpretation of the Bible but also some error that has crept in, a tendency to accommodate the Church's approach to reading the bible to an external authority, to the philosophical spirit of the time. Against this trend, I have argued that we need a method and theory of biblical interpretation that is rooted in the Bible's own authority. *The Gift of Reading – Part 1* presented such a method; here in *Part 2,* I am establishing the theory that upholds that method. In the last three chapters (part one of this book), we looked at the role of the Bible in its own interpretation and the relationship between the biblical text and meaning. In this section, part two of this book, I want to turn to the role of the reader in interpretation.

This section and the one that follows are intentional asymmetrical with the first; that is, I intend parts two and three to be together shorter than part one. The reason for this is simple: the theory unpacked in this book is text-centred, so our discussion will predominantly concern the text. However, the reader and the author still have an important role to play, so we will consider these roles in this and the following part. Here, in chapter 5, I want to consider the contribution of the reader to meaning, as we have defined it in chapter 3. Namely, I want to consider what it means for the reader to be the maker of meaning and how this creative production is governed by the text. In the following chapter (6), I want to consider for whom the Bible was written and the impact this has on interpretation.

To say that the reader is the maker of meaning may be a dangerous line to take, yet I think it is a helpful way to look at the reader's role in light of our definition of meaning in chapter 3. If meaning is a justified use of a text, then texts do not have meaning until they are read; what they have is meaning potential. A reader makes meaning by actualizing the potential of the text, by rightly applying it to specific circumstances and questions. This is the sense in which I identify the reader as a maker of meaning and the way I conceive of the role of the reader in interpretation. Their job is not to decode the Bible, to recreate its history. Instead, their job is to use it. In the many passages concerning the role of Scripture in the believer's life, this is its role; it is used by the reader under the guidance of the Holy Spirit to change actions, perceptions, and even hearts (e.g. Rom 10:14-21; 2 Tim 3:16-17, 4:1-4). Because of the Spirit at work in our lives, the Scriptures are active in their own right, convicting us of sin (e.g. Heb 4:12-13), yet the primary emphasis is on how through careful thought (meditation) we use the Scriptures in our own lives and in the lives of others, for encouragement, rebuke, instruction, teaching, etc. We are called to be meaning makers, using the Bible for the glory of God.

This role requires much creativity to anticipate and perceive how the Bible applies to our own lives and the world around us. Sometimes the application is direct and easy; at other times, it takes much effort to discern how the situations before us are analogous to and fall under the purview of the Bible. We do so, however, with the assurance that Scripture is indeed useful so that we might be fully equipped for the good works for which we were created (2 Tim 3:16-17, cf. Eph 2:10).

By identifying the reader as a maker of meaning (in the sense defined above), we are coming close to the Postmodern approaches to biblical interpretation, yet we are not entirely in agreement with them. Postmodernism has done some good in showing us that the reader has an important role to play in reading, yet they have done so within a philosophical paradigm that rejects God's authority and the authority of texts. As

Christians, we do not share these assumptions. We are self-consciously submitted to the Lordship of Christ and are obligated to honour not only him but the men and women who have written texts. That is, we have a moral obligation to submit ourselves to God and, as an extension of this submission, to seek a proper understanding of the texts and utterances of men and women created in the image of God.[1] One of the ways we do this, and here I am particularly thinking of our reading of Scripture as an act of submission to God, is to ensure that the uses we make of the text are justified. In chapter 3 and in *The Gift of Reading Part 1*, I discussed three criteria we use to determine whether a text is justified; it must be valid, appropriate, and fitting. The reader is responsible for doing due diligence in order to use the text in a justified manner, to creatively make meaning in submission to God. *The Gift of Reading Part 1* was my attempt to show how this is practically done, how we read Scripture in a way that yields justified meaning—how we use it in submission to God. We can be confident that we will be able to use the Bible in a justified manner because, as we saw in the last section, God has written the Bible to be used by and useful for his people. However, this claim is contested explicitly or implicitly among many approaches to reading the Bible, so we need to consider it to a greater depth in order to uphold our argument so far.

---

[1] See further, *The Gift of Knowing*, esp. 74-77.

6

THE AUDIENCE OF SCRIPTURE

> For whatever was written in former days was written for our instruction, that through endurance and through the encouragement of the Scriptures we might have hope. – Romans 15:4

For whom was the Bible written? This question is very important, for if the Bible was written for a distant people—separated from us by time, space, and culture—how can we be sure that what was clear for them will be clear for us? So far, I have assumed (with some proof-text evidence) that Christians today and throughout history are the intended audience of the Bible. However, the most common analyses of the Bible today do not share this assumption. For example, in their textbook *Grasping God's Word*, J. Scott Duvall and J. Daniel Hays argue that we must first understand the text within the thought-world of its *original audience* before we can apply it to us;[1] and in his book *Exegetical Fallacies*, D.A. Carson argues that we must undergo "distanciation"—an act of comprehending our distance from the original audience of Scripture—in order properly interpret Scripture.[2] Most commentaries and introductions to the Old and New Testaments by Evangelical Christians spend much time discussing the original audience of the biblical books.[3] This gets at the heart of the question: in biblical interpretation, are we concerned with the books of which the Bible is

---

[1] Duvall and Hays, *Grasping God's Word*.

[2] Carson, *Exegetical Fallacies*, 23–24.

[3] E.g. D. A. Carson and Douglas J. Moo, *An Introduction to the New Testament*, Second Edition. (Grand Rapids: Zondervan, 2005).

composed or the Bible, which can be subdivided into books? That is, is the Bible a unity that can be divided into books or books that are packaged and distributed together?

A. The Audience of the Bible

If our answer is the latter—that the Bible is a package of many different books—then our answer to the question of the audience will be varied. We can look at Romans and identify the audience as the 1st century Roman Christians; for Galatians, we can identify the audience as the 1st century Galatian Christians, etc. Even though we do not know the exact audience of Hebrews, Samuel, and Job, we can still say that these books were originally written for an audience other than us.

This is all true, but I have contended and will contend again that this is not all the Bible says about itself. It is true that the Bible originated as individual works authored by men under the inspiration of the Spirit, works addressed to specific groups of God's people in specific situations. Yet, to say that that this is how the Bible originated is not to say that this is an adequate description of what it is now. Already in our discussion, we have seen that to put a text in a new context is transformative; from the moment a letter or book of the Bible became part of the Bible, the authoritative canon God has given his church, it has taken on a new nature. We will see in the next chapter that there is strong continuity between the original and final form of these documents, but we can no longer consider them individual books that are part of the Bible; instead, they must be considered as pieces of the canonical book God has entrusted to his people. From this perspective, we need to re-evaluate the question of the audience. Fortunately, the Bible has much to say in this regard.

I argued in *The Gift of Reading – Part 1* that the bible is a unified literary work that is intended to govern God's people, a covenant document. It is not a collection of historical documents that give us insight into a past act of revelation nor a record of a revelatory act that we can access; to the contrary, it is a direct word from God to his covenant people. To see this, consider with me the way the biblical authors talk about the Old Testament and even—here and there—about the New Testament. Paul is clear that "whatever was written in former days was written for our instruction, that through endurance and through the encouragement of the Scriptures we might have hope" (Rom 15:4). For Paul, the Old Testament Scriptures were written for all Christians. This is repeated in Timothy and Corinthians;

> All Scripture is breathed out by God and profitable for teaching, for reproof, for correction, and for training in righteousness, that the man of God may be complete, equipped for every good work (2 Tim 3:16-17)

> It is written in the Law of Moses, 'You shall not muzzle an ox when it treads out the grain.' Is it for oxen that God is concerned? Does he not certainly speak for our sake? It was written for our sake.... (1 Cor 9:9-10)

> Now these things [i.e. the events recounted Exodus and Numbers] took place as examples for us, that we might not desire evil as they did.... Now these things happened to them as an example, but they were written down for our instruction, on whom the end of the age has come. (1 Cor 10:6, 11, cf. Heb 1:1)

Lest we think this only applies to the Old Testament—though that is phenomenal in and of itself—the New Testament speaks about itself in a similar way. Paul, in Colossians, indicates that his letters were not to be kept solely for a single church but to be read by the other churches (Col 4:16).[4] Peter, in 2 Peter, indicates that Paul's letters were being read by his audience as well—even that they were written for them—and equates them with Scripture, which Paul himself indicates was for all Christians to be equipped (2 Pet 3:14-16; 2 Tim 3:16-17). According to the Bible's own testimony, it was written for us on whom the end of the age has come, for Christians—those who live between the first and second coming of Christ.

The New Testament does not treat the Old Testament as an assortment of books written to other people; it treats the Old Testament as a unified document, as the abiding Word of God, written for Christians. The New Testament authors likewise treat each other's letters as messages to all Christians. As I argued in *Part 1* by analogy with the Old Testament, the Bible should be read as a single unified document; it follows from this analogy and from the explicit statements of the New Testament that it is a document written for Christians. We can be confident, therefore, that the Bible is

---

[4] It is interesting that the manuscript evidence for Ephesians suggests that it may have been a cyclical letter, with that edition written to the Ephesians and other editions of the same letter addressed to other churches.

addressed to us as much as it was addressed to them, that its audience includes us alongside the ancient Jewish and 1st century Christian people.

B. <u>Our Distance from the Text</u>

If this is true, if this is how the Bible addresses the question of audience, we must then consider what we should do about the appearance or perception of distance we experience when we read the Bible. That is, there is a reason why Carson and others discuss distanciation: there does seem to be an identifiable distance between us and the content of the text. I think we can resolve this issue, of perceived distance, with an appeal to the setting of the text, the analogy of faith, and the Christian worldview.

To begin with, consider the setting of the text. Though we are the audience of the Bible, the Bible is set across thousands of years. Genesis covers the beginning of the world until the 2nd millennium BC, so we should expect to feel some distance between ourselves and the stories there. Even Revelation, the last book of the Bible, is separated from us by 2000 years. Because the Bible is set in different times, the customs recounted within, the societal problems, and the cultures recounted are vastly different from our own. If we do not feel the distance, we are not reading the Bible rightly. Yet, if we are the intended audience of the Bible, then this distance is not an impediment to our reading. Instead, this is the setting God has chosen—and chosen because it represents the history of his people—to communicate to *us*. We can be sure that though we are distant, these situations are analogous to our own and that they are intended to teach us how to live in our own day. We may not, therefore, understand every detail as a person of that time would—the value of a "*pim*" (1 Sam 13:20), the appearance of an Ashtoreth pole, etc.—yet we can be sure that we will understand enough to receive the message God is communicating to us. I can understand what is meant in context by a "*pim*"—a unit of measure—without learning from archaeology that it means two-thirds of a shekel. I can understand from context that the Israelites erected wooden poles to worship Ashtoreth, the false goddess of the Sidonians, and that this was a visible reflection of their idolatry without understanding the dimensions or cultic function of such a pole. That we are the intended audience, and that God has given Scripture to be used for and by us, is our assurance of this fact.

The historical distance caused by the setting should be no more of a hindrance to our understanding than the mythical settings of Star Wars and the Lord of the Rings. With such novels and movies, we expect them to give us enough details of their world in order to understand what is going on. For the Bible, the analogy of faith as set out in the first section of this book indicates how the Bible functions to facilitate our interpretation of it. The Bible is vast enough in its content to give us the necessary pieces to interpret its stories and events in order to profit from them. In addition to the analogy of faith, the shared worldview of God's people brings the unity we need to interpret the Bible rightly.

If you took a 1st-century pagan Roman citizen and 21st-century person from almost anywhere in the world, the differences between them would be outstanding. Their religious practices, way of viewing the world, understanding of their purpose in life, their relationship to everyone else in society, their obligations to the state, the nature and origin of the natural world, etc. would all be very different. But a different answer would have to be given if we considered the differences between a 1st-century Greek convert in Ephesus and a 21st century convert in Vancouver, granting that they both have a firm grasp of Christianity. We could still identify things that separate them—their positions in society, their understanding of the natural world, etc.—but we would find that there is a lot more uniting them than separating them.

Both live within "the world," a kingdom consisting of all human persons, rebelling spiritual persons, and institutions who are united under Satan in futile opposition to God. Their relationship to the unbelieving world is defined by this opposition; they are called to be holy and spiritually separate from the purposes of the World. They are called to act in such a way as to point those in the world towards the Kingdom of God and its proclamation, the Gospel. Furthermore, participation in the life of the local church will have a significant role in their life, sometimes at the expense of relationships with biological family. They will worship the same God, worship on the same day where possible, and read the same Scriptures. They would have (relatively) the same understanding of the origins of the world and the way it will end. They would have the same understanding of their purpose in the world. Essentially, in as much as their beliefs conformed to the Bible (their mutual standard for faith and practice), they would have the same worldview—the same ethic, the same epistemology, the same understanding of the world in relation to God.

It is, of course, true that no Christian has a perfect understanding of God and his world, but in whatever right understanding they have, Christians throughout the generations are united. Furthermore, they are united in their efforts to ever submit their beliefs to God through Scripture, so their unity will only grow throughout their lifetime.

Because the actions commanded of and rightly performed in Scripture come forth from the same worldview we are called to have today, there is great commonality between us as the audience of the Bible and the 1st-century Christians and ancient Jewish people who originally received biblical revelation. Furthermore, because the practices and beliefs of the culture in which they lived are shaped by the same fundamental posture against God that our culture today possesses, the challenges they faced are very similar to those we face. Even though the form of idols differs, and the sins of the day may not be the same, we readily find analogous circumstances in our culture to those faced by the original recipients of biblical revelation. Together with the considerations of text setting and the analogy of faith, along with the stated audience of Scripture, we have a firm footing for reading the text as an address to us, God's covenant people.

—Part 3—
The Role of the Author

7

THE AUTHOR AND MEANING

> We have the prophetic word more fully confirmed, to which you will do well to pay attention as to a lamp shining in a dark place, until the day dawns and the morning star rises in your hearts, knowing this first of all, that no prophecy of Scripture comes from someone's own interpretation. For no prophecy was ever produced by the will of man, but men spoke from God as they were carried along by the Holy Spirit. – 2 Peter 1:20-21

In the last two chapters, we turned from considering the role of the text in reading the Bible to the role of the reader. Now, in these final two chapters, we will consider issues related to the author, namely, how the author is the originator of meaning and what it means to speak of authorship with regard to Scripture (chapter 7) and how the text and meaning relate to historical background (chapter 8)—the authors' circumstances. In this chapter, we will first consider how the author relates to meaning and who is/are the author(s) of Scripture.

A. The Author as Originator

We saw in chapter one that under Modernism, the author and his or her intentions became the most significant consideration in meaning. Under Postmodernism, the reader tends to be credited with the most significance. In the first two parts of this book, we saw that the text is rightly considered the ground or standard for meaning—which is the role given to the author under Modernism—and that Postmodernism is partially correct in identifying the reader as a key player in making meaning. It might seem, then, that the author has no role in meaning—at least as we have defined it. Yet this would go against common sense, for we intuitively perceive that intentional authorship is an essential condition for texts to mean anything.

For example, if we observed water carving out letters in a mountainside to form a sentence, such as "Bob's store is down the road," we would not give any effort to identify the meaning or usefulness of this statement; it would be pure coincidence that the rock formation resembles a coherent sentence—and maybe a case of reading more into formations than is actually there. Indeed, if there was a store down the road named after or owned by a man named Bob, we would immediately draw the conclusion that what we thought was a mindless, accidental process was actually the work of an author. Therefore, where meaning is present, we rightly infer the activity of an author; and if there is no author, we rightly infer that all semblance of meaning is an illusion.

So we know that authors have a role in meaning, yet they are not the standard of meaning—for we have no access to their mind other than the text they produced.[1] Furthermore, they are not the makers of meaning in that they do not define and intentionally prescribe every use their text may have; the reader is the maker of meaning by using the text. What is left is the role of originator or origin of meaning, or more accurately, meaning-potential. That is, when an author says something—whether it is writing a text or speaking an utterance—they create a finite body of meaning potential. Their communication (in this case, a text) is spoken in a context to say something specific. This contextually bound communication has a fixed potential for meaning—as we saw in chapter 3. Without an author acting, there would be no meaning potential and, therefore, no meaning. As the originator of meaning, the author's role is a presupposition for meaning rather than an agent in the making of meaning. We cannot understate the significance of this role: it is because an author wrote something that we have meaning at all. So by defining meaning as the product of a reader's interaction with a text, we are not excluding or diminishing the role of an author in communication.

Of specific relevance to the reading of Scripture, we can also say that the author is the seal of a text's authority. That is, no text bears authority in and of itself; authority is something possessed by persons. A text may state many things, but our judgment of the value of these statements depends on the

---

[1] Cf. Lewis, "Modern Theology and Biblical Criticism."

author. For example, if a reputable and trustworthy historian releases a book, we will trust that the text, when properly interpreted, will tell us something about the world. However, if a known forger and liar releases a history book, we know that no amount of careful study will reveal truths about past events and people. Again, it would make a big difference whether a letter came from our spouse or from our enemy—even if it said the very same thing. If a document is sent to us concerning parking on the street in front of our house and is authored by a government official with the capacity to legally bind us, we would treat this text with much more authority than the same document drafted by a neighbour with no such authority. In this way, the author as originator of meaning is also the seal of its authority. Because the Bible is authored by God himself through his chosen representatives, the Bible carries his ultimate authority in every statement, in every claim, in every command and demand. To conclude this chapter, it is worth spending a moment discussing this, for the so-called "dual authorship" of Scripture has proven to be a stumbling block for many in the discussion of hermeneutics.

B. <u>The Authorship of Scripture</u>

If we were to take the position of Modernism described in chapter 1, the question of authorship would be of profound importance, for meaning rests in what the author intended to achieve by his specific communicative act to a specific people. Moreover, the question of dual-authorship of the Bible—the Divine and human authors of its constituent documents—would prove to be quite difficult to answer. That is, if the meaning is the authorial intention, are we looking for the earthly or Divine author's intentions? Furthermore, if the meaning is singular, what do we do with situations where the text apparently said more than the human author could have reasonably intended? If, however, the approach I have offered is correct, I think these problems disappear. After considering what the Bible says about its authorship, I will outline how its claims to dual authorship do not prove problematic in light of our argument so far.

The standard Evangelical position concerning the Bible is that Scripture was written by human authors under the inspiration of the Holy Spirit with the result that every word of Scripture is that which God wanted to be written.² The result is a text that is fully human, bearing the stylistic variety of a human work, and also fully divine, being God's very words. That God is the author of all of Scripture is evident from hundreds of passages in the Bible. Some of the more significant are 2 Timothy 3:16-17, where all Scripture is said to be "breathed out" by God (leading to the theological term, *inspiration*), and 2 Peter 1:20-21, quoted above, in which Peter says that the writers of Scripture "spoke from God as they were carried along by the Holy Spirit." Several times through the Bible (e.g. Hebrews 4:7), the Holy Spirit is identified as the author of words that are ascribed to men (cf. Acts 4:25). These texts are significant in that God is not identified as the author only of passages where his direct speech is quoted (such as in Exodus and Deuteronomy) but also of psalms and narratives where the author or narrator are speaking. Now, in many of these texts, a human author is explicitly given. Therefore, there are human authors of Scripture, yet they are not its only authors; God is the ultimate author who "carried them along" in their writing in order that the product would be his very words—breathed out by him and carrying his authority (2 Tim 3:16-17; 2 Pet 1:20-21). The mechanism by which he led their writing is unknown to us, but we do not need to know it in order to confess this truth.

Now, if the meaning of a text were singular, then we would need to legitimately ask, could God have inspired a text to have a meaning that the original author did not intend when he wrote? However, this question is irrelevant on our account of meaning.

That is, the meaning potential of a text is fixed by its context, including the words of which it consists and the textual context within which it is embedded. This means that when a biblical text became part of the canon, this change in context may have enlarged its meaning potential, yet this by no means entails that there is a change in the definitions, syntax, and grammatical relationships of the text as originally penned. Because God orchestrated the writing of the original text, I think it is safe to assume that the meaning potential of a text now found in the Bible is enlarged yet in continuity with that which the earthly author originally penned.³ The question of the original

---

² This is often called "verbal plenary inspiration," God has inspired every word of Scripture.

³ On the other hand, because meaning potential is changed by context, it may not

author's intention may be relevant for historical study but not for interpreting a text. Furthermore, it is not relevant for interpreting the Bible as we have received it; the final interpretive context is not the original situation in which the writing was penned but its final canonical context, the context of the Bible as an authoritative covenant document written for our sake. If this is the case, the most significant ramification it may have is on our understanding of the role of historical evidence (extra-biblical literature, archaeological finds, etc.) on our reading of Scripture.

---

be wise to attempt to read between the lines of the final text we have and deduce conclusions about the original author and audience to which it was first written. We need to be careful here; this is not because the texts are ahistorical but because their new context is different then their original. This is only a danger to certain forms of historical-critical study, for as we have seen, God intends the final form as we have received it to be the final interpretive context within which we ascertain what is a justified reading or not. Footnote 23 on page 72 is relevant in this regard.

THE BIBLE IN HISTORY

> Now these things happened to them as an example, but they were written down for our instruction, on whom the end of the ages has come. – 1 Corinthians 10:11

Much of modern biblical interpretation revolves around the study of the Ancient Near Eastern and 1st-century Roman world in which the biblical texts were written. In the study of the Old Testament, much time is given to the study of the Hebrew Language within its context as an ancient Semitic language; there is also lots of attention given to the literary milieu in which it was written—to the Babylonian, Ugaritic, Egyptian, Assyrian, etc. texts from a similar time. In the study of the New Testament, much attention is given to the Greek literature of the late 1st century BC and the 1st Century AD to better understand Koine Greek, the dialect in which the New Testament was written. Furthermore, much attention is given to the literature of Second Temple Judaism and of the Roman world at this time to better understand the worldviews of the biblical authors, their audiences, and the circumstances which the biblical letters were meant to address. If the argument of the books in this series (*The Gift of Knowing; The Gift of Reading Part 1 & 2*) has been cogent so far, then this approach to the Bible needs to be radically revised.

First, the intention and thought-world of the author are not the basis for meaning; the text interpreted in its biblical context is the basis for meaning. Second, the audience for which Scripture was written was not the original audiences of each biblical text, an audience that might approach the text with 1st century or ANE assumptions; instead, we—Christian throughout the ages, those "on whom the end of the age has come" (1 Cor 10:11)—are its intended audience. Third, the worldview of the authors who wrote Scripture, of its original audience, and of us today are not radically different from one another—as the worldviews of the ANE, of the 1st-century Roman Empire, and of any 21st-century culture are. On the contrary, we all share the worldview revealed by the Bible and delivered to us through the community of faith that has shaped us. We are all subject to the reforming work of Scripture and bear to greater and lesser degrees its worldview, over against the worldviews that characterize the kingdom of Satan—with its assumptions of the autonomy of persons and opposition to God. We cannot, therefore, assume that an understanding of the ancient world and its languages will have the impact on our studies that it is thought to have. However, we cannot throw out this evidence either. We know from the history of interpreting the Bible that this evidence—the evidence of extra-biblical literature and archaeology—has helped us grow in our understanding of the Bible. What we need is not a wholesale rejection of extra-biblical resources but a proper understanding of their place, an understanding that appropriately relates them to the Bible as it declares itself to be—authoritative, self-interpreting, and universally relevant. For the rest of this chapter, I want to briefly outline what role I think such evidence should take in our study of the Bible.[1]

To re-phrase the problem of using extra-biblical evidence in biblical interpretation and to frame our discussion for the rest of this chapter, consider the following statement and its implications: *when a historical parallel is used to explain a text, the evidence necessary to establish a link between a piece of extra-biblical data and the text needs to be sufficient to make the point independently.*[2] That is, if the extra-biblical data is said to say something the text itself does not say, this is called imposition or eisegesis—reading into the text something that is not there. Meaning is no longer found in the text; it is found in the author's mind, in his thought processes that led to the text he wrote. However, as I have argued above, this is an inadequate view of meaning. Meaning is the use of a text governed by the text itself. If this is true, historical material is not necessary to understand a biblical *text*, which is the object of our interpretive endeavours. Historical evidence may help us to better understand the thought process of the author (if that is

---

[1] What follows is adapted from my article "The Problem with the Use of Extra-Biblical Data in Interpretation," from https://teleioteti.ca/2018/08/15/the-problem-of-extra-biblical-data/.

[2] This is the same principle used in our discussion of genre in chapter 4.

possible) and the original audience's reception of the document. It cannot, however, be used to make the text say anything that is not already there. If sufficient evidence to justify the use of historical material is only present when the text says as much as the evidence is used to say, historical material is in a significant sense redundant. If we cannot appeal to historical evidence to find meaning, for the meaning we would find is no longer that of the text, then all this evidence can really do is help us see better what the text has been saying all along. So we need to ask, what good is extra-biblical evidence after all?

Before we give an answer, a secondary point needs to be made. Much use of extra-biblical material is a fallacy sometimes called *illegitimate totality transfer*.[3] That is, every word or symbol has a semantic range that is narrowed by context to indicate something specific. When a true parallel is made between an extra-biblical item and the text, this does not justify reading the whole semantic range of that item into the text. The connection is made between two specific points on the semantic range of the text and the item; such a connection does not justify expanding from there to the whole range. For example, one may argue that Paul is using the word-group παιδεια (*paideia*, education) in Galatians 3-4 in relation to the Roman views of adoption and inheritance, of which this is a key word-group. Granted that this connection is legitimate, it would be fallacious to read any more about Roman views of adoption and inheritance into the text than Paul makes clear.

If we do not allow such a jump, from one point of the semantic context to its entirety, we are then left with our initial proposition: the text must be able to make any point extra-biblical data is used to establish.

A. The Uses of Extra-Biblical Evidence

Our discussion so far leaves us with an obvious question: What then is extra-biblical data useful for? I want to argue that it is useful for illustration, illumination, confirmation, and application. First, it is useful for illustration, helping us preach the text. That is, we can understand how Paul used the word παιδαγωγός (*paidagōgos*, guardian) in Galatians by examining the word's range of meanings within the Bible. But by drawing the connection

---

[3] Cf. Carson, *Exegetical Fallacies*, 60–61.D. A. Carson, *Exegetical Fallacies* (Grand Rapids: Baker Books, 1996), 60–61.

to the broader social context of the word, we are provided with rich illustrative material to make clear Paul's point. If a preacher or teacher can make such an illustration without implicitly teaching his audience that this material is necessary for interpreting the text—a danger this series of books have been trying to avoid—such illustrations can be very effective.

Second, extra-biblical background material is useful for illumination, useful for helping us to see the text. This is needed at times because we have cultural blinders inherited from our culture and upbringing or other limitations that prevent us from seeing what was present in the text the whole time. Historical material can unearth such things. For example, in the 19th and 20th centuries, it became popular to view the language of the New Testament as a divine language, a special Greek dialect given by God to communicate the unique content of the New Testament. However, the discovery of hundreds of Greek papyrus texts in the 20th century—letters, government documents, shopping lists, etc.—revealed that the language of the New Testament was not a divine language; it was the common language of the day, hence "Koine" or common Greek. This discovery revealed that the theories of a by-gone generation were wrong, that these theories were not rooted in anything the Bible said. This discovery was a corrective on arguing theological ideas from the absence of evidence—of violating the rule that the absence of evidence is not the evidence of absence.

Third, extra-biblical material is useful for confirmation. Sometimes there is heated debate over specific stances on interpreting a passage. There may be a case where the argument reaches a standstill and producing a piece of extra-biblical evidence will tilt the case one way or another. One instance is 1 Samuel 13:21. After telling us that the Israelites went to the Philistines to have their tools sharpened, for there was no blacksmith, we are told ... וְהָיְתָה הַפְּצִירָה פִים לַמַּחֲרֵשֹׁת ($v^e h\bar{a}yt\bar{a}h\ happ^e s\hat{i}r\bar{a}h\ p\hat{i}m\ lammah\breve{a}r\bar{e}s\bar{o}t$). The meaning of this verse is not immediately evident, for "פְּצִירָה" ($ps\hat{i}r\bar{a}h$) and "פִים" ($p\hat{i}m$) occur only here in the Hebrew Bible. The syntax, along with the probable meaning of פְּצִירָה ("fee," from פצר, psr, to urge), suggests the following rendering: "and the charge was a *pim* for the plowshare...." However, the translators of the KJV attempted read פִים with פְּצִירָה to mean "a double-edged (lit. double-mouthed) file," translating it simply as "a file"; this translation indicates that Israel had the ability to sharpen some of their tools themselves. However, this does not quite conform with the previous verse, which says that Israelites went to Palestine to have these same weapons sharpened (v. 20). Archaeological evidence confirms that פִים should be understood as a Philistine measurement, weighing about two-thirds of a shekel. This supports the first interpretation over-against the KJV. The implication is that Israel was dependent on the Philistines even for their tools, showing that they had no weapons. Some commentators argue that the price suggests they were being gouged, but this is not necessary to understand the use of the term in its context.[4] Thus, extra-biblical data helps us follow one interpretation over another; it may also have functioned in this case for illumination.

Lastly, it is useful for application. By bringing forth extra-biblical material, we expand the sphere of application for a text: we can let the item and the text interact to shed insight on, for example, a historical question. For example, by bringing forth the discovery of an inscription reading "house of David," we can use the bible to shed light on the meaning of that phrase and its relevance.

B. The Challenge of Using Extra-Biblical Data

There remains a challenge in our use of such data, namely, how we can be sure that our extra-biblical evidence is being used rightly? I want to propose one test we can use and then some challenges that need to be overcome if we are to use this data rightly.

First, the test: an interpreter must ask if they could make the point for which they are using extra-biblical evidence from the text alone. This is another implication of the statement with which we began. If the historical evidence disappeared, can you convince someone from the data available in the text? If not, this is an invalid use of extra-biblical data.

Second, the use of background data is fraught with more troubles than is commonly acknowledged. 1) There needs to be a sure connection between the data and the text, but how can one establish this? What evidence can be produced to establish this connection? Many times, dating and locating are

---

[4] Cf. V. Philips Long, "1 and 2 Samuel," in *Zondervan Illustrated Bible Background Commentary: Old Testament: Volume 2, Joshua, Judges, Ruth, 1 and 2 Samuel*, ed. John H. Walton, vol. 2 (Grand Rapids: Zondervan, 2009).

uncertain; how then can it be known that the author or audience was even aware of this particular piece of background data someone wishes to employ? The problem is compounded when we add that we are unsure of the social stratification of author and audience: if the data is right concerning time and place, how do we know they had access to and then used it? 2) This data itself needs interpretation. Because the Bible claims illumination, self-sufficiency, and truth for itself, it is a better tool in interpretation than any other piece of data. Therefore, it is more appropriate to interpret extra-biblical data by the Bible than the other way around. 3) I would raise again the problem that the extra-biblical evidence can add nothing to the text. If we judge the meaning of a text by its context and the meaning of the evidence by its context, by what do we judge our construal of their relationship? The only judge is the hypothesized mind of the author or audience, which is itself derived from one of the above. We are thus left with no standard of verification for our interpretation. We have no way of knowing if our construal of the relationship between the Bible and a piece of extra-biblical evidence is correct. However, if our use of extra-biblical data passes the test I proposed, then these challenges are no longer a problem, for our point rests in the text. Now, I can imagine that there might be some objections to the point I am making in this chapter, so in conclusion, I want to consider what I think will be the most common objections.[5]

C. Objections

First, someone might say, "the author originally wrote to an audience; do we not need to understand what this original audience would have understood?" This same argument could be made about the author. We could answer this in two ways. First, if we accept this assumption, this does not invalidate our point. The reason is this: the text is our standard of verification, so our conception of the author or audience's interpretation must always conform to the words of the text in their literary context. Thus, such an interpretation is subject to our test for verifying extra-biblical data given above. If our understanding of "what they would have understood' does not pass this test, it is invalid. And if it passes this test, it is redundant, we are just rephrasing "what the text says" as "what the author said," or "what the audience would

---

[5] These reflect objections I have encountered in discussions with my peers, pastors, professors, and in various articles and books concerning interpretation.

hear." Second, as we have seen, the Bible was written for our sake. Thus, we are the ultimate audience of the Bible and our standard for interpreting Scripture itself, so we are back with what the text says.

Second, someone may object that such an approach de-historicizes the text. By severing its relation to the external data, have we not de-historicized the Bible, made it merely an interpretation that says nothing about the facts of history? This conclusion is unwarranted. The text speaks about history from within the flow of history—it provides the true interpretation of history—and so applies to history. Yet, it is self-interpreting, written in such a way that it fully interprets history without needing external data to interpret it. It was produced in history, speaks to history, yet was shaped by God to be interpreted throughout history.

Third and finally, someone might suggest that this "disembodies" the text. That is, they might suggest that the approach given here treats the Bible as if it has fallen from heaven, free from the historical processes by which texts are usually formed. In response, we can say, first, that the points I am making are universal points of interpretation. Given a cogent text (a text not meant for insiders with extensive extra-textual knowledge), the best interpretation is the one that corresponds to the words of the text. Second, though the Bible began its life in the same way as many documents written in various circumstances, these documents were reconstituted—"reembodied"—as a New Covenant document written for a community stretching 2000 years, written to be understood and used throughout the ages. We are therefore not disembodying the text, making an unearthly entity, but properly considering the way God has chosen to embody it.

CONCLUSION

I began this book with a challenge I believe all Christians, especially pastors and teachers, face today, the erosion of the perspicuity of Scripture in contemporary biblical studies. In *The Gift of Reading – Part 1*, I set out to present an exegetical method that was derived from the Scripture's own claims to authority and intelligibility. In this second part, I have attempted to support and uphold that method by explaining at length the theory and theology behind it. In chapter 1, we briefly surveyed the history of biblical interpretation among Christians and the post-Christian world. In the following chapters, we interacted with the challenges raised in this survey.

In Part 1, we considered the role of the Bible, how it is the standard by which we measure meaning—a justified use of Scripture—and the way Scripture is self-interpreting. In Part 2, we considered the role of the reader in interpretation. We looked at the reader as the maker of meaning, the one who puts the Scripture to use, and we saw how the Bible is addressed to Christians throughout the ages, including us today. In Part 3, we considered the role of the author as the originator of meaning, the one who says something with a text and from whom a text derives its authority. In the final chapter, we considered how extra-biblical evidence plays a role in interpretation.

In the end, I believe we have seen how Scripture not only presents itself as self-interpreting but also how it functions in this way. We have seen that God has not left us without hope for hearing his voice. He has granted us a clear text that contains within itself the resources necessary to interpret and use it throughout the ages. We, like the 1st-century Christians, are those upon whom the end of the age has come, those who live as members of the new creation living within the old creation. To live for God's kingdom, to make his glory known and expand the sphere of those who confess his rule, we are deeply in need of a divine word. We need certainty amid our society's relativity; we need of hope in the place of our society's nihilism; we are in need of confidence that we are indeed united with Christ and recipients of his salvific work; and we are in need of wisdom, wisdom to make decisions every day concerning faithfulness to God and the success of his commission. Thanks be to God that he has not left us without a witness; he has provided us with all these things and more in the Scriptures. The Bible is a treasure granted to us and to our children; God in his kindness has not left us without a way to access and use this treasure. He has granted us all things pertaining to life and godliness, including the ability and resources necessary to make use of his Word.

To illustrate how this works in application, especially with problematic texts, I have included six exegetical essays (3 Old Testament, 3 New Testament) illustrating the use of biblical background material (Appendices 2 & 3), use of the Bible to resolve translations issues (Appendices 1, 2, 3, & 5), and the use of the Bible for theology (Appendices 5 & 6). In addition, my commentary on Habakkuk, to be released at the end of 2019 (God willing), illustrates the theory and method of *The Gift of Reading – Part 1 & Part 2* through the exposition of an entire biblical book.

In conclusion, we must thank the Lord with the Psalmist for the great gift that is his Word. We must seek ever to grow in our understanding and application of it;

> Oh how I love your law!
>   It is my meditation all the day.
> Your commandment makes me wiser than my enemies,
>   for it is ever with me.
> I have more understanding than all my teachers,
>   for your testimonies are my meditation.
> I understand more than the aged,
>   for I keep your precepts.
> I hold back my feet from every evil way,
>   in order to keep your word.
> I do not turn aside from your rules,
>   for you have taught me.
> How sweet are your words to my taste,

sweeter than honey to my mouth!
Through your precepts I get understanding;
   therefore I hate every false way.

Your word is a lamp to my feet
   and a light to my path.
I have sworn an oath and confirmed it,
   to keep your righteous rules.
I am severely afflicted;
   give me life, O Lord, according to your word!
Accept my freewill offerings of praise, O Lord,
   and teach me your rules.
I hold my life in my hand continually,
   but I do not forget your law.
The wicked have laid a snare for me,
   but I do not stray from your precepts.
Your testimonies are my heritage forever,
   for they are the joy of my heart.
I incline my heart to perform your statutes
   forever, to the end. (Psalm 119:97-112)

—APPENDICES—
Theory in Application: Exegetical Essays

THE SOVEREIGNTY OF GOD OVER THE REPENTANCE OF MAN: RE-READING DEUTERONOMY 30:1-14

This paper was originally prepared as an appendix to my book, *Prevenient Grace*.[1] It appears here with some adaptation. It argues against the standard translation of Deuteronomy 30:1-14. It is argued that in its context, this passage speaks of a future day when God would grant his people new hearts to believe in and love him as he had commanded them to. It is therefore a prophecy of the New Covenant and the fount of most New Covenant prophecies in the Old Testament.

The attentive reader, following along in his or her Bible, may have noticed that my interpretation of Deuteronomy 30:1-14 differs significantly from most English translations. I want to briefly defend my reading and offer a provisional translation that follows the contours of the interpretation I am suggesting. Three main issues confront the exegete in this passage; first, one must determine where the protasis (if...) ends and the apodosis (then...) begins.[2] Then the functions of the many uses of כִּי (*kî;* for) need to be determined. Finally, one must arrive at a conclusion on the tense of verses 11-14, namely, are they referring to the same time as the previous verses (future) or to the situation of those to whom Moses first wrote (present).

---

[1] J. Alexander Rutherford, *Prevenient Grace: An Investigation into Arminianism* (Vancouver: Teleioteti, 2016).

[2] In a conditional sentence (if...then), the apodosis is the main clause—what will happen (then). The protasis is the condition—when or in what circumstances this will happen (if).

From the syntax of the chapter and its context—both immediate and greater—I will argue that the text should be translated as follows,[3]

¹And *when* all these things come upon you—the blessing and the curse, which I have placed before you—then you will <u>return</u> these things to your heart[4] among all the nations where Yahweh your God scattered you. ²And you, you and your sons, will <u>return</u> to Yahweh your God and obey his voice with all your heart and with all your soul, according to all I have commanded you today. ³And Yahweh your God will <u>turn</u> your fortune[5]

---

[3] Stylistically smooth English has not been my primary focus with this translation. My translation philosophy for this passage has been somewhat akin to the ESV, attempting to be as close to the text as possible while accommodating for foreign idioms. For the sake of the following arguments, I have underlined the keyword שׁוּב and italicized the conjunction כִּי.

[4] Idiomatically, this means something like "call to mind" or "remember." I have retained the clumsier wording because of its parallels throughout the rest of the passage. Cf. ESV, NASB.

[5] This is the probable meaning of this interesting phrase; a literal rendering would be, "to turn your turning." The Vulgate and Septuagint seem to have read the Hebrew word rendered "your fortune"—שְׁבוּתְךָ ($š^eb\hat{u}t^ek\bar{a}$)—as a derivative from שׁבה ($šbh$), to take captive. God would then be turning their captivity. The LXX has rendered it as "your sin", τας ἁμαρτιας σου (*tas harmatias sou*), and the Vulgate as *captivitatem tuam*, "your captivity." Study of a cognate Aramaic phrase, from the Sefire inscription, suggests strongly that this word is indeed derived from שׁוּב ($š\hat{u}b$), to turn. Further support for this is found in our context, where *šûb* is a key word. Though God's turning of their turning—in light of history, the greater canonical context, and the immediate context—has in view his restoration of their fortunes via a return from exile, the idea of captivity is not to be derived from the word itself. With Driver, it seems best to understand the word to refer to a "*turn*, or change, in a people's fortune." With the same meaning in context, Christensen and Tigay identify it as an idiom with the specific meaning "restore," that is turn one's fortune by restoring a previous, and positive, state. Cf. Jb. 42:10.

Jeffrey H. Tigay, *Deuteronomy [Devarim]: The Traditional Hebrew Text with the New JPS Translation*, 1st ed., The JPS Torah commentary (Philadelphia, Penn.: Jewish Publication Society, 1996), 284, 399; Francis Brown et al., *The Brown-Driver-Briggs Hebrew and English Lexicon* (Peabody, Mass.: Hendrickson Publishers, 1996), 986; Ludwig Koehler et al., *The Hebrew and Aramaic Lexicon of the Old Testament*, electronic ed. (Leiden; New York: Brill, 1999), 1385–1386; Duane L. Christensen, *Deuteronomy 21:10-34:12*, vol. 6B, Word Biblical Commentary (Nashville: Thomas Nelson Publishers, 2002), 738; S. R. Driver, *A Critical and Exegetical Commentary on Deuteronomy*, 3rd ed., The International Critical Commentary (Edinburgh: T. & T. Clark, 1895), 329; Joseph A. Fitzmyer, *The*

and he will have compassion on you; he will <u>turn</u> and gather you from all the people among whom Yahweh your God has scattered you. ⁴Even if your exiles are at the edge of the heavens, from there Yahweh your God will gather you and he will take you from there. ⁵And Yahweh your God will bring you into the land which your fathers possessed and you shall possess it, and he will do good to you and make you more numerous than your fathers.

⁶And Yahweh your God will circumcise your heart and the heart of your offspring so that you will love Yahweh your God with all your heart and all your soul, so that you may live. ⁷And Yahweh your God will lay all these curses upon your enemies and upon those hating you, who persecuted you. ⁸And you will <u>turn</u> and obey the voice of Yahweh and do all his commands, which I have commanded you today.

⁹And Yahweh your God will prosper you in all the works of your hand, in the fruit of your womb, and in the fruit of your cattle and in the fruit of your land. *For* Yahweh will <u>turn</u> to rejoice over you for good, as he rejoiced over your fathers. ¹⁰*For* you will obey the voice of Yahweh your God, to keep his commandments and his precepts, the ones written in this book of the law. *For* you will <u>return</u> to Yahweh your God with all your heart and with all your soul. ¹¹*For* this commandment, which I have commanded you today, will not be too difficult for you and it will not be far away. ¹²It will not be in the heavens, that you should say, "Who will go up to the heavens and retrieve it for us and make us hear it so that we may do it?" ¹³And it will not be beyond the sea, that you should say, "Who will cross to the other side of the sea and retrieve it for us and make us hear it so that we may obey it?" ¹⁴*For* it will be very near to you, in your mouth and in your heart, so that you will do it.

To defend this translation, I will briefly address the three translation issues mentioned above. There are two main interpretations of this passage found among commentators, each reading sharing similar translations for each issue. One reading emphasizes Israel's response as the condition for God's actions—so the apodosis is understood to begin in verse 3, and the multiple instances of כִּי (*kî*) are understood to be strongly causal or conditional (because, if).⁶ The other understands the whole passage as prophetic and sees

---

Aramaic Inscriptions of Sefire, Biblica Et Orientalia 19 (Rome: Pontifical Biblical Institute, 1967), 119–120; R. Laird Harris, Gleason L Archer, and Bruce K Waltke, *Theological Wordbook of the Old Testament*, vol. 2 (Chicago, Ill.: Moody Press, 1980), 896.

⁶ On these readings, Kyle B. Wells, *Grace and Agency in Paul and Second Temple*

verse 6 as key; God's action is emphasized.⁷ My translation follows this later reading. The first reason for this is the identification of the apodosis.

A. Identifying the Apodosis of The Condition in Verse 1

In the former reading, prioritizing Israel, the apodosis is usually identified as starting in verse 3, when Yahweh is said to turn Israel's fortune. Verses 1b-2 are then understood as conditions for Yahweh's actions; he will restore Israel when the nation turns back to Him. Though this reading is syntactically possible, there is not much evidence in context favouring it. The unit of verses 1b-9 is composed of a series of vav+perfect constructions (and you/He will…); in theory, any of these vavs could begin the apodosis (then clause),⁸ but it is best to read the first vav as beginning the apodosis. A few reasons for this are as follows.

First, there is no discernible reason to start the apodosis at the third vav and not the first. Brettler shows that considering the syntax alone, neither the first nor the third vav clause is favoured as the beginning of the apodosis.⁹ Moreover, sometimes the subject shift from "you" to "Yahweh" is identified as a reason for taking verse 3 to begin the apodosis. This is not convincing,

---

Judaism: Interpreting the Transformation of the Heart, Supplements to Novum Testamentum 157 (Leiden; Boston, Mass.: Brill, 2015), 39. Block and, seemingly, Wright follow this first reading, at least to some extent. Daniel Isaac Block, *Deuteronomy*, The NIV Application Commentary (Grand Rapids, Mich.: Zondervan, 2012), 695, 700; N.T. Wright, *The New Testament and the People of God*, Christian Origins and the Question of God 1 (Minneapolis: Fortress, 1992), 289.

⁷ Wells, for example, provides possible arguments for this interpretation. Wells, *Grace and Agency in Paul and Second Temple Judaism*, 29–33. Coxhead, Brettler, and Sailhammer, for differing reasons, read it as a promise of the New Covenant. Marc Zvi Brettler, "Predestination in Deuteronomy 30:1-10," in *Those Elusive Deuteronomists* (Sheffield: Sheffield Academic Press, 1999), 171–188; Steven R. Coxhead, "Deuteronomy 30:11-14 as a Prophecy of the New Covenant in Christ," *Westminster Theological Journal* 68 (2006): 305–320; John H. Sailhamer, *The Pentateuch as Narrative* (Grand Rapids: Zondervan, 1992).

⁸ Ronald J. Williams and John C. Beckman, *Williams' Hebrew Syntax*, 3rd ed. (Toronto: University of Toronto Press, 2007), 181.

⁹ Brettler, "Predestination in Deuteronomy 30:1-10," 176–177.

for the subject first changes between 1a and 1b—from "these things" to "you."[10] If a subject change is our clue to the beginning of the apodosis, then it should begin in 1b. Subject changes aside, we must determine the beginning of the apodosis from context.

There is nothing in context that would favour suspending the apodosis until verse 3, but there are good contextual reasons to identify the shift at verse 1b. Turning from the coming of the curses in chapter 29, chapter 30 begins by casting a prophecy for the future; "when all these things have happened...." Taking verse 1b as the apodosis starts the prophecy with the promise of a time when Israel will turn back to God. They will finally be obedient, and God will prosper them. No cause would then be given for why Israel turns, just that they most assuredly will after God brings the curses upon them. The reader is immediately confronted with a tension: what has made it so that the negativity of chapter 29 changes to such a positive hope in 30? chapter 30 verse 6, the heart of this passage, will give us the answer.

In 29:1-4, Moses laments the state of the people, they have seen all the miraculous signs God has done, yet God has not given them the heart to understand it all (v. 4). The eventual rebellion and the coming of the curses in this chapter flow right out of this state (cf. 29:19). This has already been foreshadowed in Deuteronomy 5:29. Here, the people vow to follow Yahweh, but he responds with the desire that they would have this heart always, for then it would go well for them. However, the problem is that they do not have this heart always. If Israel's disobedience stems out of stubborn hearts that God has yet to change, the sudden obedience prophesied in Deuteronomy 30 should automatically beg us to ask what has changed: has God acted?[11]

This is exactly what the structure of the chapter and verse 6 point to. The syntax of verses 1b-9a, reading the apodosis in 1b with the first vav, links together a series of events that will all happen in the future, after the blessings and the curses come upon Israel. They could all be simultaneous: the syntax does not suggest that one is dependent on another. However, syntax is not our only guide; the macro-structure of the chapter and the context we have just looked at suggests that verse 6 is the key to all the prophesied future events. Many commentators have pointed out a chiasmic structure in this

---

[10] Wells, *Grace and Agency in Paul and Second Temple Judaism*, 29.

[11] Wells makes a similar point. Ibid., 38.

passage, ending it at v. 10, but there seems to me to be a few points that are forced in these structures.[12] Taking vv. 11-14 to be part of the prophecy in verses 1-10, the structure they are seeing becomes a closer parallel. With my translation, it looks like this:

> (A) and you will <u>return</u> these things to your heart... (v. 1b)
>> (B) And you will <u>return</u> to Yahweh your God and obey (v. 2)
>>> (C) and Yahweh will <u>turn</u> your fortunes... <u>turn</u> and gather you... do good to you and make you more numerous than your fathers (vv. 3-5)
>>>> (D) *⁶And Yahweh your God will circumcise your heart and the heart of your offspring, so that you will love Yahweh your God with all your heart and all your soul, so that you may live... and you will <u>turn</u> and you will obey the voice of Yahweh and you will do his commands* (vv. 6-8)
>>> (C') And Yahweh your God will prosper you... *for* Yahweh will <u>turn</u> to rejoice over you... as he rejoiced over your fathers. (9)
>> (B') *For* you will obey the voice of Yahweh your God. *For* you will <u>return</u> to Yahweh your God with all your heart and with all your soul. (v. 10)[13]
> (A') ¹¹*For* this commandment... will not be too difficult for you and it will not be far away... ¹⁴*For* it will be very near to you, in your mouth and in your heart so that you will do it." (v. 11-14)[14]

The heart of a chiasm is the point it is meant to emphasize: here it is the work

---

[12] E.g. in Block's chiasm, v. 8 is attached to v.9 as echoing vv. 3-5, but v. 7 need to be ignored in his diagramming of the chiasm for it to make sense. his chiasm also must begin at 2a, though we are seeing that 1b is the clearest beginning for the apodosis—2a is also an even more awkward point to begin the apodosis than 3. The biggest issue is the severing of vv. 12-14 from the preceding passages, which we will examine with the use of כִּי (kî). Ibid., 32; Block, *Deuteronomy*, 695; Wright, *The New Testament and the People of God*, 289.

[13] This verse is directly dependent upon v. 6, as the repetition of "all your heart and with all your soul" suggests. It is because God has worked that this is possible; the parallelism suggests that the act in v. 2 would also be dependent upon God's act in v. 6. Cf. Wright, *The New Testament and the People of God*, 289.

[14] The day will come when the people will turn to the commandments God has revealed to them, remembering them (v. 1). The parallel also emphasizes the same thing, but from a different perspective. Here, we see that it is because of God's work that the day will come when the commandments will be inside the hearts of the people.

of God to change the heart of his people with the result that they "will love Yahweh [their] God with all [their] heart and all [their] soul." Love is the heart of *covenant* faithfulness, and so this act is what enables them to be covenantally faithful; as verse 8 makes clear, this is what enables the Israelites to then return to God and obey Him. In Deuteronomy 5:29, God exclaimed, "Oh that they had such a heart as this always, that it might go well with them and with their descendants forever." Here, Moses prophesies that a day will come when this is true; the cause of this change is God, working to change their hearts.

Understanding verse 1b as the apodosis makes this future prophecy parallel in structure and emphasizes what the context has already demanded to be emphasized: God needs to act so that Israel can be faithful.

B. Translating the Conjunction Ki

The second translation issue is the use of כִּי (*kî*) in verses 9-11. כִּי in Hebrew encompasses functions that English expresses with many different words: there is no one-one equivalence in translating this word. In a helpful and much-cited paper, Aejmelaeus examines the various functions כִּי has in Hebrew, classifying them according to whether they follow or precede the main clause.[15] When כִּי (*kî*) precedes the clause, it usually has a function like a subordinate clause in English—Aejmelaeus classifies these uses as circumstantial. In these situations, the conjunction can communicate the ideas of condition (if), temporal condition (when), or causation (for/because).[16] This is seen in verse 1, where כִּי has a subordinate temporal value, functioning as the protasis of a conditional construction. However, all the occurrences of כִּי in verses 9-14 follow their main clause, and so—according to Aejmelaeus—need to be considered separately from those that precede the main clause.

---

[15] She uses main clause in a slightly idiosyncratic way: "The term 'main clause' will, however, be used in the following discussion to designate the clause to which the כִּי clause is joined, regardless of the distinction between subordination and coordination." Anneli Aejmelaeus, "Function and Interpretation of כִּ in Biblical Hebrew," *Journal of Biblical Literature* 105, no. 2 (1986): 196.

[16] Cause is used in the broadest possible sense, for כִּי can communicate cause, motivation, reason, explanation. Ibid., 196–198, 201–202.

From Aejmelaeus' analysis of these uses, it appears that כִּי following its main clause has a causal sense most of the time—in the broad sense noted above. Exceptions to this are the odd temporal or conditional occurrence, though the temporal use of כִּי following a main clause is always linked to a temporal correlate in the main clause. The only example she has of a conditional use after the main clause is earlier in Deuteronomy, where Israel's obedience is demanded by context as the condition (e.g. in the account of covenantal blessings).[17] Some have argued for the temporal reading of כִּי in our passage, suggesting that the temporal use of כִּי in verse 1 and the temporality of the main clause (and… will…) allow for this.[18] I must agree with Block that this seems forced, but a causal sense needs to be nuanced sand not treated as equivalent to a condition.[19]

Each of the uses of כִּי carries a strong causal sense, explaining the action in the previous clause. In 9b, Yahweh's act of prospering his people is the result of his turning to them and rejoicing over them. God rejoices over his people because they will finally obey his commandments (10). This is not a condition, for it is sure to happen, but it is also more than temporal. They will obey *because* they will turn to Yahweh with all their heart and soul (8). As I mentioned earlier, this verse is dependent on God's work in verse 6, as are verses 11-14. The resulting idea is that even though the cause of God's rejoicing is Israel's obedience, they turned to him because he acted first to circumcise their heart. Verses 11-14 gives the reason that Israel will finally obey and return to Yahweh: they will obey because in that future day the commandments of Moses will no longer be external and distant; the commandments will then be inside of them. This is a direct result of God's act of circumcision (30:6), and as we have seen earlier [this is a reference to the book, *Prevenient Grace: An Investigation into Arminianism*], the rest of the Old Testament and New Testament interpret it as such (cf. Jer. 31, Isa. 54:13, Rom 10:7-9). This brings us to our last translational issue, the timing of verses 11-14.

---

[17] Ibid., 207–208.

[18] E.g. Coxhead, "Deuteronomy 30:11-14 as a Prophecy of the New Covenant in Christ," 307–308.

[19] Block, *Deuteronomy*, 700. his translation in the chiasm, following the NIV, is conditional. Ibid., 695.

C. The Time of Verses 11-14

The NIV, NET, NASB, ESV, and LXX all translate verses 11-14 with verse 15ff and so separate them from what preceded, seeing a shift from the future back to the present. The breaks marked in the MT may also support his reading (with an open break [פ] between verses 10 and 11 and a closed one [ס] between vv. 14 and 15). Despite this consensus, there are good reasons to doubt this division of paragraphs.

First, verses 11-14 are made up of adjectives, participles, pronouns, and prepositional phrases, none of which communicate a time value in Hebrew. So any judgment about the timing of these verses needs to come from context.[20] This immediately lays the burden of proof upon those claiming that these verses return to the present, for everything preceding them was looking to the future. We must ask, then, if there any indications of a shift in timing. Other than the external testimony of the LXX and MT, the only other argument available is to suggest that הַיּוֹם (*hayyôm*; the day, today) in v. 11 calls the reader back to the present.[21] This is not convincing for two reasons. First, הַיּוֹם is not functioning adverbially to indicate when the commandment will be close (as in "today the commandment is close") but is part of an adjectival clause clarifying what commandment is in view: it is Yahweh's law, which Moses has delivered to the people that day, that will be close to them in the future. Second, in verses 2 and 8—both of which look to the future— הַיּוֹם (*hayyôm*) is used in the exact same way. So the use of הַיּוֹם does not anchor this text in the time of Moses.

The arguments for taking verses 11-14 with what precedes it are numerous. Wells points out that the very problem Israel suffered from in chapter 29—that God had not yet given them hearts to understand—is said to be remedied in this passage, so it must refer to Israel after God has given

---

[20] Coxhead, "Deuteronomy 30:11-14 as a Prophecy of the New Covenant in Christ," 306; Thomas O. Lambdin, *Introduction to Biblical Hebrew* (New York, N.Y.: Charles Scribner's Sons, 1971), 19.

[21] I am not spending time on the argument that this passage is directly connected to what follows, for it is begging the question to argue that because this is connected to what follows, it should be translated in the present. If the tenses are translated present, then vv. 11-14 surely goes with vv. 15ff. But if there are good reasons to take the tenses as future—such as no evidence to the contrary and both the syntax and flow of thought which suggests this—then it must go with vv. 1-10. Wells, *Grace and Agency in Paul and Second Temple Judaism*, 37.

them a heart to understand (i.e. after 30:6).²² There is also the coordination of כִּי (*kî*) clauses throughout the later verses of this chapter. Most English translations do not show this sequence of כִּי stretching from verses 9-14, a sequence without any syntactical clues that would suggest they should not be understood together. It makes most sense to take כִּי in verse 11 as marking a causal clause occurring at the same time as verse 10, as I have suggested in my explanations of the uses of כִּי above.²³ Furthermore, Paul quotes this passage in Romans 10:7-8 and understands them to be fulfilled in the New Covenant through Christ. If we read Deuteronomy 30:11-14 as referring to the future, this explains his interpretation.²⁴

Lastly, Sailhamer has demonstrated that the internal clues of verses 11-14 point away from Sinai to a New Covenant—as later prophesied by the prophets. The two question Moses says do not need to be asked are: "Who will go up to the heavens and retrieve it for us and make us hear it so that we may do it," and "Who will cross to the other side of the sea and retrieve it for us and make us hear it so that we may obey it?" Some may take these as generic references, expressing the difficulty and length of the task needing to be done. Sailhamer, in contrast, argues that in these verses the prophesied New Covenant seen in verses 1-10 is compared with the Covenant at Sinai.²⁵ These are not generic references then; they are references to the nature of the Old Covenant. Under the New Covenant, no one will have to go up to the heavens to get God's commandments—as Moses ascended Sinai to receive them from God. Showing this parallel, he writes, "At Sinai, for example, God spoke directly to the people "from heaven" (Deut. 4:36). Moses' words here also reflect the words of the people at Mount Sinai, 'You [Moses] go near and listen to all that the Lord our God says, Then tell us whatever the LORD our

---

²² Ibid., 38. The rest of the OT, as we saw earlier, also anticipates this as a future act of God. Coxhead, "Deuteronomy 30:11-14 as a Prophecy of the New Covenant in Christ," 309.

²³ Coxhead, "Deuteronomy 30:11-14 as a Prophecy of the New Covenant in Christ," 306–308. I disagree with his conclusion that כִּי in v. 11 should be taken temporally, but his arguments do show that כִּי should be joined with what came before it (v. 1-10).

²⁴ Ibid., 311–319; Sailhamer, *Pentateuch*, 474. See my paper reproduced as Appendices 4.

²⁵ Sailhamer, *Pentateuch*, 473.

God tells you' (5:27; cf. Exod 20:18-21)."[26] What was under the Old Covenant written upon stone tablets will now be etched in the hearts of God's people (Deut 30:6, 14; Ezek 36:26).[27] "Who will cross over the sea" would then be a reference to the crossing of the Red Sea on the way to Sinai.[28] Reading 30:11-14 as referring to the future also picks up the natural transition in verse 15, were "today" shifts from telling us about the commandments to focus on the present actions of Moses.[29]

I have argued here that Deuteronomy 30 should be read as a prophecy of a coming New Covenant, when God will enable his sinful people to obey and follow him by giving them a new heart. Israel's actions, their faithfulness, are not what precipitate God's actions; it is God's merciful act of heart circumcision that brings about their covenant faithfulness. Deuteronomy 30:11-14 is not, then, Moses' affirmation of the people's ability to follow the law as they were. These verses are his promise that in the future God would act as he had not yet acted (cf. 29:4) so that the people would finally be able to follow and obey him from their hearts.

---

[26] It is true that Moses does not explicitly make this connection, but there is enough evidence to show that it is intended. When God meet Moses at the mountain, God speaks to the people from heaven (Exod 20:22; Deut 4:36; Neh 9:13). In Deut 4:36, God is also said reveal himself on earth in fire and to speak from it, God comes in clouds and fire and Sinai becomes the place where heaven and earth meet (Deut 5:22-27). Furthermore, the words of Deut. 30:12-13 allude to Deut 5:27, where the people ask Moses to mediate for them (Deut 5:27, cf. Exod 20:18-22). Ibid., 474.

[27] Ibid., 473–474.

[28] Ibid., 474; Coxhead, "Deuteronomy 30:11-14 as a Prophecy of the New Covenant in Christ," 310–311.

[29] Sailhamer, *Pentateuch*, 474.

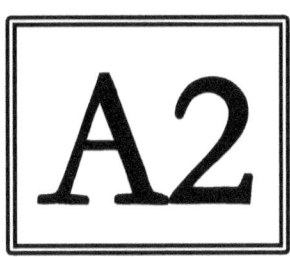

I WILL MAKE THEM LIKE THE CALF: AN EXAMINATION OF JEREMIAH 34:17-22 IN ITS LITERARY CONTEXT

This paper was originally prepared for a study on Jeremiah with Professor Tremper Longman III. It serves to illustrate the use of Scripture to resolve grammatical difficulties and how appeals to context can resolve issues that are usually resolved with appeals to archaeological material, as is the case with the self-maledictory covenant ceremony recounted in this passage.

Called from a young age, Jeremiah was God's prophet to apostate Judah. For decades he spoke of the coming judgement of God against the unrighteousness of his people. He was given the difficult task of speaking for God to a people hardened in their disobedience towards Him. Yet the book of Jeremiah is not just a giant judgment oracle; the many texts concerning judgment are punctuated by glimmers of hope and accounts of the sins that have led to Judah's dire situation. It is in the juxtaposition of hope and judgment, of God's faithfulness in fulfilling his promises and his people's adultery, that the substance of the message of Jeremiah emerges. Jeremiah, following Deuteronomy (esp., 30:1-14), presents God and his sovereign mercy as the only hope for Israel. God is consistently free, merciful, and faithful: he brings the judgment he promises yet grants mercy to the repentant; he tears down and overthrows yet will build and plant. These juxtapositions are significant for the passage that this paper will explore, 34:17-22.

In these verses we read an account of momentary repentance among the Judahites. Around the time of a short respite from Babylon's attack on Jerusalem, the leaders and people of Jerusalem covenant before God to free their slaves, in accord with a long-neglected command from Deuteronomy. Yet, shortly after fulfilling their promise, the owners of the slaves go back on the promise and repossess their slaves, possibly in response to Babylon's withdrawal.[1] In response, in 34:17-22, God pronounces judgment on these covenant breakers. The purpose of this paper will be to examine these five verses. We will look at this passage in its literary context, following God's promises (chs. 30-33) and preceding the obedience of the Rechabites (ch. 35), to see how it contributes to the theology of Jeremiah and how its placement accents the various themes found within it. To accomplish this purpose we will first look at 34:1-16 to understand the necessary context for 34:17-22, then we will take a closer look at verses 17-22, finally we will set these verses in their greater literary context and draw out some of the implications this context has for our reading of the passage. In conclusion, I will offer some ways this passage relates to the New Testament and speaks to our contemporary circumstances.

A. Jeremiah 34:1-16

Jeremiah 34 comes as somewhat of a downer after the heights of hope expressed in 30-33. Returning to the narrative under the reign of Zedekiah (28-29, 32:1-35), Jeremiah presents a message about the end of Zedekiah and Jerusalem: Zedekiah will be captured by Babylon and the city will be burned with fire (34:2-3). Yet, though Zedekiah will meet his end, a measure of mercy is found in God's prophecy concerning his future. Regarding Jehoiakim, God shows Jeremiah that there will be no royal burial or lament (22:18-19), but it is said of Zedekiah, "You shall die in peace. And as spices were burned for your fathers, the former kings who were before you, so people shall burn spices for you and lament for you, saying, 'Alas, Lord!'" (5).[2]

The following verses then revisit the same period (cf. 34:1, 6) from a

---

[1] R. K. Harrison, *Jeremiah and Lamentations*, Reprinted., Tyndale Old Testament Commentary 21 (Downers Grove, Ill.; England: Inter-Varsity Press, 2009), 148; Tremper Longman III, *Jeremiah, Lamentations*, NIBC (Peabody, Mass.; United Kingdom: Hendrickson Publishers; Paternoster, 2008), 229; J. A. Thompson, *The Book of Jeremiah*, NICOT (Grand Rapids, Mich.: WM. B. Eerdmans Publishing Co., 1980), 611.

[2] All Scripture quotations except Jer. 34:17-22 are taken from the ESV. It is noteworthy that הוֹי אָדוֹן (*hóy 'ádón*; Alas, lord!) is found in the MT only here and in Jer. 22:18.

different perspective. We are now told of a brief moment of repentance, initiated by Zedekiah, in which the people of Jerusalem move to fulfill obligations God had laid upon them in Deuteronomy 15:12. They were to set free their Hebrew slaves every 7 years, yet this had not been done (Jer 34:13); those who covenanted with Zedekiah in the presence of God were to set free the slaves they had kept far past these prescribed years (34:8). They went back on this covenant (11), so God sent Jeremiah with a message for these covenant breakers. In verses 13-16, God recounts his faithfulness and the basis for the covenant they had made: he had made a covenant with their fathers; he had taken them out of slavery in Egypt and instructed them to set their slaves free regularly. Verses 17-22 continue this message from God, giving his response to the disobedience of those who made the covenant with Zedekiah.

B. Jeremiah 34:17-22

Having recounted in 34:16 what they had done—"but then you turned and profaned my name when each of you took back his male and female slaves"—Jeremiah then presents them with the consequences of their covenant breaking:

> [17]Therefore, this is what YHWH has to say, "You yourselves have not obeyed me to proclaim liberty, each man to his brother, and each man to his neighbour." "Behold, I am proclaiming for you liberty," says the Lord, "liberty unto the sword, unto pestilence, unto famine, and I will make you a horror to all the kingdoms of the earth. [18]And I will make the men who transgressed the covenant, who did not establish the words of the covenant that they cut before me, like the calf they cut in two and between whose pieces they walked—[19]the officials of Judah and the officials of Jerusalem, the eunuchs, the priests, and all the people of the land who passed between the pieces of the calf. [20] I will give them into the hand of their enemies, into the hand of those seeking their life, and their carcasses will be food for the birds of the heavens and the beasts of the earth. [21]And I will give Zedekiah, the king of Judah, and his officials into the hand of their enemies, into the hand of those seeking their life, into the hand of the army of the king of Babylon, which has gone up from against you." [22]"Behold, I am giving the command," says YHWH, "and I will bring them back to this city and they will wage war against it and capture it and burn it with fire. I will make the cities of Judah a desolation without

inhabitants."³

In this fascinating passage, the consequences for covenant failure are seen to be dire. Significantly, we are given in this passage a glimpse of covenant making in Israel: the consequences of covenant failure are given in terms of a covenant making ritual the people of Jerusalem underwent (18-19).

Verse 17 reiterates the failure of these covenanters, furthering the message of judgment with a play on the liberty they said they would give. They said they would proclaim liberty, but took it back; God, on the other hand, would not waver in granting them liberty, though it would be a liberty to death by various means (cf. 14:12, 24:10, 32:24). Their feigned repentance had bought them no mercy; their fate remained what it had always been, if not worse (18-20).

Verses 18-19 make this judgment more specific. What is clear in these verses is the basic nature of the ritual these covenanters underwent: they cut a calf in half (18) and walked between the halves (18, 19). The meaning of the latter half of verse 18, and so the consequences they faced for their failure, is more debated.⁴ The MT text does not have an equivalent to "like" in this verse; the MT reads "I will make [lit. give, נָתַן] the men... the calf which...." To make sense of the text, the BHS suggests an emendation of הָעֵגֶל (hā'ēgel; the calf) to כָּעֵגֶל (kā'ēgel; like the calf), others reject a comparison and suggest alternate ways to understand the relation of "the calf" to the rest of the sentence.⁵ It seems to this author that neither option is optimal; instead,

---

³ This is my translation of Jeremiah 34:17-22. It is translated from the MT as represented in the BHS. No emendations were followed.

⁴ Kapelrud argues that Jeremiah has reinterpreted a non-threatening covenant ratification in a self-maledictory manner. Harrison thinks that self-imprecation is implied, but that the idea "like the calf" should not be supplied. Arvid S Kapelrud, "The Interpretation of Jeremiah 34:18ff," *Journal for the Study of the Old Testament* 22 (1982): 138–141; Harrison, *Jeremiah and Lamentations*, 149.

⁵ The LXX has translated הָעֵגֶל as an accusative, which the NETS understands to be equivalent to the Hebrew sense: "render them as the bull calf" (41:18). The vulgate follows suit, translating with the accusative *vitulum*; this may allow for a similar ad sensum construction but is rendered by Douay-Rheims adverbially ("when they cut"), with a resumptive verb in verse 20 ("And I will give the men... I will give them into...").

it is best to read the text as it stands with the comparative idea implied. The reasons for doing so are based on the syntax and sense of the passage.

Beginning with the syntax, an implied comparative is rare but not unheard of in prose (frequent in poetry). In Exodus 7:1, when God reassures Moses, he tells him that he has made (נָתַן, *nāṯan*) him "אֱלֹהִים לְפַרְעֹה" (*'ĕlōhîm lᵉp̄ar'ōh*; God to Pharaoh). No one reads this as YHWH's pledge to make Moses one of Pharaoh's gods, nor in the generic sense "a mighty one." The sense here is "I have made you like God to Pharaoh" (ESV; cf. NASB, NRSV).[6] Though "like" in Exodus 7:1 is not semantically equivalent to "like" in our passage—for in 7:1 the idea is "in the place of God as a representative" and in Jer. 34:18 as "sharing the same fate as" (in the place of)—these ideas are close enough in Hebrew, as in English, to see in this passage justification for unmarked comparisons.[7] Furthermore, without אֵת (*'eṯ*) attached, "calf" is most likely not functioning as a direct object, for Jeremiah uses the marker of the DDO consistently—especially in prose.[8]

Considering the sense of the passage, נָתַן (*nāṯan*; "make") requires some sort of complement and הָעֵגֶל (*hā'ēḡel*; the calf) is appropriate. Semantically, נָתַן involves transference: sometimes נָתַן is spatial, with the subject giving the object to someone or setting the object on or in something; in other instances, נָתַן is transformative, with the subject making the object to be something. In the latter case, a woman is given as a wife, Moses is made to be like God, and Abraham is made to be the father of many nations. Transference, whether spatial or transformative, requires a complement in the sense that what is receiving the object or what the object becomes needs to be implied or explicitly indicated. When we read in the passage that God "will make the men who transgressed…," we naturally look for that which they are to be made into. The only possible complement to אֶת־הָאֲנָשִׁים (*'eṯ-h'anāsîm;* the men) is הָעֵגֶל (*hā'ēḡel;* the calf), for every other part of the

---

[6] That Moses represents YHWH, the אֱלֹהִים, and that the text has the plural for singular אֱלֹהִים not אֵל (*'ēl*) or אֱלוֹהַּ (*'ĕlôah*) suggest that Moses will be like YHWH, the God, to Pharaoh

[7] The closest discussion I could find of this in the major grammars is the instances of understood prepositions with a verb when clarity is unaffected. Paul Joüon and Takamitsu Muraoka, *A Grammar of Biblical Hebrew*, Revised English Edition. (Pontificio Istituto Biblico, 2006), 462.

[8] Contra Harrison, *Jeremiah and Lamentations*, 149.

sentence is part of an adjectival clause. Apart from נָתַן (*nātan*; "make", there is no clause in which הָעֵגֶל could function: it is not connected to the preceding relative ("the words of the covenant which they cut before me") and the following relative modifies it adjectivally (the calf "they cut in two and whose pieces they walked between"). If we take הָעֵגֶל as part of the נָתַן clause, it is clear Yahweh is not going to turn these men into the calf. Apart from the ridiculousness of that reading, the article and the following relative clause indicate that the calf to which they are to be made like is the one they cut in half. Therefore, there is very good reason to read the text, without need of emendation, as "and I will make the men... like the calf...."

We should then understand the ceremony these men performed as one of self-malediction: by walking through the severed halves of the calf, these men indicated that they will fulfill their vow and that failure will result in their own dismembering.[9] They made this vow before God; because they failed, God now says through Jeremiah that he will be faithful on his part: they will be made like that calf; their lives will be forfeit.

Verses 20-22 then explicates the nature of the judgment they will receive. All who passed through the calf will be given into the hand of their enemies. Their bodies will be slaughtered and become a feast for the birds—a death notably worse than that promised to Zedekiah in 34:1-16. The Babylonians at this time appear to have withdrawn (21-22), yet in tremendous irony, these pagans will be obedient to YHWH's command and return to take the disobedient Zedekiah and his officials captive and to burn the city.

In summary of these verses, the repentance initiated by Zedekiah failed: the people went back on their covenant and incurred God's wrath further. Instead of receiving blessing for obedience, they would receive cursing for disobedience. The officials and the people would be made like the calf whose pieces they walked through to affirm their covenant, Zedekiah would be given into the hand of the Babylonians, and the city would burn.

C. Verses 17-22 in Context

Now, with an understanding of verses 17-22, let us consider these verses in

---

[9] So Longman III, *Jeremiah, Lamentations*, 230; Hetty Lalleman, *Jeremiah and Lamentations*, Tyndale Old Testament Commentaries 21 (Downers Grove, Ill.: InterVarsity Press, 2013), 248–249; Thompson, *The Book of Jeremiah*, 612–613.

their greater literary context, in relation to verses 1-16, chapters 30-33, and chapter 35. Beginning with the most immediately connected, it is important to note how verses 17-22 contrast the death of the covenanters with Zedekiah's promised death in verses 3-5. There is an inclusio here; the section begins and ends with Jeremiah's word that Jerusalem would be burned by the Babylonians (vv. 2, 22), his word that Zedekiah and—in the second text—his officials would be captured (vv. 3, 20-21), and a contrast between the fate of Zedekiah (vv. 4-5) and his officials (vv. 18-20). Lying between these bookends is the narrative of Zedekiah's failed attempt at initiating repentance. This suggests that part of the reason Zedekiah receives mercy whereas Jehoiakim did not is at least this attempt (cf. Jeremiah 36). Zedekiah is still to be judged, for he is consistently considered an unfaithful king, yet the portrait Jeremiah paints is of a weak and cowardly king, who seeks God's will but does not have the guts to follow it (cf. 37:2, 20-21, 38:13-28). This contributes to the greater tension within Jeremiah between God's promises to David (23:1-8, 33:14-26) and his judgment upon the Davidic line (cf. 34:1-16, 22:11-30). The act of mercy here, in contrast with judgment pronounced on Jehoiakim's line, makes it even more shocking when all of Zedekiah's children are slaughtered before his eyes (39:6) and God reveals hope in the preservation of Jeconiah, Jehoiakim's son, at the conclusion of the book (52:31-34). This contrast demonstrates the theme of Jeremiah's ministry—God's sovereign freedom and his purpose to "pluck up and to break down, to destroy and to overthrow, to build and to plant" (1:9-10)—in relation to his promises to David.

 This tension with regard to the Davidic covenant is especially heightened by the placement of this passage following the restoration oracles in chapters 30-33. In 33:14-26, God promises to raise his righteous branch from the line of David (cf. 23:1-8), concluding with his purpose to "restore their fortunes and [to] have mercy on" the offspring of Jacob and David. That the following account has a faint glimmer of mercy regarding the Davidic line is surely intentional.

 The greater significance of the location of 34:1-22 in relation to chapters 30-33 is the reinforcement the latter account provides for the promises preceding it. This is first achieved negatively; God's faithfulness is contrasted with the unfaithfulness of Judah. The actions of the wicked Judeans in breaking their covenant provides a foil for the revelation of God's enduring purpose to be faithful to his covenants with David and the patriarchs (33:23-

26). In concluding the restoration promises, God compares his faithfulness to this covenant with his faithfulness to the covenant he made with creation and affirmed with Noah—as the day and night endured, so would these promises. In the account of 34:1-22, this is set against the background of Judah's inability to maintain even the most basic commitments of their covenant with God: they promise to make up for their neglect and only reap further condemnation.

The reinforcement of the promises made in 30-33 is also achieved positively in this passage. In contrast with the faithfulness of the officials of Judah, God through Jeremiah reminds them of the reason for the command to release the slaves: God was faithful to deliver his people from slavery as he had covenanted[10] and proceeded to make a covenant with their fathers to do the same. God's faithfulness was demonstrated in Egypt and became the foundation for the requirement to release Hebrew slaves regularly. Furthermore, those who passed through the calf did so before YHWH in his temple (34:15, 18); they vowed that they would do this or pay the consequences. When they failed to keep up their end of the deal, God demonstrated his faithfulness in judgment, revealing that the Babylonians will return and that the unfaithful covenanters will pay the consequences of their broken oath. This account of a covenant made under Zedekiah is, then, perfectly placed after the promises of restoration in 30-33 to draw attention to Judah's failure, continue Judah's indictment, and emphasize even more God's faithfulness and trustworthy character.

We have considered our passage in relation to some of the greater themes unpacked across Jeremiah and in light of what precedes, all that remains is to consider 34:17-22 with what follows in chapter 35. chapter 35 takes us back to the days of Jehoiakim; we are given an account of Jeremiah's interaction with the Rechabites. In short, Jeremiah contrasts the disobedience of Judah with the obedience demonstrated by the Rechabites. The Rechabites are a family of Jews who undertook an oath from their fathers to abstain from certain practices, such as drinking or building and living in a house. When Jeremiah places before them wine, they are obedient to their oath and refuse

---

[10] It is surely not coincidental that when God performs the self-malediction ceremony on behalf of his servant Abraham (Genesis 15), he promises to deliver his people from slavery in Egypt, as this ceremony involves their vow to release the slaves.

(35:5-6). This family is faithful to the words of men, says Jeremiah, how much more should Judah be faithful to God's covenant? The folly of Judah's disobedience is magnified when set next to the faithfulness this family showed to their fathers.

The result for the Rechabites is God's promise to preserve them, "Jonadab the son of Rechab shall never lack a man to stand before me" (35:19). But concerning Jerusalem God says, "I am bringing upon Judah and all the inhabitants of Jerusalem all the disaster that I have pronounced against them" (35:17). This example of obedience provides, of course, a sharp contrast with the disobedience of Judah displayed in 34.[11] God's mercy and faithfulness are also demonstrated in that he blesses the Rechabites for their obedience. The message received by the reader is that Judah has no one to blame for their end but themselves. God is ever faithful to bless obedience but equally faithful to curse disobedience; God will tear down Judah for their disobedience, but he will build up the Rechabites for their obedience.

D. Conclusion

The purpose of this paper was to examine Jeremiah 34:17-22 in its literary context. We first examined the words of Jeremiah given in 34:1-16, an account of the making and breaking of covenant made by the people of Jerusalem to set free Hebrew slaves. This prepared us for our discussion of verses 17-22, in which God's judgment on the covenant breakers is pronounced. There, after weighing the evidence, we saw that the people undertook a self-maledictory covenant ceremony and, after failing to keep their promise, brought upon themselves God's sure judgment: they would be made like the calf they cut in two, slaughtered at the hands of their enemies. Considering these verses in their literary context, we then saw how the account in 34:1-22 was perfectly placed to emphasize Jeremiah's themes through a contrast and comparison of God's faithfulness in the promises of restoration (chs. 30-33) and the Rechabites' obedience (ch. 35) with Judah's unfaithfulness is chapter 34. Having understood Jeremiah 34 in its context, we must now—to conclude this paper—ask how it relates to the New

---

[11] Only Kidner explicitly comments on this literary contrast. Derek Kidner, *The Message of Jeremiah: Against Wind and Tide*, The Bible Speaks Today (Leicester, England ; Downers Grove, Ill.: Inter-Varsity Press, 1987), 116–119.

Testament and our contemporary situation.

Regarding our text and the New Testament, the faithfulness of God that Jeremiah is eager to emphasize ultimately finds its fulfillment in Christ. In our passage, God was seen to be faithful in cursing disobedience and his faithfulness to his promises was highlighted in context; both facets of God's faithfulness find their consummation on the Cross, as does the promise of blessing contrasted in chapter 35. On the Cross, God is shown to be perfectly faithful in his justice, poured out on Christ in our stead; he is also shown to be faithful with regard to his promises of restoration, providing in Christ the new heart his people needed (John 6:44-45), and raising up the Righteous Branch and true Davidic Messiah (shockingly, a descendent of Jeconiah). With regard to blessing, God is faithful to honour Jesus' perfect covenantal obedience, rendering to his people the benefits of right covenant relationship achieved by Him.

Regarding our contemporary situation, we are in as much need as the original recipients of Jeremiah of the faithfulness of God, who is consistent in fulfilling his promises and blessing obedience. Concerning the former, we as Christians are a people waiting for the fulfillment of God's promises. In Christ, he has given the new heart and provided the forgiveness of sin promised (31:31-34), but we still await Christ's return and the fullness of the kingdom of God in the new creation. That God is ever faithful is the encouragement we need to stay vigilant as we wait for Jesus' return. Concerning the latter, that God rewards obedience and punishes disobedience is a reminder of what Christ accomplished in his life and death. Because he took our disobedience upon himself, we can have assurance and we can praise God that there is now no condemnation for those in Christ Jesus: the curse has been removed. Because he fulfilled all obedience, we can be assured that we now take part in and will soon experience the fullness of the covenant blessings God has prepared for those in right covenant with Him. Lastly, though it would be wrong to reduce this text to a moralistic passage about keeping our promises, surely in our pursuit of Christlikeness, God would ask nothing less of us than mirroring his faithful character in being people of our word, fulfilling our commitments, oaths, and promises.

THE LAMENT OF THE AFFLICTED: A TRANSLATION OF JOB 30

This paper was originally prepared for Professor Andrew Lewis to meet the requirements for a graduate level advanced Hebrew course. It has been adapted for this context. It explores the issues of translation and the sufficiency of Scripture for textual/linguistic challenges in interpretation.

In a matter of days, Job lost his children and his wealth; at the hands of Satan—by God's permission—Job lost everything. Compounding this, the friends who came to comfort him fail to reckon that Job may not be suffering for his wickedness. For chapter after chapter, we read the accusations and self-styled remedies proffered by these friends. As these speeches draw to an end with the poem to wisdom in chapter 28, the narrator presents three final speeches from Job in chapters 29-31. Job moves from contemplating his past condition in chapter 29 to his present state in chapter 30; chapter 31 concludes this series of speeches with a defence of his innocence. Though each of these chapters is worthy of study, the present paper will focus on chapter 30, presenting a translation which aims to communicate the meaning potential of the Hebrew text with as much of the poetic effect of the original as possible. Thus, an effort will be made to follow the form and particular emphasis of the Hebrew text in readable English, the goal not being good English literature but Hebrew literature that is comprehensible to the English reader and that achieves the emotive effect of the original.

Before considering my translation, a word on the form of evidence and argumentation employed is necessary. Like many books of the Hebrew Bible, scholarly translation and interpretation of Job regularly involves significant emendation of the Masoretic Text.[1] By their very nature, such emendations are speculative. Even on the level of explicit reasoning, without addressing theological presuppositions, one may take issue with this approach.[2]

An emendation is only invoked when the present text is considered suspect to the interpreter, yet what is suspect to one interpreter may not be so for another. Such suspicions may be a product of the reader rather than the text, of unfamiliarity with Hebrew, or of an overly constrictive understanding of language (e.g. an author is not credited with the freedom to create new constructions and grammatical combinations using rules exhibited elsewhere).

Because of the speculative nature of emendation, the practice of the present author is to seek an explanation in the possible sense "awkward" texts may have when considered in light of similar grammatical and syntactical combinations found elsewhere in Scripture. Because we have no a-priori reason to doubt the Masoretic text we have received, and we have significant a-posteriori evidence to trust it, this author will accord the MT the benefit of the doubt, leaving the burden of proof on the one who seeks to prove that their emendation is better than the received text. The principle of parsimony also favours any reading that explains the text as it stands, without need of multiplying explanations. Furthermore, because it is impossible to prove that the present text is unintelligible, no one being fluent enough in ancient Hebrew to make such a definitive judgment, any proof resting on "better sense" will be rejected, for this is a subjective judgment based on limited knowledge (i.e. that it makes no sense to us says nothing about its comprehensibility for the original author or audience). According to the definition of emendation given above, such claims of awkwardness or incomprehensibility are the only possible evidence in favour of consonantal

---

[1] "Emendation," as used here, encompasses everything from the subtle changes of revocalization to the insertion of consonants and supposedly missing words *without manuscript warrant*. Emendation does not encompass the comparison of variant readings, which are measured by the canons of textual criticism.

[2] Of course, to not talk about such presuppositions is not to say they do not matter nor that they are not influencing the following discussion. It is only to say that I will not explicitly argue for the beliefs presupposed below, though I have in the present book, and will not directly address the presuppositions of those who disagree. Cf. J. Alexander Rutherford, *The Gift of Knowing: A Biblical Perspective on Knowing and Truth*, God's Gifts for the Christian Life Part 1 - The Christian Mind I (Vancouver: Teleioteti, 2019).

emendation, so such emendations will be rejected.

Proposed revocalizations will be considered not on the basis of "better sense," for the reasons stated above, but on the basis of analogous misreadings in the present tradition and alternative textual evidence, thus being considered on the basis of a textual criticism as with consonantal emendation. For these reasons, the Masoretic Text will be given priority.[3]

Concerning lexica, evidential priority for the interpretation of *hapax legomena* and other rare words will be given, in order of priority, to the canonical biblical text, other Hebrew texts, Aramaic texts, and then other Semitic language texts. The canonical text will be given priority, for it forms a single body of intelligible language and exerted an influence on itself over the course of its writing (e.g. the Pentateuch and its language influenced the following works). Because extra-biblical Hebrew texts share the same language and vocabulary where they can be compared, appeals to words that are present in these texts to explain those rare in the biblical corpus are substantiated by this shared lexical stock. Aramaic clearly influenced the authors of the biblical texts, including demonstrable borrowing of vocabulary, and is present in the biblical text, so appeals to Aramaic of relatively the same period as the text under consideration are considered legitimate. Other Semitic languages yield many insightful parallels in lexical stock, yet one must tread carefully for it is impossible to be certain of the influence of a particular language and its vocabulary on the author or audience of a particular book, an issue compounded when the provenance and date of a book such as Job is unknown—despite the best speculations concerning the nature of its language.[4] On the basis of these considerations, an interpretation is to be preferred when it can be supported by the context,

---

[3] A full text critical analysis of the text falls beyond the scope of this paper, yet it should be noted that many of the appeals made to alternate manuscripts and translations violate the canon of *lectio difficilior*.

[4] Cf. Aaron Hornkohl, "Periodization," in *Encyclopedia of Hebrew Language and Linguistics: Volume 1; A-F*, ed. Geoffrey Khan, vol. 1, 4 vols. (Leiden; Boston: Brill, 2013); Jan Joosten, "The Distinction Between Classical and Late Biblical Hebrew as Reflected in Syntax," *Hebrew Studies* 46 (2005): 327–339; Choon Leong Seow, "Orthography, Textual Criticism, and the Poetry of Job.," *Journal of Biblical Literature* 130, no. 1 (2011): 63–85; Ian Young, "Is the Prose Tale of Job in Late Biblical Hebrew?," *Vetus Testamentum* 59, no. 4 (2009): 606–629.

analogous uses of syntax and grammar,[5] and inter-biblical lexical appeals. On this basis, the following translation is proposed.

A. Job 30

a. Strophe 1 – I Am Mocked by Wretches[6]

Stanza 1

¹But now, men younger[7] than I laugh at me,
   whose fathers I refused
   to put with the dogs of my flock.[8]
²Yes, the strength of their hands, what use was it to me?
   men whose vigour had perished![9]

---

[5] "Analogy" is not restricted to identical grammatical and syntactical combinations (syntagms) but comparable uses of the same morphological (e.g. noun patterns), grammatical (clause level: e.g. a noun in a construct relationship with an adjective), or syntactical (sentence level: e.g. כִּי functioning to subordinate a clause) patterns.

[6] "I will employ the terms 'strophe' and 'stanza' in a particular way…: I employ these terms to describe greater and lesser sense units, respectively, made up of groups of colons (the smallest sense unit of poetry, a grouping of lines). Strophe in my use would be roughly equivalent to a 'verse' in contemporary lyrical poetry, the broadest division of a poem or song. Stanzas are the smaller units that make up a strophe." J. Alexander Rutherford, *The Book of Habakkuk: An Exegetical-Theological Commentary on the Hebrew Text*, A Teleioteti Old Testament Commentary 1 (Vancouver, BC: Teleioteti, Forthcoming), 52.

[7] צָעִיר can have connotations of social inferiority, which appears to be the case here (cf. DCH, HALOT).

[8] This is read as enjambment, with the infinitive completing מָאַס.

[9] This line appears to be describing further the "fathers" in the previous lines, so a past tense is appropriate in translation. Two problems concern us here; the first is the meaning of כֶּלַח ("vigour"). כֶּלַח occurs only here and in Job 5:26. In Job 5:26, Eliphaz expounds the rewards of one who responds rightly to God's corrective discipline; this man will "go to the grave in *kelaḥ*." The idea would be that he will die while he still has strength, or vigour. HALOT identifies it as a collocation of לֵחַ and כֹּה, supporting this, contra David J. A. Clines, *Job 21 - 37*, ed. Bruce Manning Metzger et al., Word Biblical Commentary 18a (Nashville: Nelson, 2007), 944.. The following line uses the imagery of a sheaf gathered at the appropriate time,

Stanza 2

³Because of want and barren hunger,[10]
>they were those who gnawed[11] at the parched land
>—only yesterday it was ruined and devastated—[12]
⁴who broke off the mallow from its bush,
>and the root of shrubs for their food.[13]

---

supporting the English idiom used by the ESV "ripe old age." What this means, though, appears to be the same as the previous line: "you will die at a good time, not too early nor will your life stretch on unnecessarily." This idea of vigour, the vitality of life, thus works in 5:26 and here in 30:2—these men are useless, their vitality is long gone. כָּלַח is used for its assonance with the initial כֹּחַ.

The second problem concerns the use of עַל here. Hartley, in agreement with DCH, suggests it means "from"; yet the lexical evidence for this meaning is lacking. John E. Hartley, *The Book of Job*, NICOT (Grand Rapids: Eerdmans, 1988), 396. Clines argues that it is better understood according to the so called "pathetic" sense (advantage/disadvantage), yet the meaning this yields is not readily apparent to this author (a problem Clines acknowledges when he identifies it as "untranslatable"). Clines, *Job 21 - 37*, 944. Clines' interpretation further requires an implied possessive connecting "them" to "vigour," a connection which עַל suffices to make. By analogy with אֶל (concerning), with which עַל is often interchanged, עַל here means "concerning them, vigour has perished." This is equivalent semantically and emphatically with "men whose vigour had perished."

¹⁰ "Barren" seems to emphasize their hunger while adding the idea of hopelessness, that it will not be satisfied.

¹¹ The article on the participles in vv. 3 and 4 indicates that they are functioning substantivally, further describing the fathers of those who now mock Job. ערק only appears twice (also in Job 30:17), yet the meaning "gnaw" seems clear from context and is supported by Syriac and Arabic cognates (cf. the Vulgate's *rodo*). The LXX's "flee" is contextually unlikely. Similarly, Clines, *Job 21 - 37*, 945.

¹² The pair of nouns here appears to be in apposition with צִיָּה ("parched land"), describing it as it was when these men were alive. אֶמֶשׁ ("yesterday"), which usually refers specifically to the previous night or generally to the previous day, is being used much like the English idiomatic use of "yesterday" for a period some time ago that seems much more recent. The land was at this time—as if only yesterday—ruined and devastated.

¹³ לַחְמָם is either a verbal form "to warm themselves" (חמם) or לֶחֶם with a 3mp pronominal suffix. The verbal form would require a revocalization or it would be an anomalous infinitive form (Isaiah 47:14 has the same form; HALOT suggests a revocalization, yet the line could be read as "this [fire] is no hot coal fire for *their food*, no fire to sit before!" that is, it is no campfire). The form in the MT is a standard

Stanza 3

⁵They were driven from the community

—they shouted against them as thieves!¹⁴

⁶So they dwelt in the slopes of wadis,¹⁵

in holes of the ground and among rocks.¹⁶

⁷In the midst of bushes they bray,

under nettle they huddle together.

⁸Sons of lowly wretches,¹⁷

—yes, they are men without names—

---

form for לָחֶם and is best read as such.

"Shrub" is usually identified as "broom," the roots of which are inedible, yet this should not be used either to dismiss the possibility that the root could be food (contra Clines, *Job 21 - 37*, 946; Marvin H. Pope, *Job: Introduction, Translation, and Notes* (Garden City: Doubleday, 1973), 220.) or to read too much into the line—such that the inedibility of broom-root emphasizes their desperate state. Either of the two possibilities above is plausible, yet it is not clear in context that either is intended. Whether mallow or saltwort, מַלּוּחַ is not a preferable food option; the context indicates that the root of this broom shrub—inedible or not—was likewise not preferable (cf. Franz Delitzsch, *Job: Two Volumes in One*, Commentary on the Old Testament in Ten Volumes IV (Grand Rapids: Eerdmans, 1978), 142–143.).

¹⁴ The shift in verbal subject in the second line creates a disjunction, a rapid change of perspective, best communicated with an emphatic parenthesis.

¹⁵ "Wadi" refers to stream beds that are dry until the rainy season, when heavy rains fill them.

¹⁶ Neither חֹר ("hole") nor כֵּף ("rock") has a preposition: the בְּ from the first line is assumed. This could be read as "in holes of dust and of rocks" or "in holes of the dust and in rocks." A decision here is difficult, yet the second reading seems slightly more likely because the collocation of rocks and holes in the ground as hiding places for the destitute appears elsewhere (cf. 1 Sam. 13:6, 14:11; Isaiah 1:19).

¹⁷ בֵּן plus a noun is often used attributively or substantively; with an adjective, this construct makes the adjective a substantive. When בֵּן is in a construct relationship with an adjective, it is almost always with a gentilic adjective (15/18 times). In two other cases, the adjective is an indefinite substantive (אֶבְיוֹן, one who is needy [Ps. 72:4]; עֶלְיוֹן, (the) Most High [Ps. 82:6]). This leaves only Job. As with the two instances in the psalms, the adjective is indefinite, suggesting that it should be read as substantive genitive of relationship: "children of a lowly wretch." נָבָל has usually been understood as "fool" (senseless, unwise), yet it is employed elsewhere in opposition with נָדִיב (noble; Pr. 17:7, Isa. 32:5): the sense seems to be "lowly of status" with negative connotations of the dregs of society (Isa. 32:6) or foolish people (Deut. 32:6) depending on the context.

they were violently driven from the land.[18]

b. Strophe 2 – I Am a Byword to the Unrestrained

Stanza 1
⁹But now I have become their sons' song[19]
    I am a byword to them.
¹⁰They abhor me and keep themselves far from me;
    yet from my face they withhold not their spit.[20]

Stanza 2
¹¹Because he loosed my cord[21] and humbled me;
    they cast off all restraint in my presence;[22]
¹²At my right hand the rabble arises;
    they shove my feet
    and raise against me

---

[18] נָכָא is an alternate form for the more common נָכָה (to strike; cf. DCH, HALOT). An adjective נָכֵא (stricken) with these consonants is found in Proverbs 15:13, 17:22, and 18:44, with a meaning related to נָכָה (cf. the adj. נָכֵה). נָכָא in the Niphal, therefore, means "to be struck"; followed by מִן, the idea is to be struck resulting in movement away, thus "to be violently driven from."

[19] נְגִינָה, a musical composition, doesn't necessarily have negative connotations; yet elsewhere it is contextually clear that a "mocking song" is intended (Lam. 3:14, 3:63). Heb., "their," referring not to the fathers that were being described previously but their sons introduced in v. 1.

[20] Clines objects that it is logically incoherent to say that they keep themselves far from Job but also spit on his face. Clines, *Job 21 - 37*, 948. This is not necessarily the case: both spitting and keeping their distance are actions of disdain and disrespect; Job envisions the young mockers at times giving him a wide berth and at others drawing near only to spit upon him. Therefore, the uses of מִן concluding the first line and opening the second are visually and semantically parallel.

[21] יֶתֶר refers to a piece of material used for various functions for which we would use a "string" or a "cord" (e.g. "bowstrings" Ps. 11:2). The idea here is not readily apparent to the contemporary reader, yet we can surmise from context that for God to loose Job's "cord" was to bring about the humiliating and oppressing circumstances under which he now finds himself.

[22] Lit., "they cast off reins in my presence": because God has afflicted Job, these young men act towards him without any sort of restraint.

> their calamitous ways[23]
>
> [13]They break up[24] the path before me[25]
> and profit from my destruction—
> they have no need of help.[26]
>
> [14]As through a wide gap they come,
> beneath a calamity[27] they roll on.[28]
>
> [15]Sudden terrors are turned upon me,[29]

---

[23] Clines describes סלל ארחות as "technical language for throwing up a siege-ramp"; I was unable to find any evidence for this contention. Clines, *Job 21 - 37*, 950. A noun from the root סלל (סֹלְלָה) does mean "siege ramp," yet this noun is never used with the verb. The verbal form is used elsewhere with synonyms of אָרַח (Job 19:12, Isa. 62:10) and is used absolutely for building a road (Isa. 57:13, 62:10). Another use of סלל describes the piling up of corpses (Jer. 50:26), which is similar in idea if "building a road" involves the piling of stones. Cf. the verbs used for siege ramps in Hab. 1:10 and Ezek 4:2. It is probable, then, that the idea here and in Job 19:12 is not the making of a siege ramp but of establishing a way of acting towards someone that is intent on their destruction (corresponding to the well-established metaphorical extension of אֹרַח and דֶּרֶךְ as a way of behaviour). "The paths of their calamity" is "their paths of calamity," a descriptive genitive, and so equivalent to "their calamitous paths."

Each of these four lines is brief, forming an almost staccato description; this echoes the unrestrained, rebellious "rabble" it describes.

[24] נָתַס (break up) is a hapax, best explained as an alternate form of נָתַץ, cf. HALOT, DCH, BDB.

[25] Lit., "my path."

[26] Lit., "there is no helper for them": contextually the idea is not that they have no helper and need one, but that they have no helper because they are succeeding so well in the afflictions they administer.

[27] DCH lists שׁאָה as a hapax, yet it is better taken as a defectively written form of שׁוֹאָה (cf. v. 3; so HALOT). The sense of "roll on" is obscure, but in light of use of גלל to describe the movement of rocks and the flowing of water, it probably has a sense of unyielding power.

[28] At first these lines are opaque, but it seems that "calamity" and "wide gap" are parallel: Job envisions these young men assailing him during or after a disaster has wrought its destruction.

[29] The written form is a Hophal, the only such instance for this verb; some conjecture a Niphal, yet the Hophal makes contextual sense. It emphasizes the terror while keeping the subject doing the turning in the background, fitting for a context in which Job expounds his suffering with reference to those who are assaulting him.

they chase away my nobility like the wind;³⁰
my salvation passes away like a cloud.

c. *Strophe 3 – I Am Afflicted by God*

Stanza 1

¹⁶And now my life is poured out before me,
  days of affliction seize me!
¹⁷The night digs out my bones from me,
  and my gnawing pains do not sleep;
¹⁸With great violence it disguises itself as my garment;³¹
  like the neck of my tunic, it clings tightly to me.³²

Stanza 2

¹⁹He throws me to the mud,
  I become like dust and ashes.
²⁰I cry to you for help and you do not answer me,
  I stand to my feet and you just look on me;

---

³⁰ Some emend תרדף, a Qal 3fs verb, to a Niphal, "my nobility is chased away." Hartley, *The Book of Job*, 399. This is, however, unnecessary: though it is awkward to have a plural subject in the first line ("terrors") paired with a singular verb in the second ("it chases away"), this is not unheard of and is to be preferred over the suggested emendation. The resulting sense would be, "Sudden terrors are turned upon me, the terrors chase away my nobility like the wind."

³¹ לְבוּשׁ (garment) is translated with a comparative value. This function is often marked by the preposition כְּ; there are, however, exceptions where the comparative is unmarked. In poetry, unmarked comparisons are common and in prose at least two examples can be presented (e.g. Jer. 34:18, Exod 7:1; cf. Appendix 2). Reading the first line in this way allows us to make sense of the following line, which is often translated at odds with the first line (cf. ESV, NET). The masculine subject probably refers neither to "night" (a feminine noun) nor God (contra NET), but the night personified and collocated with עָרְקִי (my pains): the night-pain, equivalent to v. 16's "affliction," wraps close like his garments.

³² These two lines are difficult, yet the second line seems to presuppose as its subject not לְבוּשׁ (garment) but לַיְלָה or עָרְקִי. Neither of these readings is ideal, yet the idea is clear enough: "the afflictions (associated with the night) cling close to me, like my very garment they force themselves on me." The usual reading (ignoring emendations) that his clothing disguises itself—i.e. distorts itself—is lexically difficult (the word does not have this extension elsewhere) and one struggles to make sense of it with the following line (though the image of tossed clothing fits well with the previous lines).

²¹You have changed, become cruel towards me;
> with your powerful hand, you harass me!

²²On the wind you raise me and cause me to ride;
> you attain success causing me to melt.³³

Stanza 3

²³But I know that you will turn me to death,³⁴
> to the home appointed for all the living—

²⁴surely he would not stretch a hand against a ruinous heap,
> if in his misfortune he utters a cry for these things!³⁵

²⁵Though I did not weep for the man facing a difficult day,³⁶
> my soul now³⁷ grieves as a needy man.

²⁶For I hoped for good,
> but calamity has come

---

³³ Or "with great competence (or wisdom) you melt me." This follows the qere, תּוּשִׁיָּה (sound wisdom or success), translated as an adverbial accusative, "with success." Many translations and commentators reject the qere as nonsensical; e.g. Robert L. Alden, *Job*, The New American Commentary v. 11 (Nashville: Broadman & Holman, 1993), 293–294; Clines, *Job 21 - 37*, 956; Delitzsch, *Job: Two Volumes in One*, 161–163; Hartley, *The Book of Job*, 402; Pope, *Job: Introduction, Translation, and Notes*, 223.

"Cause me to melt" translates the verb מוג: the meaning is either that Job is like earth washed away by the wind and rain (cf. Ps. 65:11) or that God's attack melts away Job's courage, his strength, his resolve (cf. Isa. 14:31, Jer. 49:23, Ezek 21:20). The latter fits well with Job's contemplation of death in the following verses.

³⁴ שׁוּב does not mean here "bring me to where I once was" but " turn me towards a new place."

³⁵ The identity of "these things" is the pressing question of this line. It seems that the cry uttered by Job, describing himself as a "ruinous heap," is directed to "death" and "home" in the previous verse. Cf. Alden, *Job*, 295, ft. 53.

³⁶ Lit: "difficult of day," functioning substantively. A few possibilities present themselves for these two lines: looking back on a difficult day, Job remembers his endurance, yet now as things have soured even further, he is broken; or, the initial *lamed* indicates the object for which one weeps and the second a comparison with one who grieves. Cf. v. 4, Deut. 9:21; Bruce K. Waltke and Michael Patrick O'Connor, *An Introduction to Hebrew Syntax* (Winona Lake, Ind.: Eisenbrauns, 1990), 206–207. On the second approach, interpreting "difficult" as a substantive, Job's position has been reversed.

³⁷ Though not explicit, the apodosis functions as a temporal contrast with "the difficult day" in the previous line.

and I waited for light,
> but darkness has come.

Stanza 4

²⁷My bowels are in turmoil and are not silent,
> days of affliction meet me;

²⁸I go about blackened, but not by the heat of the sun;
> I get up in the assembly and cry for help,

²⁹But I have become a brother to the jackals
> and a neighbour to the ostrich's children.[38]

³⁰The skin upon my flesh has blackened,
> my bones burn with heat.

³¹My lyre is now for mourning,
> my flute for the sound of those weeping.

---

[38] The Hebrew does not have a conjunction opening v. 29, yet the relationship with what precedes and what follows implies the adversative relationship provided by "but." The sense is that the blackening of his skin, his diseased state, results in his cries for help falling on deaf ears: he is rather like the animals of the wild deserts, alone and rejected.

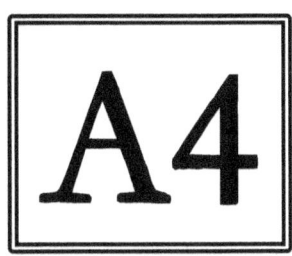

DO NOT SAY IN YOUR HEART: AN EXPOSITION OF ROMANS 10:1-8 IN THE CONTEXT OF 10:1-13

This paper was originally prepared for Professor Doug Moo to meet the requirements of graduate-level study on Romans. The parameters of this assignment restrained the amount of conversation partners with which I could dialogue, yet this does not take away from the strength of the arguments presented herein. This paper illustrates the theory and method unpacked above with particular attention to the question of the New Testament's use of the Old.

In a pluralistic society like ours, nothing is more offensive than the proclamation of Christ as Lord, the sole King and way to God. Christ as *the* way to God precludes any other. Despite the 1st century's own pluralism, the offense of Jesus was not his exclusivity over against other religions, but the exclusivity, the superiority, of Christ over the Old Covenant. Jesus' exclusiveness is offensive to all societies, yet the problem was particularly compounded for Paul in light of God's promises to Israel—how can they not be saved? Paul, in Romans 9-11, takes on this challenge: he wrestles with the question of what God's ultimate work in Jesus means for Israel.

At the middle of this section, in 9:30-10:13, Paul looks at the culpable failure of Israel that resulted in their condition. Paul expounds how in ignorance they rejected God's climactic work in Christ and so needed salvation (10:1-13). This section is important, yet difficult. In 10:5-8, Paul boldly juxtaposes Moses' own words in Leviticus and Deuteronomy to show that the Jews, in seeking their own righteousness, repudiated God's ultimate provision of righteousness in Christ.

This paper will seek to expound this most difficult section. It is broadly acknowledged that 9:30-10:13 is a single unit in Paul's argument.[1] I, with some commentators, recognize a further subdivision between 9:30-33 and 10:1-13.[2] For the purposes of this paper, I intend to concentrate on verses 1-8 in this subsection. It is my intent to expound the argument and unity of this text, with particular attention paid to Paul's use of Deuteronomy 30:11-14.[3] To relate my exposition, I will offer my proposed outline and then present my exegesis of Romans 9:1-8, with an excursus on Deuteronomy 30:11-14.

Before turning to our text, let us consider the argument's flow in 30:1-13:

I. <u>Israel's Need for Salvation (10:1-13)</u>
    1. Israel Needs Salvation, Having Rejected God's Righteousness (10:1-4)
    2. God's Righteousness Is Not the Law-Righteousness Israel Seeks: It is by Faith through Jesus (10:5-13)
        A. *Moses wrote of a law-righteousness (10:5)*
        B. *Faith-righteousness is God's near, New Covenant, work, received by faith and confession (10:6-13)*
            i. God's faith-righteousness is not of the distant Old Covenant but the near New Covenant (10:6-8)
                a. *Faith-righteousness is not the distant law (10:6-7)*
                b. *Faith-righteousness stands upon New Covenant faith (10:8)*
            ii. Confession and faith are the way for all to receive salvation. (10:9-13)

---

[1] Douglas J. Moo, *Encountering the Book of Romans: A Theological Survey*, 2nd ed., Encountering Biblical Studies (Grand Rapids, Mich.: Baker Academic, 2014), vii; Thomas R. Schreiner, *Romans*, Baker Exegetical Commentary on the New Testament 6 (Grand Rapids, Mich.: Baker Books, 1998), 533.

[2] F. F Bruce, *The Epistle of Paul to the Romans: An Introduction and Commentary* (Grand Rapids, Mich.: Wm. B. Eerdmans Publishing Co., 1963), 68; Moo, *Encountering*, 144; Schreiner, *Romans*, 534.

[3] Cf. Appendix 1.

A. Exegesis

a. *Israel Needs Salvation, Having Rejected God's Righteousness (10:1-4)*

Brothers, my heart's desire and prayer to God for them is that they may be saved. ²For I bear them witness that they have a zeal for God, but not according to knowledge. ³For, being ignorant of the righteousness of God, and seeking to establish their own, they did not submit to God's righteousness. ⁴For Christ is the end of the law for righteousness to everyone who believes.[4]

Verse 1. Paul's use of the vocative "Brothers" signals a shift to another facet of the present topic.[5] Having explained Israel's failure to attain righteousness in the preceding verses, Paul now reiterates his heart concerning Israel, first expressed in 9:1-4,[6] in light of this failure: he desires their salvation. He focuses on the human cause of their apostasy, further explaining Israel's failed pursuit of a law leading to righteousness (9:30-33).

Verse 2. In verse 2 we encounter the first occurrence of the conjunction γαρ (*for*) in these verses (also 3, 4, 5, 10, 11, 12, 13). Most of these uses are explanatory. Here, Paul begins to explain his desire for Israel's salvation: they are not saved; their zeal for God is in ignorance of his accomplishment. Paul testifies that they have zeal, yet it is misplaced. Their ignorance is expounded in what follows.

Verse 3. Paul now provides further explanation (γαρ) on verse 2. "[B]eing ignorant" (αγνοουντες) and "seeking" (ζητουντες) translate two participles that explain Israel's failure to submit.

First, they were ignorant of God's righteousness: it is not that they did not have access to but that they disregarded this truth. Though Paul often uses this word αγνοεω to refer to a lack of knowledge (Rom. 1:13, 1 Cor. 10:1,

---

[4] Scripture quotations are from the ESV. Quotations from Deut. 30 are my translation.

[5] Douglas J. Moo, *The Epistle to the Romans*, NICNT (Grand Rapids: Eerdmans, 1996), 631.

[6] Here, with anguish over their damnation.

12:1), he also uses it with the sense of the culpable rejection of truth (Acts 13:27, 1 Cor. 14:38). This latter sense is intended here (cf. vv. 5-8, 14-21).

Second, this wilful ignorance is coupled with the pursuit of personal righteousness. In light of Paul's salvific focus, individual—not corporate—righteousness is surely in view (cf. 10:1, 9, 10, 13).[7] From the rest of Paul's argument, s is law-righteousness (cf. 1:16-17, 3:21-4:12). So Paul continues a series of contrasts begun in 9:30-31 between law-righteousness and faith-righteousness.[8] Law-righteousness is not God's faith-righteousness, to which they have failed to submit (3). The righteousness they seek is by works (5), God's is by faith (6); the first is distant, of the Old Covenant (5), God's is near, of the New (6-13).

Verse 4. Paul now explains how Jews have failed to submit to God's righteousness, and so are in need of salvation. In Paul's compact argument, the connection between vv. 3-4 is not immediately clear.[9] Unpacking his argument, he is saying that the Jews have no righteousness and, therefore, are not saved (10:1, 3), because "Christ is the end of the law for righteousness to everyone who believes." It is because they reject Jesus and the New Covenant in his blood that they are without righteousness and damned. The righteousness of God in verse 3 is then that which God has made available through faith in Jesus. The introduction of the law here prepares us for the following contrast between law-righteousness (5) and faith-righteousness (6-13). However, the controversies over this text must detain us a moment longer.

In which sense Christ is the "end of the law" and the relation of "for righteousness" to this sentence are controversial. Beginning with the former, the semantic range of τελος, translated "end," suggests that Jesus is the goal of the law or that he ends it—some argue that both senses coincide in this word. Because both are true theologically (Matt 5:17-20, Luke 24:44, Rom 7,

---

[7] Personal faith and confession in context also support an individual reading. Moo, *The Epistle to the Romans*, 634; James R. Lowther, "Paul's Use of Deuteronomy 30:11-14 in Romans 10:5-8 as a Locus Primus on Paul's Understanding of the Law in Romans" (Doctoral Dissertation, Southwestern Baptist Theological Seminary, 2001), 101–102..

[8] Moo, *Encountering*, 142

[9] Schreiner, *Romans*, 547.

Gal 3:24-25, Heb 8), context is our only guide. Following Moo, I interpret τελος to refer to Jesus completing the law in that he is the goal towards which it moved. As a race has the finish line for its goal and end, so also the law has Christ. With the finish line reached, the Law has ended.[10]

My main reason for this interpretation is Paul's argument in the following verses. In 10:5-8, we will see that Deuteronomy 30:11-14 anticipates the end of the Sinai covenant and its Law. Furthermore, through his Christological application, he shows that this text—and so the Law as written revelation and the Law as an inadequate covenant—anticipates the need for and the coming of Christ (Christ as its goal). To this we can append Moo's arguments: first, the language of "attaining" and "pursuing" in 9:31-32a suggests that *end* refers to the *goal*. Christ, as the righteousness to which the law would lead, is that goal which Israel was pursuing with the law but missed. Second, in support of the temporal aspect ("it has ended"), Paul is consistent in his focus on the salvation-historical transition from Law to Christ resulting in the Law's end (3:21ff; 6:14, 15; 7:1-6): here, he maintains discontinuity between the law-righteousness sought by the Jews and God's righteousness.[11] Last, Moo argues that many similar New Testament uses of τελος bear this dual nuance of "an end that is the natural or inevitable result of something else."[12]

Against this, Schreiner identifies the emphasis to be on Israel's subjective failure (3): the law, then, has not had a complete, objective end but has ended subjectively, ended as a way for righteousness.[13] However, though the Jews are seeking their own righteousness, this is part of the wilful rejection of God's righteousness: they have rejected the salvation-historical shift.

We would be remiss if we did not now address the debate over what "for righteousness" modifies. Our discussion above assumes, and is evidence, that "for righteousness" modifies the whole initial clause.[14] We can add as evidence for our interpretation that it is supported by the contextual arguments made above and by verses 5-13, where Christ has made

---

[10] Moo, *Encountering*, 144–145; James D. G Dunn, *Romans 9-16*, Word Biblical Commentary 38b (Dallas, Tex.: Word Books, 1988), 589.

[11] Moo, *The Epistle to the Romans*, 622–626, 640.

[12] Ibid., 641.

[13] Schreiner, *Romans*, 547.

[14] Contra Ibid.

righteousness available through faith by ending the law.[15]

In summary, Paul shows the need for Israel's salvation by juxtaposing their sinful pursuit of law-righteousness with God's provision of righteousness in Christ as the Law's goal and end. In verses 5-8, Paul will now explain this by contrasting two OT passages.

b. God's New Covenant Righteousness Ended the Law (10:5-8)

⁵For Moses writes about the righteousness that is based on the law, that the person who does the commandments shall live by them. ⁶But the righteousness based on faith says, "Do not say in your heart, 'Who will ascend into heaven?'" (that is, to bring Christ down) ⁷"or 'Who will descend into the abyss?'" (that is, to bring Christ up from the dead). ⁸But what does it say? "The word is near you, in your mouth and in your heart" (that is, the word of faith that we proclaim).

Verse 5. Paul connects this verse as an explanation of what has preceded with γαρ (*for*). Moo interprets this verse as the grounds for verse 4 only—Christ as the end of the law.[16] I take verses 5-13 as an explanation of all of verses 1-4, that is, it shows the nature of Israel's ignorance in missing Christ as the end of the law and so their culpability and need for salvation. This is unavoidable if my interpretation of verse 4 as the summary and conclusion of 1-4 is maintained.

Paul begins this section (5-8) by showing what Moses said about law-righteousness, which the Jews sought. With a quotation from Lev. 18:5, it is seen that law-righteousness is by works: The one who *does* will live—in context, be saved.[17] This verse invokes one side of a tension in the OT between God's gracious promise (Gen 12:1-7; 26:4-5) and the need for

---

[15] Moo, *The Epistle to the Romans*, 637–638.

[16] Ibid., 645.

[17] Paul's use is supported in the OT. Habakkuk 2:4, juxtaposing Gen. 15:6 and Lev. 18:5 with regard to covenant life—not just physical blessing—shows that life could be regarded in an extended manner in the OT. See Rutherford Forthcoming; Rutherford 2016c, cf. Douglas J. Moo, *Galatians*, Baker Exegetical Commentary on the New Testament (Grand Rapids: Baker Academic, 2013); Moo, *The Epistle to the Romans*.

Israel's obedience (e.g. Gen 19:5-6, Deut 3:26). Having already shown that life by works is impossible (1:18-3:20), it is by faith (1:17), Paul introduces Leviticus 18:5 as a foil for God's ultimate act of grace in Christ, ending the tension. The Law pointed beyond itself; it was penultimate: the ultimate has come in Christ. In what follows, Paul will demonstrate this. To do so, Paul turns to Deuteronomy 30:11-14.

iii. Excursus: Deuteronomy 30:11-14 in Context

Because most interpreters argue that these verses refer to the Law, Paul's quotation is obscured: has he used the Law to combat the Law? When understood in its context, I argue that this text is not a challenge to obey the Law: it is a prophecy of the New Covenant.[i]

Occurring in Moses' third speech, between accounts of the curses Israel will incur, Deuteronomy 30 is the glimmer of hope amidst the darkness of Israel's future.[ii] Assuming the failure of Israel, Moses looks to the future (30:1) and sees a day when Israel will turn to YHWH and prosper. By carefully using a chiasm, Moses identifies God's act to circumcise their hearts (30:6-8, reversing 29:4) as the reason for this turning of fortunes (30:3). Deuteronomy 30:11-14 concludes this chiasm: echoing 1b, it identifies Israel's remembrance as the result of a future heart-circumcision provided by God. These verses look to this future, gracious work of God. No longer would there be a distant, mediated covenant (vv. 12-13). Instead, God would circumcise their hearts and they would have the commandment close to heart and mouth.

Moo mentions this interpretation but rejects it. He gives as evidence for rejecting it "a clear transition" from the future restoration in 30:1-10 to the present situation of Israel in 30:11ff, signaled by the end of the waw+perfect pattern in verse 11.[iii]

I have argued elsewhere for reading verses 11-14 with 1-10; here I will summarize two of those arguments.[iv] First, verses 11-14 are made up of nominal and participle clauses; these do not convey time, adopting it from context. Those who argue for a return to the present in verses 11-14 need to provide evidence for a significant disjunction between verses 10-11, justifying this temporal shift. Evidence against this shift is found in the sequence of the Hebrew word כִּי (*kî, for*) through verses 9b, 10a, 10b, 11a, and 14. The end of the chain is not in verse 10 but in verses 11 and 14. Moses grounds the future return of Israel in verses 11-14, connecting these verses with God's circumcising work in verse 6. Second, heart circumcision, the very thing needed (29:4) and which God will provide (30:6), is seen to be fulfilled here (30:11-14, cf. Jer. 31:31-34). However, does the shift in verb usage introduce the needed disjunction?

For two reasons I argue that it does not. First, Moses has not begun to use the perfect conjugation as he does in other present addresses (e.g. ch. 29, 30:15ff); he employs nominal and participle clauses throughout these verses, with indicatives only in direct speech (vv. 12-13). Second, the nature of the clauses argues against an intentional disjunction. The clauses making up these verses (excepting the direct speech) are all describing the commandment, clauses which, in Hebrew, are most naturally expressed with predication. Furthermore, Moses would not have used waw+הָיָה (*hāyāh*, to-be) for predication in future time: nominal clauses are equally adequate to indicate future time, and הָיָה is not used as regularly for predication (in Deut. 30, הָיָה is only used twice).[v] So, our interpretation is well within the boundaries of Hebrew syntax.

In conclusion, there is sufficient evidence to conclude that Moses intends verses 11-14 to continue 1-10: the present is only reintroduced in verses 15 with the use of an imperative and a perfect verb. We can then suggest, for our reading of Romans 10:6-8, that Paul has identified this text as a New Covenant prophecy.[vi]

---

[i] Cf. Christopher Wright, Deuteronomy, NIBC (Peabody, Mass.: Hendrickson Publishers, 1996), 290; Eugene H. Merrill, Deuteronomy, The New American Commentary 4 (USA: Broadman & Holman Publishers, 1994), 390–391; Daniel Isaac Block, Deuteronomy, The NIV Application Commentary (Grand Rapids, Mich.: Zondervan, 2012), 706.

[ii] Chs. 28-29, 31-32; N.T. Wright, "Romans," in *The New Interpreter's Bible*, ed. Robert W Wall and J. Paul Sampley, vol. X (Nashville: Abingdon Press, 2002), 659.

[iii] Moo, *The Epistle to the Romans*, 652.

[iv] See appendix 1.

[v] Once as a predicate in a condition.

[vi] One may inquire why Paul has quoted the LXX in v. 8 if he reads it in this manner. Often the NT writers will quote the Septuagint when it disagrees with MT if it makes an appropriate application of the Hebrew for their circumstances, as it does here. E.g. Acts 13:41, Heb. 10:37-38.

Verses 6-7. Paul, in verses 6-13, intends to explain the righteousness of God as the righteousness available through Jesus, ending the Law and bringing the New Covenant, in contrast with the law-righteousness Israel pursued. Paul begins this contrast here, using the common minor adversative conjunction δε (*de*). In verses 5-8, Paul will focus on Jesus as the end of the law, connecting this to faith-righteousness in verses 8-13. He has already shown throughout Romans that faith, even in the Old Testament (1:17, 4:1ff), is the means by which one is righteous before God: here he will tie this truth into the New Covenant through Deuteronomy 30:11-14, demonstrating that faith-righteousness is the goal and end of the Old Covenant Law. This will then demonstrate Israel's dire state, for in pursuing the hopeless demand of Leviticus 18:5, Israel has missed God's very provision for salvation, the goal to which the Law has pointed all along.

To make this point, Paul personifies faith-righteousness and places in its mouth four quotes from Deuteronomy. The first three describe faith-righteousness by saying what it is not. Paul's first quote, "Do not say in your heart…" (Deut 9:4), is perfectly matched to his present purposes.[18] In Deuteronomy 9:4, Moses warns the Israelites: they are not to think that their righteousness has earned them life; they have stubborn hearts. They are receiving the land because of the nations' wickedness and God's faithfulness (9:4-5). By introducing Deuteronomy 30 with this quote from 9:4, Paul wants us to read what follows in terms of this rebuke against earned righteousness.[19]

Paul's quote from Deuteronomy 30 is less clear: with few exceptions, the various interpretations have all supposed that Deuteronomy 30:11-14 describes the Law in Moses' day. Paul's thought is clarified by our

---

[18] Moo, *The Epistle to the Romans*, 652.

[19] Ibid., 651; Schreiner, *Romans*, 558. The connection between 9:4-6 and 10:12-22, 30:6-14 make it especially fitting.

interpretation of these verses. In Deuteronomy 30:12-13, the lines that Paul quotes describe the future "word" negatively. The New Covenant will not be like the Old:[20] "It will not be in the heavens, that you should say, 'Who will go up....' And it will not be beyond the sea, that you should say, 'Who will cross to the other side of the sea....'" That is, this commandment will not be distant—there will be no need for a human mediator to go up Sinai. It will be near, easy. Paul interprets this Christologically: "'Who will ascend into heaven' (That is, to bring Christ down) or 'Who will descend into the abyss?' (that is, to bring Christ up from the dead)."[21]

Paul's Christological interpretation indicates that the New Covenant has come through Jesus's incarnation and resurrection. With the arrival of the New Covenant, Paul shows that the Old has ended (no longer will they say, "Who will go up?"), and he equates Moses' commandment with Jesus; he is near through God's work. This thought is finished in verse 8 with another quote from Deuteronomy.

Verse 8. In verse 8, faith-righteousness speaks again, describing the present reality: "But what does it say? 'The word is near you, in your mouth and in your heart' (that is, the word of faith that we proclaim)." Having equated Jesus with the commandment in verses 6-7, Paul effectively equates Jesus here with "the word," which is "the word of faith that we proclaim." Jesus, and the whole of his accomplished work, is the message Paul preaches, one that calls for faith, not works.[22] The Law's goal was Christ; now that he is here, it is has become obsolete.

---

[20] In Deuteronomy, it is not described as the New Covenant, but its interpretation and fulfillment throughout Scripture identifies it as such, e.g. Jer. 31:31-34, Ezek 36:22-37:28, Heb. 8. See further the first chapter of Rutherford, *Prevenient Grace*.

[21] The Septuagint likewise has "sea." Schreiner and Moo argue cogently that Sea and the Abyss (Hebrew, 'the deep') overlap in semantic range. Though the original context alludes to the crossing the Red Sea, the emphasis lays on the distance and difficulty it illustrates. Here, he has sacrificed this allusion in the second line to make clear his application. Moo, *The Epistle to the Romans*, 655–656; Schreiner, *Romans*, 558–559..

[22] That the message's content is faith is ruled out by the equation with Jesus in the previous verses and the following emphasis on faith as a response to the message. Schreiner argues that it is really a 'both-and;' this is true in as much as the message of Jesus has within it a message of faith (Hab. 2:4 in Rom. 1:17). Moo, *The Epistle to the Romans*, 656–657; Schreiner, *Romans*, 559.

In these verses then, Paul has shown that Jesus has fulfilled Moses' prophecy of a future where God's word, his demands, would be internalized and his people would be able to follow Him. In showing this, Paul has proved that Christ has ended the law and shown that Israel has wilfully rejected God's revelation to stubbornly pursue their own righteousness. Because of this, they are in need of salvation. Paul further connects this in verses 8-13 through the language of easiness, nearness, heart, and mouth to the Righteousness of God revealed in Christ—this is the ultimate fulfillment of the law and Moses' prophecy.

B. Conclusion

In this paper, I have only been able to scratch the surface of this passage, arguing for this exposition mostly through the demonstration of its explanatory value—how it makes coherent sense of the texts and contexts of Romans and Deuteronomy. The purpose of this paper has been achieved, shedding fresh light on this difficult passage via careful exegesis of the Deuteronomy quotations. Paul's pertinent use of Moses' prophecy substantiates his argument in verses 1-4 by showing the nature of Israel's culpable rejection of God's plan and explaining Israel's need for salvation. We may summarize these verses as an explanation of Israel's need for salvation, expounded in terms of their rejection of God's climatic and exclusive provision of righteousness through Christ—the end of the law—attained by faith.

This passage, interpreted in this manner, offers many insights. For our pluralistic society, this passage reinforces the exclusiveness of the Gospel. If anyone were to be saved apart from Christ, it would be Israel. Paul testifies that they are zealous, yet the Jews are in need of salvation because their zeal is misplaced. With a misplaced object, zeal achieves nothing. God has made his righteousness easily available in Jesus, yet this is also the only source of righteousness. For the Church, the exclusiveness of Christ testifies to the great treasure of the salvation God has given us—we should give everything to pursue it. It also speaks to the urgency of our mission: with Paul, we must pray and seek the salvation of all who are perishing apart from Christ the saviour. This is a challenge for me as it is for the Church generally—to give my all for Jesus and seek the salvation of the lost.

This passage also provides an intellectual challenge for the Christian. If my proposed exposition holds true, it serves as reminder that God knows better than us: instead of supposing with some that Paul was wrong in his uses of the OT, we see again that much thought and diligent prayer in submission to God's Word and his Spirit can show us the true genius of his Scriptures. Paul's intertextuality is a vivid witness to the theological cohesion of God's revelation. Theologically, this text contributes to the greater biblical theology of the New Covenant in Christ and reveals further the intertextual web that contributes to our understanding of it (to Jeremiah, Isaiah, and Ezekiel, now Deuteronomy 30: to John and Hebrews, now Romans 10).

2 THESSALONIANS AND HELL: SEPARATION FROM OR WRATH COMING FORTH FROM GOD?

This paper was originally written for Teleioteti.ca. I wrote it to address a trend I was finding among Evangelicals as I researched and wrote on the doctrine of Hell. It appears that many evangelicals are adopting a view of Hell that is primarily characterized by absence from God and not his active presence for judgment. This paper was written to address one specific text used to uphold such a view.

Many writers and preachers today speak about Hell as, among other things, eternal separation from God. Hell, it is said, is receiving what the sinner wanted all along, freedom from God, the absence of his goodness. Such a state would be horrifying indeed—the One who is Goodness, Love, our Joy himself completely absent!—yet is this what the Bible pictures? The text often cited in this regard is 2 Thessalonians 1:9: "to those who do not know God and to those who do not submit to the gospel of our Lord Jesus, who will receive as punishment eternal destruction *from* the presence of the Lord and *from* the glory of his might."[1] The key word here is "from," the Greek preposition απο (*apo*). It is often understood in terms of separation, "eternal destruction separated from the presence of the Lord and separated from the glory of his might." Though this is a valid and a common sense of απο (e.g. Matt 8:30, Matt 11:25, 1 Thess 4:3), I will argue that the immediate context, Paul's use of απο elsewhere, and the greater perspective of Scripture indicates that the text means "coming forth from" (preposition indicating location

---

[1] My translation unless indicated otherwise

from which something comes).²

Our first consideration is the context in which verse 9 is found: the context indicates overwhelmingly that this final judgment the unbeliever faces is the active judgment of God, the pouring out of his wrath. In 1 and 2 Thessalonians, Paul is interested in explaining the day of the Lord, arguing that God will repay those who presently afflict believers when Christ returns and that those who have died will not miss out on the resurrection. Thus, Paul is interested in the two sides of the Day of the Lord: the resurrection to eternal life and the final judgment, beginning with Christ return. In 1 Thessalonians, Paul explains that the day of the Lord, Christ's return, will come quickly and be inescapable. The salvation the Thessalonians await is contrasted with the wrath unbelievers await (5:9). Then in 2 Thessalonians, Paul explains further this "wrath." In 1:5-7 Paul explains that in the final judgment, God in justice will repay with affliction those who presently afflict the Thessalonians; this will begin when "the Lord Jesus will be revealed from heaven with his mighty angels³ in flaming fire, dealing out retribution" (1:7-8 ESV). Thus, God's righteous wrath against unbelievers manifests in his active judgment against sinners, retribution. This then brings us to verse 9, which is expanding upon verse 8. The end of verse 8 tells us that Jesus is dealing out retribution to those who do not know God and to those who do not "submit to the Gospel of our Lord Jesus"; verse 9 then describes further the retribution they will receive: "[they] will receive as punishment eternal destruction *from* the presence of the Lord and *from* the glory of his might." In the context of Christ coming for judgment from the throne of God, απο (*apo*) clearly does not indicate *separation from* God's presence but the horrifying truth of judgment pouring *forth from* God's presence. This is consistent with Paul's use of απο throughout 1 and 2 Thessalonians.

Consider this (ridiculous) sentence, "to *bear* arms is part of the great responsibility we, as citizens, *bear;* we *bear* many burdens in our lives as responsible citizens, this is why we *bear* resemblance to our forefather." The first three uses of "bear" represent the sense "to carry," the latter two of which do so metaphorically; the fourth has a different sense, "to bear

---

² Both uses of απο indicate separation, but the former is static; the latter involves movement away from.

³ Or "with the angels of his host (i.e. army)."

resemblance." In this context, the switch in sense is quite obvious, but if it was more ambiguous ("this is why we bear the image of our forefather"), the consistent use of one sense of "bear" (to carry) would suggest that we read "bear" in this sense and not the other: "this is why we [carry] the image of forefather."[4] This idea, that a writer will avoid ambiguity if he is using a word in a different way than it was consistently used before, lies behind my first argument.

Paul uses απο (apo) 15 times in 1 and 2 Thessalonians. Of the 8 uses in 1 Thessalonians, only 2 have the idea of separation without movement from— and both of these are signalled by the verb they accompany ("to abstain"). Of the seven uses in 2 Thessalonians, four uses (other than v. 9) indicate movement away from (1:2, 7; 2:2; 3:2). The first two of these come immediately before our verse and refer to the same subject or sphere (peace comes forth from God in v. 2, Jesus from heaven in v. 7). This suggests to me that, in the absence of any clear indication of a shift in sense, the "ambiguous" use in 1:9 should be taken in the same way—"[coming] forth from the presence of the Lord and from the glory of his might." That Hell is the experience of God's wrath and not his absence is consistently attested elsewhere in Scripture

Three other Scripture should serve to confirm this. In Matthew 10:28, Jesus instructs the Twelve not to fear man, but rather "fear him who can destroy both soul and body in hell" (ESV). That is, Jesus looks to hell as the place where God will actively (he will do something) destroy[5] the body and soul in Hell. Furthermore, in Romans 2:8 Paul contrasts eternal life with "wrath and fury" towards unbelievers: wrath and fury both are active, they are something inflicted. This is affirmed in Revelation 14:9-10,

> And another angel, a third, followed them, saying with a loud voice, "If anyone worships the beast and its image and receives a mark on his

---

[4] We of course do not read it in this manner because even in this example, it is not ambiguous—context makes it pretty clear—and the idea of carrying around an image of an ancestor or predecessor is not common.

[5] Some suggest that "destroy" here means that Hell will have an end, but the horrifying truth is that to destroy something immortal (resurrected for judgment) is to subject it eternally to the forces that would ordinarily end mortal life. Thus, the horror of hell is underscored: we must be passionate to rescue unbelievers from this fate through the preaching of the Gospel.

forehead or on his hand, he also will drink the wine of God's wrath, poured full strength into the cup of his anger, and he will be tormented with fire and sulfur in the presence of the holy angels and in the presence of the Lamb. And the smoke of their torment goes up forever and ever, and they have no rest, day or night, these worshipers of the beast and its image, and whoever receives the mark of its name. (ESV)

This is horrifying language, but it is consistent with 2 Thessalonians 1:9. In all three of these Scriptures we see that final judgment is not being left in one's own misery, to be finally separated from God, but to have God excruciatingly present in judgment: even in Sheol, God cannot be escaped (cf. Ps 139:8, Job 26:6).

This is no trivial issue; this is not merely academic discussions of the minute details: it is deadly serious! 1 and 2 Thessalonians, and the rest of Scripture, teach that Hell is horrifying: it is the place where God's wrath is poured out in judgment against both the body and the soul! This is what Scripture teaches, and it does so for a reason. The doctrine of Hell in all its horror underscores two key Christian teachings: the nature of our God and the necessity of vigorous evangelism.

God is just, all Scripture testifies to this. This means that God has to punish sin; Hell demonstrates the seriousness with which he takes sin. Yet God sent his Son to save us from that reality; therefore, to properly understand Hell is to properly understand the cross. When Jesus cried out to the Father, "My God, My God, why have you forsaken me," he was not lamenting the absence of his Father. Jesus was expressing the agony of his Father turning the weight of his wrath towards him, wrath which he had patiently withheld for thousands of years. Jesus was experiencing the Father orientated towards him with pure white-hot wrath against sin. He was experiencing there on the cross the equivalent of an eternity of burning fire, of darkness so deep it hurts. He was experiencing eternal destruction—destruction pouring forth from the throne of God.[6] Jesus suffered that for you, for me: he suffered God's wrath against sin that we who believe might be forgiven and sanctified, glorified as members of his bride the Church.

---

[6] The description comes from the language of Hell; that Christ bore our punishment in our place, the punishment we would have faced in Hell, is testified throughout Scripture: e.g. Isa. 53:4-6, 10-12; Rom. 3:25; 2 Cor. 5:21; Gal. 3:10-14; 1 John 2:2, 4:10.

Yet there are those of whom this cannot be said: members of my family and old friends face that fate. Everyone who has not confessed Jesus Christ as Lord, who has not believed that God raised him from the dead after he was crucified (Rom 10:5-17), faces this fate: that is why the great commission, to go out into all the world with the message of the Gospel, is as vital today as it was 2000 years ago. People need to hear God's truth desperately; their lives are on the line. But how can they hear if no one goes, if no one tells them? The doctrine of Hell is absolutely horrifying, yet it is the truth.

Jesus teaches it; Paul and John teach it. They teach it so that we would go out and fulfill this commission. 2 Thessalonians 1:9 teaches that God is active for judgment in Hell: this means that we must be active in our mission to save people from this fate through the preaching of the glorious good news that Jesus Christ came and gave his life for sinners on the Cross. We must be bold in proclaiming the good news that Christ rose again on the third day, victorious over death and the grave, and now reigns at the right hand of the Father and through his people on earth. People need to hear the good news that sin has an answer, his name is Jesus Christ. They need to hear that in him alone our hope, our joy, and our future is found—and found in him abundantly.

CONVINCED OF BETTER THINGS: AN EXPOSITION OF HEBREWS 6:1-12

This paper was originally prepared for professor Doug Moo for a graduate-level study on Hebrews. It contributes to this book by showing how we use the text to argue for theological truths and application.

Many of us have faced times of disinterest, of stagnation in our faith, when all that remains is a faint vestige of its once vibrant genesis. When we, or those we know, look away from the glory of God in the face of Jesus to the fake glory of worldly satisfaction, what are we to make of our state? Are we near unto damnation, drifting away into a state irreversible? Are we about to discover the faith we once held was a sham? Such questions surface when considering the difficult warning of Hebrews 6:1-12, a text where the author seems to teach that it is impossible for a Christian who falls away, whose faith snaps and breaks, to return. It appears that no one can restore such a person to repentance.

Many have sought to argue this impossibility is not universal—impossible for man but not for God—or to soften it to a "difficulty" and others that true Christians are not the intended audience of this warning. The burden of this paper is show from the argument of the author of Hebrews (now abbreviated AOH) that Hebrews 6:1-12 is indeed addressed to Christians and that it teaches the impossibility of restoration for one who apostatizes. I maintain, as the thesis of this paper, that the author exhorts his believing audience to press on to mature Christian faith through a warning grounded in the irreversible nature of apostasy and a statement of assurance grounded in the gracious provision of God. In this way, the author balances human responsibility with divine sovereignty in a warning that serves his audience's needs and coheres with the rest of the NT canon; that is, his exhortation is firmly grounded in the compatibilist worldview assumed throughout Scripture.[1]

To argue this, I will elucidate the context of Hebrews 6:1-12 and discuss the passage according to its three sections (vv. 1-3, 4-8, and 9-12) in dialogue with Wayne Grudem's essay *Perseverance of the Saints*.[2] In conclusion, I will offer a brief reflection on the passage's theological implications.

A. Exegesis

Some consider Hebrews to be one of the most difficult books in the NT, even comparing it to a puzzle: there is no certainty concerning the author, audience, date of writing, or necessitating circumstances.[3] The book's unique structure and pervasive use of the OT compounds its difficulty. Yet, despite such uncertainty, the letter's themes and argument are largely clear. We can determine that the author is exhorting a Jewish audience to press on to mature Christian faith and that the Hebrews faced three dangers; the subtle drift characterizing a lack of forward progress (2:4), possible rebellion against Christ and the New covenant (3:12-13; 10:26-29), and external trials exacerbating these dangers (2:18, 4:16).[4] The author mounts an extensive argument from the OT for the superiority of Jesus and the New Covenant

---

[1] Compatibilism, in Philosophy, is the belief that human responsibility is not negated when a free decision is determined (when the outcome is certain). It stands opposed to Libertarianism, which maintains that a responsible human decision must not be necessitated—it must be contingent, indeterminate. I have argued elsewhere the Bible assumes compatibilism, as have numerous Calvinist authors; cf. Rutherford, *Prevenient Grace*, 111–137, 281–290, 309; Jonathan Edwards, *Freedom of the Will* (Mineola, N.Y.: Dover Publications, 2012); John M. Frame, *The Doctrine of God*, A Theology of Lordship (Phillipsburg: P&R Publishing, 2002).

[2] Wayne A. Grudem, "Perseverance of the Saints: A Case Study from the Warning Passages in Hebrews," in *Still Sovereign: Contemporary Perspectives on Election, Foreknowledge & Grace*, ed. Thomas R. Schreiner and Bruce A. Ware (Grand Rapids: Baker, 2000), 133–182.

[3] Donald Alfred Hagner, *Encountering the Book of Hebrews: An Exposition* (Grand Rapids: Baker Academic, 2002), 20; William L. Lane, *Hebrews 1-8*, ed. David A. Hubbard, Glenn W. Barker, and Ralph P. Martin, vol. 1, Word Biblical Commentary Vol. 47,A (Nashville: Word Books, 1991), xlvii.

[4] Paul Ellingworth, *The Epistle to the Hebrews: A Commentary on the Greek Text*, NIGTC (Grand Rapids: Carlisle: W.B. Eerdmans ; Paternoster, 1993), 78–80.

inaugurated in his blood, interspersed with warnings and exhortations to move on to maturity. The author argues both from the superior nature of Jesus, the covenant representative, (1:4-4:13, 11:1-13:19) and from the New Covenant and its cult (4:14-7:38; 8:1-14; 9:1-10:39) for the superiority of the New Covenant salvation over against the Old Covenant.[5] The main idea of the book, then, is that the unmatchable Jesus, mediator of a superior covenant, ensures a superior salvation from which one dare not depart.

Our passage occurs at the beginning of the author's prolonged exposition of Psalm 110:4; AOH pauses his exposition to address the Hebrews' present spiritual state. In 5:11-14, the author explains that they are far from where they should be, given the time passed since their conversion (5:12). Though they should already be mature enough for a diet of solid spiritual food, they are infants still needing milk. One commentator explains this as irony: it is not that they are not mature, have not received mature teaching, but that they are acting like they are not.[6] I am not convinced this explanation does justice to the connection between 5:11-14 and 6:1-12. In 6:1, the author does not exhort them to return to a maturity they once had or live in a way fitting their true state (act mature, not infantile!). Instead, he exhorts them to press on to maturity: the warning, then, functions to move the audience from their infant stagnation into the maturity they must display. He has "much to say, and it is hard to explain" because of their present state (5:11),[7] but saying it is exactly what they need. Presenting them with solid food accompanied by exhortation and warning, is exactly the means by which he intends for them—with God's permission—to move on to maturity. Thus, AOH begins chapter 6 with the exhortation to move on with him to solid food.

a. *Hebrews 6:1-3*

With the exhortation in 6:1-3 to move on from milk to maturity, AOH indicates he does not intend to give them the milk they have heard so often but to press on to the hard-to-explain things. Before he does so, though,

---

[5] Several exegetes recognize the centrality of covenant, including Philip Edgcumbe Hughes, *A Commentary on the Epistle to the Hebrews* (Grand Rapids: Eerdmans, 1977), 3; Ronaldo Guzman and Michael W. Martin, "Is Hebrews 5:11-6:20 Really a Digression?," *Novum Testamentum* 57, no. 3 (2015): 303.

[6] Lane, *Hebrews*, 1:135.

[7] All quotations, unless otherwise stated, taken from the ESV.

AOH begins a dire warning, extending from verse 1-12, intended to spur the Hebrews on to maturity. These beginning three verses introduce an exhortation to which the warning in verses 4-8 will add dreadful urgency.

Verse 1-2 By introducing this section with διο (*dio*, therefore), our author indicates a close logical connection between this exhortation and his indictment of the Hebrews in 5:11-14. Having identified them as spiritual infants who live on milk, he now calls them to move past this to the solid food more fitting their objective age. Within verse 1, ἀρχης (*archēs*) and θεμελιον (*themelion*) are both semantically parallel, the former referring to a temporally early state ("beginning") and the latter a physically base state ("foundation"). They correspond clearly to chapter Five's metaphorical "milk." The six items in verses 1-2 following "foundation" have engendered no small amount of scholarly debate over their precise nuances, yet it should suffice for our purposes to identify their collective function. The string of genitives is clearly dependent upon θεμελιον, giving the author's outline of the "milk" upon which they have been living; these are, for AOH's purposes, the first things of Christianity. What deserves our further attention, though, are the author's exhortations to "leave" and "go on."

Within the semantic range of ἀφιημι (**aphiēmi**), translated "leave," are various senses communicating absolute departure ("leave behind"); yet this is, in context, not what the author has in mind. The author is not calling his audience to abandon the basics but to build upon the basis they have. To communicate this, that they are not to reject the basic teachings from which they are to move on, Lane translates ἀφιημι "leave standing."[8] That this is correct is supported by the use of θεμελιον (*themelion*, "foundation") alongside the verb καταβαλλομενοι (*kataballomenoi*, lay [a foundation]) to describe these initial "elementary" teachings. AOH describes a foundation that is already in place and so can now be built upon; it needs no further work. Therefore the sense here is, as a metaphorical extension of "leaving behind," "to stop concerning yourself with something"—to mentally leave it behind.[9]

---

[8] Lane, *Hebrews*, 1:131, 139.

[9] Frederick W. Danker, *A Greek-English Lexicon of the New Testament and*

Our last consideration in these first verses is the hortatory subjunctive φερωμεθα (pherōmetha, "let us... go on"), from which the participle αφιημι gets its hortatory force. Though many translations render φερω (pherō) "go on" or some variation thereof (e.g. NASB, NIV 1984), many commentators follow the NIV 2011 in rendering φερω as a passive of its regular sense "to bear," resulting in the translation, "let us... be taken forward."[10] The NIV's translation would suggest they are to surrender to God's work;[11] this is, however, contextually unlikely and not the only possible understanding of φερω. Considering the context, the very charge levelled at the Hebrews is that they are being passive: they are in danger of "drifting away"; they are not pressing on to maturity. The exhortations are not framed as challenges to stop resisting God's Spirit but to pay closer attention to the message (2:1), to strive (4:11), to endure (10:36-39), and to run (12:1). Bruce describes the sense here, possibly drawing on 2 Kingdoms 18:27 (L manuscript), as "swift and energetic movement."[12] All examples of φερω used intransitively suggest vigorous movement, so the force of the φερω in this context is probably "let us press on [with vigour] to maturity!"

Verse 3. Having exhorted his audience to vigorous pursuit of maturity, AOH declares this is indeed what "we," himself and the Hebrews, "will do," given God's permission. He may have in mind the permission envisaged in James 4:15, but he predominately appears to be grounding their hope for a successful attainment of maturity in God's gracious provision, their

---

Other Early Christian Literature, 3rd ed. (Chicago: University of Chicago Press, 2000), 156–157.

[10] R. T. France, "Hebrews," in *The Expositor's Bible Commentary*, ed. Tremper Longman and David E. Garland, Rev. ed. (Grand Rapids: Zondervan, 2006), 81; Brooke Foss Westcott, ed., *The Epistle to the Hebrews the Greek Text with Notes and Essays*, 3d ed. (London: Macmillan, 1903), 145; Hughes, *Hebrews*, 194.

[11] France, "Hebrews," 81.; cf. Daniel B Wallace, *Greek Grammar Beyond the Basics: An Exegetical Syntax of the New Testament With Scripture, Subject, and Greek Word Indexes* (Grand Rapids: Zondervan, 1996), 440–441.

[12] F. F. Bruce, *The Epistle to the Hebrews*, NICNT (Grand Rapids: Eerdmans, 1964), 110. Muraoka's LXX lexicon gives the same sense for this text and gives other examples of the passive functioning intransitively (e.g. Isa. 28:15, 18; Dan. 9:21; 2 Macc. 3:25, 14:45) T. Muraoka, *A Greek-English Lexicon of the Septuagint*, Rev. ed. (Louvain ; Walpole, MA: Peeters, 2009), 713.

dependence on which receives great emphasis from the emphatic marker of a condition in 6:3b (εανπερ, *eanper*). This pressing on to maturity which God may permit includes, but should not be restricted to, the rest of the author's argument unpacked in chapters 6-7.[13] God's role is made clearer in verses 9-12 and is echoed in the benediction (13:20-21); the emphasis on God's gracious provision also coheres well with the emphasis provided by Jesus and Peter on God's role in perseverance (John 10:25-30; 1 Peter 1:3-7).[14]

b.   Hebrews 6:4-8

Having concluded his initial exhortation with a sense of uncertainty, AOH now turns up the heat in these verses: he underscores the urgency of their situation by declaring the irreversible nature of falling away from the faith.

Verses 4-8. He intensifies the warning by introducing the main verb in verse 4 and withholding its infinitive complement until verse 6: the result is a rhetorical flourish emphasizing the identity of the verbal object, described by five participles. The Christian readers wait a foreboding moment to discover what is "impossible"; in that moment they are confronted by a picture of themselves as those who could, possibly, face this dire impossibility. Many would disagree with this interpretation in at least two ways: some would contend "impossible" really means difficult, and others would not agree that the participles describe Christians.

The first is the easiest disagreement to resolve. There is really no good reason to soften the usual force of ἀδυνατος (*adunatos*) to "difficult"; this would, in fact, defeat the author's rhetorical purpose. Though Louw and Nida define ἀδυνατος as "impossible," they explain the force in our text as "an instance of hyperbole" and so justify the translation "it is extremely difficult." They give no reason, however, why it should be read in this way.[15] Hagner

---

[13] Bruce, *Hebrews*, 118.

[14] In the 13:20, AOH identifies Jesus as "the great shepherd of the sheep," an image particularly associated with preservation (Ps 23; John 10:2, 11-16; 1 Pet 2:25).

[15] Johannes P. Louw and Eugene Albert Nida, *Greek-English Lexicon of the New Testament: Based on Semantic Domains*, electronic ed. of the 2nd edition. (New York, N.Y.: United Bible Societies, 1996), 1:668.

similarly holds open the possibility God might restore an apostate, identifying the force here as "no return can be guaranteed."[16] Lexically, "impossible" is the obvious meaning; thus the burden of proof lays on those seeking to mitigate its force. Nothing in context does this; in fact, the urgency and severity of the warnings throughout the book (especially 10:26-39, 12:25-29) suggest his warning should be taken at face value. And, though it can hardly be debated that God *could* restore an apostate if he so desired, nothing in Scripture suggests he will; thus, there is no reason to soften the author's words on the basis of such a possibility.

The force of ἀδύνατος (*adunatos*) emphasizes the finality of abandoning their salvation, and thus the incredible danger of their current state.[17] This is reinforced in verse 6 when this impossibility is said to be because "they are crucifying once again the Son of God… and holding him up to contempt."[18] Thus, the author teaches the impossibility of repentance for one who falls away.

The second point of disagreement—the identity of those who face this impossibility—is more contentious. Are "those who have once been enlightened" Christians of genuine faith or do they merely look like Christians, having only apparent faith?[19] The standard Arminian view, and of

---

[16] Hagner, *Encountering*, 90–91.

[17] Bruce, *Hebrews*, 118; Peter Thomas O'Brien, *The Letter to the Hebrews*, Pillar New Testament Commentary (Grand Rapids.; Nottingham: Eerdmans; Apollos, 2010), 219; Thomas R. Schreiner, *Commentary on Hebrews*, ed. Andreas J. Köstenberger, T. Desmond Alexander, and Thomas R. Schreiner, Biblical Theology for Christian Proclamation (Nashville: B&H, 2015), 180.

[18] Delitzsch and others have suggested this be interpreted temporally, yet the placement of the participles at the end of the clause and the context suggest a causal sense—"since" or "because." Bruce writes of Delitzsch's interpretation, "To say that they cannot be brought to repentance so long as they persist in their renunciation of Christ would be a truism hardly worth putting into words." Ellingworth seconds his judgment. Bruce, *Hebrews*, 124; Ellingworth, *Hebrews*, 323–325.

[19] Among so-called "free grace" theologians this passage challenges Christians with a potential loss of rewards, not salvation. On this position, there is no distinction between "genuine faith," faith that endures (Heb 3:14) and produces fruit (Jas 2:14-26), and "apparent faith," bare assent that shows initial zeal but disappears quickly (Matt 13:20-22). All that is required for salvation is intellectual assent, but rewards are contingent upon conduct and perseverance (e.g. 1 Cor. 3:14-15). Space does not

many others, is that the first four participles describe in detail the experience of regenerate Christians, with the last participle indicating the falling away of such people. Many Calvinists, on the other hand, understand this passage as describing those who by all appearances are Christians but are not truly regenerate.[20] Wayne Grudem does an admirable job representing this view.[21] The thrust of his argument is *"the terms by themselves are inconclusive,"* are ambiguous; thus context is determinative as to whether these are true Christians or only apparent Christians.[22] Most commentators follow Grudem in giving much space to the exposition of each term. However, such an extensive task is beyond the scope of this paper and, I believe, unnecessary for understanding the author's point and seeing that these participles are meant (contra Grudem) to be a detailed description of a true Christian's experience. The phrases taken collectively, not abstracted from each other, and read in the present context give no reason to suppose these are not believers. That is, the burden of proof lies on those arguing that a group of terms that could describe genuine Christians and are found in a letter that has all appearances of being written to genuine Christians do not describe genuine Christians. Grudem offers three arguments for his view. Addressing these in order, we shall see the context indicates no such thing.

He argues, firstly, that stating the impossibility of restoring one to

---

permit a thorough interaction with this position, but many works adequately address this position. E.g. Craig L. Blomberg and Mariam J. Kamell, *James: Zondevan Exegetical Commentary on the New Testament*, Zondervan Exegetical Commentary Series on the New Testament v. 16 (Grand Rapids: Zondervan, 2008), 125–141; D. A. Carson, "Reflections on Assurance," in *Still Sovereign: Contemporary Perspectives on Election, Foreknowledge & Grace*, ed. Thomas R. Schreiner and Bruce A. Ware (Grand Rapids: Baker, 2000), 247–276; D.A. Carson, *The Cross and Christian Ministry: Leadership Lessons from 1 Corinthians*, pbk. (Grand Rapids, Michigan: Baker Books, 2004); Thomas R. Schreiner and Ardel B. Caneday, *The Race Set before Us: A Biblical Theology of Perseverance & Assurance* (Downers Grove: InterVarsity, 2001).

[20] John Calvin, *The Epistle of Paul the Apostle to the Hebrews and the First and Second Epistles of St Peter*, ed. David W. Torrance and Thomas F. Torrance, trans. William B. Johnston, Calvin's Commentaries (Eerdmans: Grand Rapids, 1963); John M. Frame, *Systematic Theology: An Introduction to Christian Belief* (Phillipsburg: P&R Publishing, 2013), 1000–1001.

[21] Grudem, "Perseverance."

[22] Ibid., 152–153.

repentance who has fallen away "does not necessarily imply that [AOH] thinks true Christians could fall away." Supporting this, he claims that the author is writing to those whose spiritual status is unclear.[23] Yet this is by no means evident; in fact, this assumes the very point Grudem is attempting to prove. He has moved from evidence for lexical ambiguity—that the four participles may describe a Christian or an apparent Christian—to actual ambiguity, that there is a question whether some of the Hebrews are Christians or only apparent Christians. However, the fact that the terminology by itself is ambiguous does not prove that actual ambiguity is being considered. Grudem takes these verses to present a test and challenge to the Hebrews. If they persevere, they are truly believers. If not, they are only apparent believers, thus they must strive for maturity so they may know their state. Yet, no evidence is given that the author questions the current salvific state of the Hebrews. Therefore, Grudem assumes by saying "he is especially writing to warn those whose spiritual status is not yet clear" that this is the question at hand and thus assumes without proof the burden of his interpretation. His following arguments build upon but do not provide proof for this assumption.[24]

Grudem argues, secondly, the illustration of the field in verses 7-8 demonstrates there was no initial saving faith. He contends that AOH uses this illustration to show that the response of the ground to the rain reveals what type of land it was: bad fruit reveals truly bad land. Against the supposition that the land once was good, he argues there is no indication the land once produced good fruit and the present participles suggest a continuous activity incompatible with land that once produced good but now produces bad fruit.[25] Again, Grudem's argument begs the question: he supposes the illustration is meant as a test, to reveal what the land was initially via its end result. This presupposes his interpretation of the passage, that it reveals endurance as the measure of true faith. He fails to give evidence that this is the purpose of the illustration. On the contrary, the author appears to illustrate with agricultural imagery two responses to God's blessing, explaining (γαρ, *gar*, for) the warning: one response receives blessings (enlightenment, etc. from vv. 4-6) and produces the intended crop; the other

---

[23] Ibid., 154.

[24] Ibid.

[25] Ibid., 155–156.

receives the same blessings and produces thorns and thistles. The end of the latter is the point the author seeks to make: if they fall away, they will face eternal condemnation—being cursed and burned.[26] This illustration, then, heightens the warning with a vivid portrayal of the end of one who falls away.

Furthermore, Grudem fails to ask what the crop in context refers to, assuming it is—as in the Gospels—good works throughout a believer's life, such that a transition from belief to unbelief would involve the transition from producing good fruit to thorns and thistles. Though the author of Hebrews employs imagery similar to other texts, he may have a more restricted intent for the "crop" in context. The end which the author seeks for the Hebrews throughout this section and the letter is endurance until the end: read in this context, the image of "crop" in contrast with "thorns and thistles" suggests a contrast between maturity resulting in perseverance and unbelief that fails to press on. Therefore, this imagery may be consistent with Grudem's view, but cannot prove it. The imagery does not rule out that those considered in the previous verses are genuine Christians; it only illustrates the end of an apostate—one who does not prove useful for those for whom he or she is cultivated.

Grudem argues, thirdly, the better things in verse 9 of which the author has confidence for his readers are good fruits evidencing salvation, better evidence than the ambiguous experiences in verses 4-6. For this, he offers four supporting arguments. We will examine these arguments below when we consider verses 9-12, but for now we can point out that Grudem again begs the question: he supposes the author's description is intentionally ambiguous in verses 4-6, in need of supplementation to prove *these are true Christians*. It is this contention he has not yet proven: though the words themselves may be ambiguous, Grudem has not shown the author intends their collective force to be likewise ambiguous (he has not met the burden of proof). Furthermore, as I will argue below, Grudem's arguments and interpretation of verses 9-12 do not withstand scrutiny. If my reasoning below is sound, Grudem fails to demonstrate that the author intends verses 4-6 to be ambiguous. We may, then, ask what the author does intend.

---

[26] The warnings elsewhere, especially in ch. 10, reinforce that eternal condemnation is indeed in sight. S. McKnight, "The Warning Passages of Hebrews: A Formal Analysis and Theological Conclusions," *Trinity Journal* 13, no. 1 (1992): 21–59.

The first four participles describe a genuine conversion experience, for "*The* sign that one was a Christian in the NT was the Reception of the Holy Spirit…. the Spirit is 'center-stage' here."[27] Though the individual terminology may be ambiguous, their collective force is unavoidable: with no contextual clues contrariwise, the Hebrews would recognize themselves in this initial description. They would recognize themselves, that is, until the final participle, "and then have fallen away"; here is where the author's rhetorical suspension is felt. His suspension of the infinitive complement allows him to describe those facing the impossibility in terms that described the Hebrews, until this final descriptor: the warning invites them to see themselves in this danger if they only have this final experience. "Fall away" itself is being used to describe a decisive movement away from New Covenant faith, as demonstrated by the parallel warning passages and immediate context.[28] Though Hewitt suggests it is being used as a counter-factual condition—if they fall away, and they will not—it is syntactically functioning as an adjective grouped with the others under τους (*tous*, the) in verse 4.[29]

Thus the author, in verses 4-6, presents a terrifying proposition for the Hebrews to consider: to experience what they experienced and fall away, like they were in danger of doing (2:4, chs. 3-4), is irreversible, with no possibility to be renewed to repentance. They are challenged to press on to maturity, to pay close attention to what they heard, lest this become their reality. In verses 7-8, the author then illustrates this danger with a picture from agriculture: having received the rain of God, two options remain, to press on to maturity and produce the crop they were intended to produce, or to produce thorns and thistles and be utterly destroyed. To produce a crop, in this context, would be to enter into maturity; to produce thorns and thistles would be to fall away. At the moment it was their choice—God permitting of course (verse 3).

---

[27] Schreiner, *Hebrews*, 185.

[28] McKnight, "The Warning Passages"; Lane, *Hebrews*, 1:142.

[29] Thomas Hewitt, *The Epistle to the Hebrews, an Introduction and Commentary*, 1st ed., The Tyndale New Testament Commentaries (Grand Rapids: Eerdmans, 1960), 110–111; T. K. Oberholtzer, "The Warning Passages in Hebrews : Part 3 (of 5 Parts): The Thorn-Infested Ground in Hebrews 6:4-12," *Bibliotheca Sacra* 145, no. 579 (1988): 332..

c. Hebrews 6:9-12

Having set out such serious stakes, AOH now revisits his statement in verse 3: will God permit them to press on to maturity? AOH has great confidence that God will not neglect the good works they have done, that they will obtain better things than fiery destruction (v. 8). Before transitioning in 6:12-20 back to the argument introduced in 5:10, AOH concludes his warning with an exhortation to show the same eagerness in the pursuit of maturity they have shown for good works.

Verse 9. The concessive statement opening this verse in the ESV describes the entire warning in verses 4-8.[30] The following clause is where Grudem's final argument comes into play: he argues "better things" should be understood as the resolution of the ambiguity in verses 4-6. The better things are the indisputable fruits of Christian living described in the following verses contrasted with the ambiguous terms in verses 4-6. He presents four arguments to demonstrate this: (1) "better" in Hebrews is usually used to contrast a good thing with something better; (2) a singular "a better thing" would be more suiting a contrast with final judgment; (3) the better things are present not future; (4) and AOH had "no need to assure them that they had not yet fallen away."[31] Verse 9, for Grudem, "provides a crucial key for understanding this whole passage." If "better things" are sure evidence of true faith contra the ambiguous experiences in verses 4-6, then those in verses 4-6 cannot be saved: there would be no need to be confident in sure signs of salvation for those who are saved.[32] Therefore verse 9 indicates those described in verses 4-6 are not believers, yet AOH is confident the Hebrews are true believers. None of these four arguments withstand close scrutiny, examining them shall serve to elucidate a more evident reading of verse 9.

Concerning his first argument, "better" is a key word in the book of Hebrews, frequently used to contrast Jesus and the New Covenant with the Old and its cult, and in many of its occurrences something good is contrasted with something better. However, this is not so for every occurrence: in 7:7 κρειττων (*kreittōn*) offers neither a positive nor a negative comparison;

---

[30] Ellingworth, *Hebrews*, 329; Schreiner, *Hebrews*, 193.

[31] Grudem, "Perseverance," 158.

[32] Ibid., 159.

instead, it is a substantive meaning "superior". In 11:16, the land the patriarchs left is contrasted with God's promise, with no evaluation given of the former land. In 12:24, "the better word" Jesus' blood speaks is one of promise whereas the "blood of Abel" is a cry for justice: the contrast is not between something good and something better, but something negative and something better because it is positive.[33] This last example is also instructive because it lies outside of the letter's main argument: contrasting Jesus' and Abel's blood does not further the New Covenant/Old Covenant contrast that is the main argument, showing that κρειττων does not necessarily compare something good with something better or an Old Covenant institution with a New Covenant one. 6:9 lies outside the main argument like 12:24 and, therefore, does not necessarily contrast something good with something better.

Grudem's second argument likewise fails. He contends that a singular "better thing" would be more suitable for a contrast with final judgment, that a singular adjective is more fitting if the author intends the better thing to be salvation. If the author were intending to contrast judgment with salvation, a singular adjective would indeed be more fitting, yet this is not the standard interpretation. The contrast is not between an abstract final judgment and final salvation, but between the ends of burning (v. 8) and of blessings (v. 7). The author is drawing explicitly on the previous illustration: he is convinced of better things than a curse and burning, using the article (τά) to refer to the end of the first field—which receives God's blessings.[34] The presence of the article rules out Grudem's interpretation.[35] The appositional phrase "things that belong to salvation" confirms this reading: these better things are not those accompanying apostasy but the better blessings of salvation (the promises in v. 12).

---

[33] Bruce, *Hebrews*, 379.

[34] Ἐυλογιας (*eulogias*, blessings) is probably an accusative plural. Μεταλαμβανω (metalambanō, receive) can take an accusative or a genitive; with genitive it has the sense "take part in," "receive a share of"; with the accusative the sense is "to experience" or "receive" (L&N "experiences blessings from God"). In Heb. 12:10, when used with the genitive, the sense is quite different; this suggests the accusative should be read here. Cf. George Wesley Buchanan, ed., *To the Hebrews*, 1st ed., Anchor Bible 36 (Garden City, N.Y: Doubleday, 1972), 85; Ellingworth, *Hebrews*, 327; Louw and Nida, *Greek-English Lexicon*, 1:805.

[35] Ellingworth, *Hebrews*, 329.

Grudem argues, thirdly, from the present tense of ἐχομενα (*echomena*, "that belong to") that these "better things" are present and not future experiences. There are at least two reasons why this argument does not succeed. Despite disagreements over the details, NT scholars agree time in the Greek verb is at the very least secondary, especially in the case of non-indicatives. Thus, the present tense here indicates only that the better things are contemporary with "salvation," they are pertaining to and accompanying it. Second, salvation in Hebrews is mainly considered a future concept (e.g. 9:28); therefore the better things accompany salvation is consistent with the imagery of verses 7-8, where the field is blessed when it produces the intended crop.

Grudem's fourth argument misses the point of alternative interpretations: the author is not telling his audience they have not yet fallen away; he is confident they *will not* fall away. The exegetes that differ from Grudem's rely upon the future orientation of salvation in Hebrews. We see in this verse, then, AOH's confidence that the Hebrews will persevere, despite his warnings. In the following verses he grounds this confidence in God's justice.

Verse 10-12. In verse 3, the author suggested the Hebrews will only attain maturity if God permits it; here, with "for," he grounds his confidence that the Hebrews will do so in God's justice. He is confident that God will give permission. Verse 10, then, forms an inclusio with verse 3, resolving the earlier verse's uncertainty. Looking at their past good deeds, the author is confident that God is not unjust to neglect their faith evidenced by their works, implying that God will be just to do his part in ensuring they attain maturity. AOH concludes this section with a final exhortation to eagerly move on to maturity, being earnest "to have the full assurance of hope until the end." With a reference to those who inherited the promises before, the author begins a transition back to his main argument and anticipates the so called "hall of faith" in chapter 11.

B. Conclusion

We see, then, AOH is confident his readers will press on to maturity, to which he intends to lead them in the following chapters. Our passage contains a severe warning—falling away is irreversible—coupled with great confidence grounded in God's just recognition of their faith-filled response of good works. Bringing together the threads of our exegesis, the key idea of Hebrews

6:1-12 is "to fail to move forward is to move back towards the final and fatal state of apostasy": phrased as an exhortation, "press on to maturity lest your sluggish immaturity lead you to fall away and be lost forever." This is the author's main idea, yet he does not leave the Hebrews with an overwhelming sense of doom. Without diminishing the threat he has given, he encourages them with Divine sovereignty: God will indeed permit them to press on. By juxtaposing Divine sovereignty and human responsibility, AOH places himself firmly within the compatibilist worldview shared by the rest of the NT, offering us a potential solution to the theological tension this passage, and those like it, introduce.

While the rest of the NT will not allow us to follow Arminianism here, exegesis will not allow us to go the typical Calvinist direction. Our exegesis reveals, though, a third solution, one which allows us to affirm the rest of the NT evidence without softening the hard words of the text. The problem, I contend, with Calvinists and their exegesis is they are not consistent with their own worldview: by accepting the Arminian argument that such a warning is merely "hypothetical," pointless, unless there is no guarantee of final perseverance, they fail to consider the solution compatibilism may provide to this exegetical-theological dilemma. The compatibilist view of free will allows us to hold together the genuine possibility of an action, such as believing or falling away, and the guarantee that an action will or will not be performed by a specific person in a specific situation: responsibility or freedom and determination (necessity) are compatible. Applied to our passage, then, compatibilism allows us to affirm both that true Christians are able to fall away and that God will never allow these—or any—Christians to do so. This is the point our author makes: press on, for falling away is devastating and irreversible; yet God is not unjust to neglect you.

I confess this interpretation is a reversal of previous printed support I have given Grudem's argument.[36] After careful examination of the passage, it is my judgment that the interpretation presented here better explains the author of Hebrews' argument. For the complacent Christian, the one who is content to confess the faith but is not willing to press on to a deeper delight in and knowledge of God and his ways revealed in Scripture, Hebrews 6:1-12 offers a dire warning: press on or drift away. There is no alternative. To

---

[36] Rutherford, *Prevenient Grace*, 250.

turn away from the faith is a decisive and permanent decision, a decision which stagnation will bring to reality. The only option is to press ever onwards towards the great promises God has given in Christ Jesus our Lord.

WORKS CITED

Aejmelaeus, Anneli. "Function and Interpretation of כי in Biblical Hebrew." *Journal of Biblical Literature* 105, no. 2 (1986): 193–209.

Alden, Robert L. *Job.* The New American Commentary v. 11. Nashville: Broadman & Holman, 1993.

Ames, William. *The Marrow of Theology.* Translated by John D. Eusden. Grand Rapids: Baker Books, 1997.

Barth, Karl. *Church Dogmatics.* Vol. 1.1. Peabody, Mass: Hendricksen, 2010.

———. *The Word of God and the Word of Man.* New York: Harper & Row, 1957.

Beale, G.K. *The Book of Revelation: A Commentary on the Greek Text.* NIGTC. Grand Rapids; Carlisle: Eerdmans; Paternoster, 1999.

Block, Daniel Isaac. *Deuteronomy.* The NIV Application Commentary. Grand Rapids, Mich.: Zondervan, 2012.

Blomberg, Craig L. *1 Corinthians.* NIVAC. Grand Rapids: Zondervan, 1994.

Blomberg, Craig L., and Mariam J. Kamell. *James: Zondevan Exegetical Commentary on the New Testament.* Zondervan Exegetical Commentary Series on the New Testament v. 16. Grand Rapids: Zondervan, 2008.

Boersma, Hans. *Heavenly Participation: The Weaving of a Sacramental Tapestry.* Grand Rapids, Mich.: W.B. Eerdmans Pub. Co, 2011.

———. *Sacramental Preaching: Sermons on the Hidden Presence of Christ.* Grand Rapids: Baker Academic, 2016.

Brettler, Marc Zvi. "Predestination in Deuteronomy 30:1-10." In *Those Elusive Deuteronomists*, 171–188. Sheffield: Sheffield Academic Press, 1999.

Brown, Francis, S. R Driver, Charles A Briggs, James Strong, and Wilhelm Gesenius. *The Brown-Driver-Briggs Hebrew and English Lexicon*. Peabody, Mass.: Hendrickson Publishers, 1996.

Bruce, F. F. *The Epistle of Paul to the Romans: An Introduction and Commentary*. Grand Rapids, Mich.: Wm. B. Eerdmans Publishing Co., 1963.

Bruce, F. F. *The Epistle to the Hebrews*. NICNT. Grand Rapids: Eerdmans, 1964.

Buchanan, George Wesley, ed. *To the Hebrews*. 1st ed. Anchor Bible 36. Garden City, N.Y: Doubleday, 1972.

Bultmann, Rudolf. *New Testament and Mythology and Other Basic Writings*. Translated by Schubert Miles Ogden. Philadelphia: Fortress Press, 1989.

Calvin, John. *The Epistle of Paul the Apostle to the Hebrews and the First and Second Epistles of St Peter*. Edited by David W. Torrance and Thomas F. Torrance. Translated by William B. Johnston. Calvin's Commentaries. Eerdmans: Grand Rapids, 1963.

Carson, D. A. *Exegetical Fallacies*. Grand Rapids: Baker Books, 1996.

———. "Is the Doctrine of Claritas Scripturae Still Relevant Today?" In *Collected Writings on Scripture*, edited by Andrew David Naselli, 179–193. Wheaton: Crossway, 2010.

———. "Reflections on Assurance." In *Still Sovereign: Contemporary Perspectives on Election, Foreknowledge & Grace*, edited by Thomas R. Schreiner and Bruce A. Ware, 247–276. Grand Rapids: Baker, 2000.

Carson, D. A., and Douglas J. Moo. *An Introduction to the New Testament*. Second Edition. Grand Rapids: Zondervan, 2005.

Carson, D.A. *The Cross and Christian Ministry: Leadership Lessons from 1 Corinthians*. Pbk. Grand Rapids, Michigan: Baker Books, 2004.

Childs, Brevard S. *Introduction to the Old Testament as Scripture*. Philadelphia: Fortress, 1979.

Christensen, Duane L. *Deuteronomy 21:10-34:12*. Vol. 6B. Word Biblical Commentary. Nashville: Thomas Nelson Publishers, 2002.

Clines, David J. A. *Job 21 - 37.* Edited by Bruce Manning Metzger, John D. W. Watts, Ralph Philip Martin, and David J. A. Clines. Word Biblical Commentary 18a. Nashville: Nelson, 2007.

Coxhead, Steven R. "Deuteronomy 30:11-14 as a Prophecy of the New Covenant in Christ." *Westminster Theological Journal* 68 (2006): 305–320.

Culler, Jonathan. *On Deconstructionism: Theory and Criticism after Structuralism.* Ithaca, N.Y.: Cornell University, 1982.

Danker, Frederick W. *A Greek-English Lexicon of the New Testament and Other Early Christian Literature.* 3rd ed. Chicago: University of Chicago Press, 2000.

Delitzsch, Franz. *Job: Two Volumes in One.* Commentary on the Old Testament in Ten Volumes IV. Grand Rapids: Eerdmans, 1978.

Driver, S. R. *A Critical and Exegetical Commentary on Deuteronomy.* 3rd ed. The International Critical Commentary. Edinburgh: T. & T. Clark, 1895.

Dunn, James D. G. *Romans 9-16.* Word Biblical Commentary 38b. Dallas, Tex.: Word Books, 1988.

Duvall, J. Scott, and J. Daniel Hays. *Grasping God's Word: A Hands-on Approach to Reading, Interpreting, and Applying the Bible.* 3rd ed. Grand Rapids: Zondervan, 2012.

Edwards, Jonathan. *Freedom of the Will.* Mineola, N.Y.: Dover Publications, 2012.

Ellingworth, Paul. *The Epistle to the Hebrews: A Commentary on the Greek Text.* NIGTC. Grand Rapids: Carlisle: W.B. Eerdmans ; Paternoster, 1993.

Elwell, Walter A., and Robert W. Yarbrough. *Encountering the New Testament: A Historical and Theological Survey.* 2nd ed. Encountering biblical studies. Grand Rapids, Mich: Baker Academic, 2005.

Fitzmyer, Joseph A. *The Aramaic Inscriptions of Sefire.* Biblica Et Orientalia 19. Rome: Pontifical Biblical Institute, 1967.

Frame, John M. *A History of Western Philosophy and Theology.* Phillipsburg: P&R Publishing, 2015.

———. *Perspectives on the Word of God: An Introduction to Christian Ethics.* Eugene, Or.: Wipf and Stock, 1999.

———. *Systematic Theology: An Introduction to Christian Belief.* Phillipsburg: P&R Publishing, 2013.

———. *The Doctrine of God.* A Theology of Lordship. Phillipsburg: P&R Publishing, 2002.

———. *The Doctrine of the Christian Life.* A Theology of Lordship 4. Phillipsburg: P&R Publishing, 2008.

———. *The Doctrine of the Knowledge of God.* A Theology of Lordship. Phillipsburg: P&R Publishing, 1987.

France, R. T. "Hebrews." In *The Expositor's Bible Commentary*, edited by Tremper Longman and David E. Garland. Rev. ed. Grand Rapids: Zondervan, 2006.

Fuhrer, Therese. "Allegorical Reading and Writing in Augustine's Confessions." In *In Search of Truth. Augustine, Manichaeism and Other Gnosticism*, edited by Jacob Albert van den Berg, Annemaré Kotzé, Tobias Nicklas, and Madeleine Scopello. Leiden, The Netherlands: Brill, 2010.

Geisler, Norman L. "Appendix B: Explaining Hermeneutics: A Commentary on the Chicago Statement on Biblical Hermeneutics Articles of Affirmation and Denial." In *Hermeneutics, Inerrancy, and the Bible*, edited by Earl D. Radmacher and Robert D. Preus, 163–190. Grand Rapids: Zondervan, 1984.

Gentry, Peter John, and Stephen J. Wellum. *Kingdom through Covenant: A Biblical-Theological Understanding of the Covenants.* Wheaton: Crossway, 2012.

Goldsworthy, Graeme. *Gospel-Centered Hermeneutics: Foundations and Principles of Evangelical Biblical Interpretation.* Downers Grove: InterVarsity Press, 2006.

Grudem, Wayne A. "Perseverance of the Saints: A Case Study from the Warning Passages in Hebrews." In *Still Sovereign: Contemporary Perspectives on Election, Foreknowledge & Grace*, edited by Thomas R. Schreiner and Bruce A. Ware, 133–182. Grand Rapids: Baker, 2000.

Gunkel, Herman. *Genesis.* Trans. of the 1910 ed. Macon: Mercer University, 1997.

Guzman, Ronaldo, and Michael W. Martin. "Is Hebrews 5:11-6:20 Really a Disgression?" *Novum Testamentum* 57, no. 3 (2015): 295–310.

Hagner, Donald Alfred. *Encountering the Book of Hebrews: An Exposition*. Grand Rapids: Baker Academic, 2002.

Harris, R. Laird, Gleason L Archer, and Bruce K Waltke. *Theological Wordbook of the Old Testament*. Vol. 2. 2 vols. Chicago, Ill.: Moody Press, 1980.

Harrison, R. K. *Jeremiah and Lamentations*. Reprinted. Tyndale Old Testament Commentary 21. Downers Grove, Ill.; England: Inter-Varsity Press, 2009.

Hartley, John E. *The Book of Job*. NICOT. Grand Rapids: Eerdmans, 1988.

Hewitt, Thomas. *The Epistle to the Hebrews, an Introduction and Commentary*. 1st ed. The Tyndale New Testament Commentaries. Grand Rapids: Eerdmans, 1960.

Hirsch, Jr., Eric D. "Meaning and Significance Reinterpreted." *Critical Inquiry* 11, no. 2 (1984): 202–225.

———. *Validity in Interpretation*. 9. print. New Haven: Yale Univ. Press, 1979.

Hornkohl, Aaron. "Periodization." In *Encyclopedia of Hebrew Language and Linguistics: Volume 1; A-F*, edited by Geoffrey Khan. Vol. 1. Leiden; Boston: Brill, 2013.

Hughes, Philip Edgcumbe. *A Commentary on the Epistle to the Hebrews*. Grand Rapids: Eerdmans, 1977.

Joosten, Jan. "The Distinction Between Classical and Late Biblical Hebrew as Reflected in Syntax." *Hebrew Studies* 46 (2005): 327–339.

Joüon, Paul, and Takamitsu Muraoka. *A Grammar of Biblical Hebrew*. Revised English Edition. Pontificio Istituto Biblico, 2006.

Kähler, Martin. *The So-Called Historical Jesus and the Historic, Biblical Christ*. Vancouver: Regent College Pub., 1998.

Kaiser, Walter C. "The Single Intent of Scripture." In *The Right Doctrine from the Wrong Texts?: Essays on the Use of the Old Testament in the New*, edited by G. K. Beale. Grand Rapids: Baker Books, 1994.

Kapelrud, Arvid S. "The Interpretation of Jeremiah 34:18ff." *Journal for the Study of the Old Testament* 22 (1982): 138–141.

Kidner, Derek. *The Message of Jeremiah: Against Wind and Tide*. The Bible Speaks Today. Leicester, England; Downers Grove, Ill.: Inter-Varsity Press, 1987.

Klein, William W, Craig L. Blomberg, and Robert L. Hubbard Jr. *Introduction to Biblical Interpretation*. Edited by Kermit A. Ecklebarger. Dallas: Word Publishing, 1993.

Koehler, Ludwig, Walter Baumgartner, M. E. J. Richardson, and Johann Jakob Stamm. *The Hebrew and Aramaic Lexicon of the Old Testament*. Electronic ed. Leiden; New York: Brill, 1999.

Lalleman, Hetty. *Jeremiah and Lamentations*. Tyndale Old Testament Commentaries 21. Downers Grove, Ill.: InterVarsity Press, 2013.

Lambdin, Thomas O. *Introduction to Biblical Hebrew*. New York, N.Y.: Charles Scribner's Sons, 1971.

Lane, William L. *Hebrews 1-8*. Edited by David A. Hubbard, Glenn W. Barker, and Ralph P. Martin. Vol. 1. 3 vols. Word Biblical Commentary Vol. 47,A. Nashville: Word Books, 1991.

Lewis, C S. "Modern Theology and Biblical Criticism." *BYU Studies Quarterly* 9, no. 1 (1969): Article 5.

Long, V. Philips. "1 and 2 Samuel." In *Zondervan Illustrated Bible Background Commentary: Old Testament: Volume 2, Joshua, Judges, Ruth, 1 and 2 Samuel*, edited by John H. Walton. Vol. 2. Grand Rapids: Zondervan, 2009.

Longman III, Tremper. *Jeremiah, Lamentations*. NIBC. Peabody, Mass.; United Kingdom: Hendrickson Publishers; Paternoster, 2008.

Louw, Johannes P., and Eugene Albert Nida. *Greek-English Lexicon of the New Testament: Based on Semantic Domains*. Electronic ed. of the 2nd edition. New York, N.Y.: United Bible Societies, 1996.

Lowther, James R. "Paul's Use of Deuteronomy 30:11-14 in Romans 10:5-8 as a Locus Primus on Paul's Understanding of the Law in Romans." Doctoral Dissertation, Southwestern Baptist Theological Seminary, 2001.

Luther, Martin. "Dr. Martin Luther's Answer to the Superchristian, Superspiritual, Superlearned Book of Goat Emser of Leipzig." In *Works of Martin Luther*, translated by A. Steimle. Vol. 3. Albany, Ore: AGES Bible Software, 1997.

———. *Sermons by Martin Luther: Volume 1; Sermons on Gospel Texts for Advent, Christmas, and Epiphany*. Edited by John Nicholas Lenker. Vol. 1. Albany, Ore: AGES Bible Software, 1997.

———. *The Bondage of the Will*. Edited by J. I Packer and O. R Johnston. Grand Rapids: Fleming H. Revell, 2003.

McKnight, S. "The Warning Passages of Hebrews: A Formal Analysis and Theological Conclusions." *Trinity Journal* 13, no. 1 (1992): 21–59.

Moo, Douglas J. *Encountering the Book of Romans: A Theological Survey*. 2nd ed. Encountering Biblical Studies. Grand Rapids, Mich.: Baker Academic, 2014.

———. *Galatians*. Baker Exegetical Commentary on the New Testament. Grand Rapids: Baker Academic, 2013.

———. *The Epistle to the Romans*. NICNT. Grand Rapids: Eerdmans, 1996.

Muller, Richard A. *Post-Reformation Reformed Dogmatics Volume 2: Holy Scripture: The Cognitive Foundation of Theology*. Vol. 2. Grand Rapids: Baker Book House, 1987.

Muraoka, T. *A Greek-English Lexicon of the Septuagint*. Rev. ed. Louvain ; Walpole, MA: Peeters, 2009.

Myers, Ched. *Binding the Strong Man: A Political Reading of Mark's Story of Jesus*. Maryknoll, N.Y.: Orbis, 1988.

Oberholtzer, T. K. "The Warning Passages in Hebrews : Part 3 (of 5 Parts): The Thorn-Infested Ground in Hebrews 6:4-12." *Bibliotheca Sacra* 145, no. 579 (1988): 319–328.

O'Brien, Peter Thomas. *The Letter to the Hebrews*. Pillar New Testament Commentary. Grand Rapids.; Nottingham: Eerdmans; Apollos, 2010.

Osborne, Grant R. "Genre Criticism: Sensus Literalis." *Trinity Journal* 4, no. 2 (1983): 1–27.

Osborne, Grant R. *The Hermeneutical Spiral: A Comprehensive Introduction to Biblical Interpretation*. Downers Grove, Ill.: InterVarsity Press, 1991.

Packer, J.I. "Infallible Scripture and the Role of Hermeneutics." In *Scripture and Truth*, edited by D. A. Carson and John D. Woodbridge, 321–356. Grand Rapids: Baker, 1992.

Patte, Daniel. *What Is Structural Exegesis?* Philadelphia: Fortress, 1976.

Payne, Philip Barton. "The Fallacy of Equating Meaning with the Human Author's Intention." In *The Right Doctrine from the Wrong Texts?: Essays on the Use of the Old Testament in the New*, edited by G. K. Beale. Grand Rapids: Baker Books, 1994.

Pope, Marvin H. *Job: Introduction, Translation, and Notes.* Garden City: Doubleday, 1973.

Poythress, Vern S. *Reading the Word of God in the Presence of God: A Handbook for Biblical Interpretation.* Wheaton, Illinois: Crossway, 2016.

Poythress, Vern Sheridan. "Divine Meaning of Scripture." In *The Right Doctrine from the Wrong Texts?: Essays on the Use of the Old Testament in the New*, edited by G. K. Beale. Grand Rapids: Baker Books, 1994.

———. *God Centered Biblical Interpretation.* Phillipsburg, N.J.: P&R Publishing, 1999.

———. *In the Beginning Was the Word: Language: A God-Centered Approach.* Wheaton: Crossway Books, 2009.

———. *Symphonic Theology: The Validity of Multiple Perspectives in Theology.* Grand Rapids: Academie Books, 1987.

Provan, Iain W. *The Reformation and the Right Reading of Scripture.* Waco, Texas: Baylor University Press, 2017.

Provence, Thomas E. "The Sovereign Subject Matter: Hermeneutics in the Church Dogmatics." In *A Guide to Contemporary Hermeneutics: Major Trends in Biblical Interperation*, edited by Donald K. McKim. Grand Rapids: Eerdmans, 1986.

Radmacher, Earl D., and Robert D. Preus, eds. "Appendix A: The Chicago Statement on Biblical Hermeneutics." In *Hermeneutics, Inerrancy, and the Bible.* Grand Rapids: Zondervan, 1984.

Roberts, A., and J. Donaldson. *Ante-Nicene Christian Library: Translations of the Writings of the Fathers Down to A.D. 325.* Ante-Nicene Christian Library: Translations of the Writings of the Fathers Down to A.D. 325 v. 10. T&T Clark, 1895.

Ruether, Rosemary Radford. "Feminist Interpretation: A Method of Correlation." In *Feminist Interpretation of the Bible*, edited by Letty M. Russell, 111–124. Philadelphia: Westminster John Knox, 1985.

Russell, Letty M., ed. *Feminist Interpretation of the Bible*. Philadelphia: Westminster John Knox, 1985.

Rutherford, J. Alexander. "An Investigation into the Role of Context in Interpretation." *Teleioteti*, January 16, 2018. Accessed January 24, 2018. https://teleioteti.ca/2018/01/16/investigation-role-context-interpretation/.

———. *God's Kingdom through his Priest-King: An Analysis of the Book of Samuel in Light of the Davidic Covenant*. A Teleioteti Technical Study 1. Vancouver: Teleioteti, 2019.

———. *Prevenient Grace: An Investigation into Arminianism*. Vancouver: Teleioteti, 2016.

———. *The Book of Habakkuk: An Exegetical-Theological Commentary on the Hebrew Text*. A Teleioteti Old Testament Commentary 1. Vancouver, BC: Teleioteti, Forthcoming.

———. *The Gift of Knowing: A Biblical Perspective on Knowing and Truth*. God's Gifts for the Christian Life Part 1 - The Christian Mind I. Vancouver: Teleioteti, 2019.

———. "Towards a Biblical Theology of Imputation: A Consideration of an Old Testament Root for Christ's Imputed Righteousness in Romans," 2016. https://teleioteti.ca/resources/papers/.

———. "Towards an Evangelical Hermeneutic: A Critique of the Chicago Statement on Hermeneutics (1982)." *Teleioteti*, December 2016. Accessed January 23, 2018. https://teleioteti.ca/resources/papers/.

———. "Christ Is Preeminent over False Religion: An Investigation of the Colossian False Teaching," August 29, 2016. https://www.academia.edu/29216349/CHRIST_IS_PREEMINENT_OVER_FALSE_RELGION_AN_INVESTIGATION_OF_THE_COLOSSIAN_FALSE_TEACHING.

Sailhamer, John H. *Introduction to Old Testament Theology: A Canonical Approach*. Grand Rapids: Zondervan, 1995.

———. *The Pentateuch as Narrative*. Grand Rapids: Zondervan, 1992.

Schaff, Philip. *A Select Library of the Nicene and Post-Nicene Fathers of the Christian Church: St Augustin's City of God and Christian Doctrine*. Vol. 2. A Select Library of the Nicene and Post-Nicene Fathers of the Christian Church. Buffalo: The Christian Literature Company, 1887.

Schreiner, Thomas R. *Commentary on Hebrews*. Edited by Andreas J. Köstenberger, T. Desmond Alexander, and Thomas R. Schreiner. Biblical Theology for Christian Proclamation. Nashville: B&H, 2015.

———. *Romans*. Baker Exegetical Commentary on the New Testament 6. Grand Rapids, Mich.: Baker Books, 1998.

Schreiner, Thomas R., and Ardel B. Caneday. *The Race Set before Us: A Biblical Theology of Perseverance & Assurance*. Downers Grove: InterVarsity, 2001.

Seow, Choon Leong. "Orthography, Textual Criticism, and the Poetry of Job." *Journal of Biblical Literature* 130, no. 1 (2011): 63–85.

Silva, Moisés. *Biblical Words and Their Meaning: An Introduction to Lexical Semantics*. Rev. and Expanded ed. Grand Rapids: Zondervan, 1994.

———, ed. *Foundations of Contemporary Interpretation*. Grand Rapids: Zondervan, 1996.

Ska, Jean Louis. *"Our Fathers Have Told Us": Introduction to the Analysis of Hebrew Narratives*. Subsidia Biblica 13. Roma: Editrice Pontificio Instituto Biblico, 1990.

Soulen, Richard N., and R. Kendall Soulen. *Handbook of Biblical Criticism: Now Includes Precritical and Postcritical Interpretation*. 3rd Revised and Expanded. Louisville; London: Westminster John Knox, 2001.

Steinmetz, David C. "The Superiority of Precritical Exegesis." In *A Guide to Contemporary Hermeneutics: Major Trends in Biblical Interperation*, edited by Donald K. McKim. Grand Rapids: Eerdmans, 1986.

Thompson, J. A. *The Book of Jeremiah*. NICOT. Grand Rapids, Mich.: WM. B. Eerdmans Publishing Co., 1980.

Thompson, Mark. *A Sure Ground on Which to Stand: The Relation of Authority and Interpretive Method in Luther's Approach to Scripture*. Carlisle; Waynesboro, GA: Paternoster, 2004.

Tigay, Jeffrey H. *Deuteronomy [Devarim]: The Traditional Hebrew Text with the New JPS Translation*. 1st ed. The JPS Torah commentary. Philadelphia, Penn.: Jewish Publication Society, 1996.

Van Til, Cornelius. "Has Karl Barth Become Orthodox." *The Westminster Theological Journal* 16, no. 2 (May 1954): 135–181.

VanGemeren, Willem. *Interpreting the Prophetic Word: An Introduction to the Prophetic Literature of the Old Testament.* Grand Rapids: Zondervan, 1996.

Vanhoozer, Kevin J. *Biblical Authority after Babel: Retrieving the Solas in the Spirit of Mere Protestant Christianity.* Grand Rapids: Brazos, 2016.

———. *Is There a Meaning in This Text?: The Bible, the Reader, and the Morality of Literary Knowledge.* Grand Rapids: Zondervan, 1998.

———. *The Drama of Doctrine: A Canonical-Linguistic Approach to Christian Theology.* 1st ed. Louisville: Westminster John Knox, 2005.

Wallace, Daniel B. *Greek Grammar Beyond the Basics: An Exegetical Syntax of the New Testament With Scripture, Subject, and Greek Word Indexes.* Grand Rapids: Zondervan, 1996.

Waltke, Bruce K., and Michael Patrick O'Connor. *An Introduction to Hebrew Syntax.* Winona Lake, Ind.: Eisenbrauns, 1990.

Watson, Francis. *Text and Truth: Redefining Biblical Theology.* Edinburgh: T&T Clark, 1997.

Wells, Kyle B. *Grace and Agency in Paul and Second Temple Judaism: Interpreting the Transformation of the Heart.* Supplements to Novum Testamentum 157. Leiden; Boston, Mass.: Brill, 2015.

Westcott, Brooke Foss, ed. *The Epistle to the Hebrews the Greek Text with Notes and Essays.* 3d ed. London: Macmillan, 1903.

Williams, Ronald J., and John C. Beckman. *Williams' Hebrew Syntax.* 3rd ed. Toronto: University of Toronto Press, 2007.

Wright, N. T. *Scripture and the Authority of God.* Society for Promoting Christian Knowledge, 2005.

Wright, N.T. *The New Testament and the People of God.* Christian Origins and the Question of God 1. Minneapolis: Fortress, 1992.

Young, Ian. "Is the Prose Tale of Job in Late Biblical Hebrew?" *Vetus Testamentum* 59, no. 4 (2009): 606–629.

Younger, K. Lawson. *Ancient Conquest Accounts.* Journal for the Study of the Old Testament Supplement 98. Sheffield: Sheffield Academic Press, 1990.

"Mirror Reading." *Andy Naselli.* Last modified May 30, 2011. Accessed April 26, 2019. http://andynaselli.com/mirror-reading.

"Review of the So-Called Historical Jesus and the Historic Biblical Christ." *Teleioteti*, July 25, 2018. Accessed April 26, 2019. https://teleioteti.ca/2018/07/25/review-of-the-so-called-historical-jesus-and-the-historic-biblical-christ/.

ABOUT TELEIOTETI

Teleioteti (Τελειοτητι, te-ley-o-tey-tee)—meaning "unto maturity"—is dedicated to faithful, thoughtful ministry. We create resources for Christian discipleship, resources that address theological and pastoral concerns from a biblical worldview. Our purpose is to see Christ's Church mature in its understanding of God and his Word. We do this through the production of Gospel-centred materials that connect the Bible with the heads, hearts, and minds of Christians. We hope to enable Christians from all walks of life to better understand and glorify God through service in his Church.

To achieve this purpose, Teleioteti publishes online materials and books researched with academic rigor yet based upon biblical presuppositions. That is, we are neither academic nor lazy. We use methods, or epistemology, informed by the Bible along with the hard work usually associated with professional research and study. We produce resources directed towards all Christians, but most of our resources are directed towards students, pastors, and theologically inclined lay Christians.

To learn more about us and what we are doing, please visit us at https://teleioteti.ca or contact us at info@teleioteti.ca. If you have found this resource helpful, prayerfully consider supporting us by giving a review on the web (e.g. Amazon, Goodreads, etc.), praying with and for us, or giving financially so that we can produce more resources like this one. For more information on how you can support us, visit us at https://teleioteti.ca/about/partner/ or at our page on Patreon, https://www.patreon.com/teleioteti.

Other Books by J. Alexander Rutherford

Prevenient Grace: An Investigation into Arminianism (Teleioteti, 2016)

When a building is built on a poor foundation, the inevitable result is its collapse. But this isn't a book on architecture; foundations are found in thought structures as well as in material structures. In theology, a bad foundation will produce results as catastrophic as a bad foundation in architecture. How we think about God and his work in the world will profoundly affect how we live and work out our Christian faith; is your foundation strong? This book evolved from the conviction that a prominent theological system rests on fragile foundation.

Believe the Unbelievable: A Study in the Book of Habakkuk (Teleioteti, 2018)

What would we do if our prayers for justice, our prayers that God's will be done in our nation, were answered with a vision of desolation, of utter destruction?

When Habakkuk prayed for salvation, a prayer for justice amid chaos, violence, and suffering, that was God's answer. He revealed in a vision the invasion of the vicious armies of Babylon. God's answer contradicted everything Habakkuk thought he knew. Yet in the end, he praised God and trusted him for this horrid salvation.

What do we do when God's actions or words contradict our understanding, contradict what we have believed? The book of Habakkuk answers this question in the face of the Babylonian invasion of Judah. Habakkuk is a book of discipleship, a book written to bring its reader to a deeper faith in Yahweh in the presence of his unthinkable deeds.

Using study questions addressing the text, theology, and application of Habakkuk and explanatory comments on difficult themes, *Believe the Unbelievable* seeks to realize this purpose for the contemporary reader.

Endorsements:

James Rutherford is a capable and creative thinker, well equipped to tackle tough projects, such as the book of Habakkuk. In this study guide, Rutherford has produced a very useful resource for individual or group study. He combines theological acumen and well-honed linguistic and literary skills to discover and then to present, in highly understandable fashion, the riches of this not so "minor" Minor Prophet.

- V. Philips Long, PhD Cambridge
  Professor of Old Testament, Regent College

My good friend, James Rutherford, has given the church a gift. He has taken his love for God's Word and focused it on an Old Testament book that most Christians know very little about. The result is a study in Habakkuk that brings together deep insight and real relevance. Habakkuk is a voice among the Biblical chorus that believers need to hear today. Thank you, James, for helping us to hear it clearly and faithfully.

- Fredrick Eaton
  Pastor, Christ City Church, Kitsilano

The Gift of Knowing: A Biblical Perspective on Knowing and Truth (Teleioteti, 2019)

To any attentive observer, the Western world is in serious trouble. It shows the signs of languishing under a devastating disease. This is clearer nowhere else than in the realm of epistemology, the study of truth and how we attain it. Here, the belief in human autonomy—the freedom of individual men and women to interpret the world and live within it as they see fit—has slowly eroded any foundation for knowledge or morality. The result is a society adrift, floating wherever the tide might take it.

If the disease ravaging our society is the belief in human autonomy, the cure is submission once again to the God who created this world, at least that is the argument of the Gift of Knowing. The author argues that apart from submission to God as he has revealed himself in the Christian Bible, there is no firm foundation for truth or a trustworthy way of attaining it. However, through his revelation in Scripture, God has given his people a foundation for knowing the world he has created and living within it.

God's Kingdom through his Priest-King: An Analysis of the Book of Samuel in light of the Davidic Covenant

Endorsements:

In the present environment of high interest in the Book of Samuel, this contribution by James Rutherford is most welcome. Rutherford is well versed in current scholarship on Samuel, but his work moves well beyond this scholarship to contribute fresh insights, not least in respect of the priestly character of King David. And concerning its structure, Rutherford argues that the Book of Samuel as a whole is arranged and narrated so as to draw attention to the centrality of the Davidic Covenant of 2 Samuel 7. Having myself studied 1 and 2 Samuel for decades now, I was nevertheless benefitted at numerous points from Rutherford's creative interpretive suggestions. His is a work well conceived, well written, and worthy of a serious read.

- V. Philips Long
  Professor of Old Testament, Regent College

This thesis argues that by weaving references to God's promises made to King David throughout his narrative, the author of Samuel reveals God's will to strip away all human pretension by bringing his promises to fulfillment through a lowly man whose ascension to kingship and endurance therein is entirely owing to God. In this way, the Samuel author fulfils his purpose of demonstrating God's sovereign working in history to establish his kingdom on earth through his chosen priest-king, a descendant of David. The thesis represents an excellent piece of work that does a great job of bringing together into one coherent argument, focused on the Davidic covenant, much of the best recent narrative-critical research on 1-2 Samuel, and from this point of view represents a distinctive contribution to the field of Samuel studies.

- Iain Provan
  Marshall Sheppard Professor of Biblical Studies, Regent College

www.ingramcontent.com/pod-product-compliance
Lightning Source LLC
Chambersburg PA
CBHW020526080526
44583CB00013B/753